JoAnne Alter

A Part-Time Career for a Full-Time You

HOUGHTON MIFFLIN COMPANY
BOSTON
1982

Library of Congress Cataloging in Publication Data

Alter, JoAnne.
A part-time career for a full-time you.

Bibliography: p.
Includes index.
1. Vocational guidance — United States — Handbooks,
manuals, etc. 2. Part-time employment — United States —
Handbooks, manuals, etc. I. Title.
HF5382.5.U5A65   650.1'4   81-6911
ISBN 0-395-31284-1   AACR2
ISBN 0-395-31868-8 (pbk.)

Printed in the United States of America

S 10 9 8 7 6 5 4 3 2 1

A Part-Time Career for a Full-Time You

Cowell

To my parents, Florence and Jerry Bresler, who always taught me that I could do anything in life that I really wanted to do. And to my husband, Fran Alter, whose encouragement and support have made my work and my life ever more fulfilling.

Acknowledgments

———————◆>————————

A Part-Time Career for a Full-Time You could never have been written without the help of hundreds of men and women who offered information, provided critical insights, and in many cases suggested still other people who might be of assistance. I thank each and every individual who agreed to be interviewed and to share personal experiences. Their generosity is all the more remarkable in view of the fact that not one person mentioned or quoted in this book asked that his or her name be changed or omitted.

I am grateful to the dozens of college placement officers, union officials, employers, representatives of professional associations, and spokespersons for federal, state, and local government agencies who provided information cheerfully, and in some cases frequently. A special thanks belongs to three such individuals. Solidelle Wasser, an economist with the U.S. Department of Labor's Bureau of Labor Statistics, for years guided me through a seemingly endless maze of statistics, charts, and microfiche — and always kept an eye out for new studies on women in the work force, career opportunities, and part-time work. Ellen Russell of the Office of Personnel Management in Washington, D.C., answered countless questions and continuously updated information and source lists for contacts within the federal government. Gurley Turner of Catalyst made that organization's extensive files accessible to me on numerous occasions.

I thank the leaders of organizations dedicated to helping women in general and part-timers in particular. Barney Olmsted, Nancy Inui, Marcia Kleiman, and Carol Parker contributed far more than the quotes that are attributed to them. Each of them must know how I appreciate their encouragement and enthusiasm.

I am particularly indebted to the editors of *Family Circle* magazine, and especially to editor-in-chief Arthur Hettich, for giving me the opportunity to write numerous articles on the subject of part-time work, careers, and work-at-home enterprises, and for permitting me to use these pieces as the basis for several sections of *A Part-Time Career for a Full-Time You*. Arthur deserves special thanks for suggesting that I write a book on part-time work.

Sue Maushart, an extremely bright, resourceful, and hard-working young woman, assisted me in all phases of gathering information. I thank Sue for top-notch interviewing and researching and for being a good and supportive friend, particularly when it seemed the book would never get done. Dorothy Holsberg has my gratitude for typing hundreds of pages of manuscript, often on extremely short notice.

Finally, I'd like to express thanks to Anita McClellan, my editor at Houghton Mifflin, for her abiding faith, patience, and sensitivity throughout the year and a half that this book was being researched and written.

Contents

Introduction

———•———

FUELED BY an ongoing energy crisis over the past decade, inflation has brought about enormous changes in the way we live. It has prompted millions of women to become working mothers. It has forced students to look for ways to subsidize their studies, retired people to seek supplementary income, and several million employed individuals to find second jobs. Hardly any family or any person has been untouched by the effects of a runaway cost of living. Indeed, inflation has created a situation in which today's families must earn more than twice the amount of money they earned ten years ago, just to maintain the same standard of living they enjoyed at that time.

How to earn that extra income? For millions of Americans, the answer has been a part-time job. Part-time work has offered not only the opportunity to bring in more money, but the chance to do so while taking advantage of the ever-widening array of life choices, educational opportunities, and leisure activities that have also presented themselves during the past decade. For example, studies have revealed that women haven't forsaken the idea of having and raising children. Rather, many have found that working at a paid part-time position provides them with the opportunity to spend most of their time with their children, to earn much-needed income, and to enjoy the challenge and satisfaction that a job outside the home can bring. Men, too, have been exposed to more choices in their day-to-day lives. Many have begun to experience the joys of caring for their young children as well as the satisfactions of their careers. Others now feel free to change careers during mid life, or to forsake high-pressured or unrewarding jobs they had once felt doomed to endure until retirement. Part-time work has enabled many women and men to earn money while they study to enter new fields, or simply to experiment with career alternatives at various stages of their lives.

While inflation continues to eat away at our pocketbooks, forcing more people of all ages to seek paid employment, certain developments seem certain to make both work and leisure opportunities more plentiful in the future. Experts predict that the birthrate will continue to decline and that more jobs will be available for those who want them. Technology will continue to expand our horizons and capabilities. We will live longer and remain healthier. The challenge to growing numbers of men and women of all ages will be not whether or how to find work, but how to balance work with all of the other activities that combine to create rewarding, fulfilling lives.

Whenever government, business, labor, and academic leaders get together to contemplate ways to create employment opportunities for women, youth, minorities, the elderly, and the handicapped, they determine that flexible work scheduling, including the option to work part-time, is a good way to meet the needs of those who are unable to work a full week or who are already in the work force and who wish to improve the quality of their lives with a part-time schedule. Such experts invariably come to the conclusion that not only would countless American workers and their families benefit, but employers stand to gain in terms of lower turnover, reduced absenteeism and lateness, less overtime, better safety performance, a higher level of job satisfaction among employees, and greater productivity.

Most companies still resist career-level part-time work. The idea of job sharing, for example, remains unfamiliar to many employers. Flexible work schedules stand to improve living and working conditions for millions of Americans, now and in the years to come. Yet far fewer good part-time jobs are available than are people who seek them. Finding a part-time job that offers both a good salary and the promise of a bright future therefore takes both time and effort.

Helping to spread the word to public- and private-sector employers of the advantages of alternative work schedules, and particularly of shortened work weeks for those who need or want them, is certainly one of the aims of *A Part-Time Career for a Full-Time You.* Throughout the following pages, and particularly in the first several chapters, you'll see repeated references to studies on part-time work that may help to dispel many of the misconceptions employers continue to hold about the value and motivation of part-time workers. Several of the top part-time advocacy groups have published extensive bibliographies and guides for prospective employers which should create a more positive attitude among employers toward would-be part-timers. See "Organizations That Help Part-Timers" and "Recommended Reading" on pages 361 and 367.

Primarily, however, *A Part-Time Career for a Full-Time You* tries to provide a solid nuts-and-bolts guide for the person who wants to find a good part-time or shared job — whether that individual is a student, a woman at home with young children or seeking to re-enter the work force after a long absence, a person who is handicapped or at or approaching retirement age, or someone looking for time to pursue educational, professional, or recreational activities.

A Part-Time Career for a Full-Time You also aims to help you land the part-time job that's right for you. The only way to find any good job, and particularly a good part-time job, is to be well skilled and well prepared and to carry out a well-planned job-hunting campaign.

The opening sections of the book explain who works part-time and why, as well as the pros and cons of part-time work as it exists today. Next, the fields in which there is high demand for qualified people are discussed, along with where the greatest opportunities for would-be part-timers lie. You'll learn which employers are most likely to give alternative scheduling and particularly the part-time options a chance.

"Landing a Good Part-Time Job" covers everything from time-tested job-hunting basics to ways to propose a job-sharing arrangement to a skeptical employer. Finally, there's a brief look at the option of working at or from your own home.

A growing number of resources are available to help you in your search for a good part-time job, many of them listed in "Resources," beginning on page 361. Take advantage of every one that might be of assistance. Also rely on people and organizations in your own community. The more thought and preparation you put into the search for a good part-time position, the more easily you will find the type of job you seek. Anything or anyone that helps you plan an effective, well-focused job hunt will maximize your chances of success.

The perfect part-time position won't land in your lap, but with a copy of *A Part-Time Career for a Full-Time You,* a well-directed strategy, and a bit of perseverance, you *can* find a part-time job that fits your needs and desires. Good luck!

A Part-Time Career
for a Full-Time You

❧ 1 ❧

The
Part-Time
Alternative

———————◆———————

IN THIS SECTION, we'll take an overall look at what it means to be a part-timer in the United States today. We'll begin by taking up the matter of how much time is considered "part" time. (You may be surprised at how many different views there are on the subject.) Next, we'll look at who today's part-timers are, why they choose the schedules they do, and what kinds of jobs they hold. Finally, we'll explore the advantages and disadvantages of part-time work — those factors that make having a part-time job the best of all possible work arrangements for some people and a source of continuing frustration for others.

Throughout this section, you'll meet a number of men and women who hold various part-time jobs and who candidly express their views on what's good, and bad, about choosing a reduced work schedule. If you already work part-time, you're sure to recognize the pros and cons they mention. If you're planning to look for part-time work, their insights will give you an idea of what you can realistically expect to find as you begin your search for a rewarding, well-paying part-time job.

How Much Time Is Part Time?

That depends on whom you ask. The broadest definition, though seemingly vague, is quite useful for many researchers who study large-scale labor patterns. It goes something like this: Part-time work is "regular voluntary employment . . . carried out during working hours distinctly shorter than normal."[1]

As you can see, this definition covers all bases, since for one company "normal" may mean a thirty-two-hour-week, and for another, forty hours or more. What this also means, as you'll soon see, is that a man or woman putting in thirty-five hours will be considered a full-timer at one company and a part-timer at another. Confused? Hang on a minute. It gets even more complex.

The U.S. Department of Labor offers a somewhat more limited definition which for our purposes, I believe, is the most useful one. A voluntary part-timer, according to the Labor Department, is anyone who works fewer than thirty-five hours per week and who does so by choice. That's it; nice and simple. Whether the worker puts in one hour or thirty-four hours, he or she is a part-timer.

Like any description of people and their activities, the Labor Department's definition is subject to interpretation —even within the federal government. For example, a key provision of the Employees Retirement Income Security Act of 1974 (known as ERISA) is that part-time as well as full-time workers be given access to company pensions. Specifically, ERISA requires every private company that has a pension plan to allow workers to participate in that plan if they work more than one thousand hours per year. Even without using your calculator, you can easily figure that a thousand hours per year works out to roughly twenty hours per week. However, the actual weekly schedules of workers are irrelevant under the terms of ERISA.

---

1. See Stanley Nollen, *New Patterns of Work* (Scarsdale, N.Y.: Work in America Institute, 1979), p. 1. This is the definition used by the International Labor Office.

To complicate matters further, when Congress enacted the Federal Employees Part-time Career Employment Act of 1978, a law that set forth plans for expanding part-time work opportunities in the federal government, it defined part time as anything from sixteen to thirty-two hours per week. Later, however, the Office of Personnel Management explained that under certain circumstances, *less* than sixteen hours' work would also be covered under the terms of the new law.

If the government's varying standards aren't enough to confuse you, consider several of the different arrangements that corporations and other employers describe as part-time. One national restaurant chain considers anyone who works more than twenty-four hours a week a full-time employee. A Florida hospital refers to full-timers as those who work over thirty-two hours a week. Some firms think of part-time workers as the employees who show up two or three full days each week. Others consider the part-timers to be those who work several hours each day, or only in the mornings or afternoons.

When asked about their use of part-time workers, many companies answer that they maintain what they call "contingent lists" or "ready work forces" composed of men and women who are available to work for a day or two here and there, whenever they're needed, or who come in for a set period of a few weeks at a time — say, during a Christmas or summer vacation. And some firms say they hire part-timers to work one week out of every three or four, throughout the year. (Most labor analysts refer to the thirty-five-hours-a-week-but-only-for-a-while work pattern as *temporary* rather than *part-time*. While the distinction is certainly a legitimate one, many companies and employees continue to lump the terms *part-time* and *temporary* together. For that reason, I believe it is useful to include temporary work among the part-time options outlined in this book, and to discuss opportunities not only for the under-thirty-five-hours-a-week group, but also for those people who wish to work thirty-five or even forty hours a week but only for a certain period of time.)

Clearly, there are lots of ways to divide the standard work week, or for that matter the year. We'll consider the more common ones in the chapter on "Your Options." For now, though, it seems only fitting that, having looked at the different government and corporate views on what is and what isn't part time, we consider part-time work from the viewpoint of those men, women, and young people who call themselves part-timers.

How much time is part time to them? Usually, between fifteen and thirty hours each week. The national average: eighteen hours.[2]

Who Are Today's Part-Timers?

The answer is, many women, some men, and lots of young people under the age of twenty. The fact is almost all of us are likely to seek part-time work at some point in our lives.

To get an idea of who today's part-time workers are, we will consider the overall numbers of people who work fewer than thirty-five hours each week. Then we will look at general breakdowns according to sex, age, and marital status. Finally, we will consider the reasons people choose to work part-time, which, of course, further helps to describe today's part-timers.

The Numbers (or, Lots and Lots of Statistics)

As of February 1980, there were over 15 million Americans working fewer than thirty-five hours a week by choice. Add another 8 million men and women who either moonlight at part-time jobs to augment their full-time earnings[3] or work part-time because they can't find full-time jobs, and you have over 23 million Americans holding part-time jobs right now.

---

2. "Worktime: The Traditional Workweek and Its Alternatives," *1979 Employment and Training Report of the President,* prepared by the Employment and Training Administration of the U.S. Department of Labor (Washington, D.C.: Government Printing Office, 1979), p. 85.

3. In 1979, the total number of moonlighters was 4.7 million, according to figures compiled by the Census Bureau and analyzed by the Bureau of Labor Statistics (BLS). About 1.4 million individuals, or roughly 30 percent of the moonlighters, were women.

That's one out of every five people employed in the United States.[4]

That number is steadily growing. Since 1954, the number of part-timers has risen at the rate of 4 percent a year. The overall growth rate since then has been about 140 percent, compared to a rise of 50 percent in the number of people working full-time, according to the BLS.[5] In the last decade alone, the ranks of part-timers have grown *three times* as fast as the ranks of full-timers.[6]

WOMEN: THE LARGEST GROUP

When experts refer to the rapid growth of the labor force in general, they're usually talking about the growth of one particular group within the labor force: women. The same is true when they discuss the increase in the number of part-time workers.

4. U.S. Department of Labor, Bureau of Labor Statistics, *Employment and Earnings, March 1980* (Washington, D.C.: Government Printing Office, 1980), p. 45.

5. See William V. Deuterman, Jr., and Scott Campbell Brown, "Voluntary Part-time Workers: A Growing Part of the Labor Force," *Monthly Labor Review* 101 (June 1978): 3–4.

6. See Joann S. Lublin, "Mutual Aid: Firms and Job Seekers Discover More Benefits of Part-Time Positions," *Wall Street Journal*, October 4, 1978.

At the end of 1980, almost 45 million adult women, or roughly 50 percent of all females over the age of sixteen, worked outside the home. Over 9 million, or about 20 percent of them, worked part-time by choice. If you also count females who work part-time because they can't find full-time jobs, however, the proportion of women working fewer than thirty-five hours per week increases.

Of course, female part-timers come from all age, racial, religious, and economic backgrounds. However, if there were such a hypothetical person as the typical female part-timer, she would most likely be a white high-school graduate between thirty-five and forty years old. She would be married and the mother of preschool or school-age children. Her husband would most likely be employed full-time, and she would be putting in between fifteen and thirty hours a week at a white-collar job.[7]

Though the typical female part-timer is married, a significant number of women who work part-time are not. One out of every six is separated, divorced, or widowed; one out of seven is single.

Now let's look at their male counterparts.

FEW MEN CHOOSE TO WORK PART-TIME

Adult males make up the smallest proportion of part-timers: about 19 percent of those voluntarily working fewer than thirty-five hours per week, and 16 percent of those working part-time for all reasons. Yet at certain times in their lives, men actually do seek part-time positions in greater numbers. According to statistics compiled by the BLS in May 1978, those periods are when they're under twenty-four and over sixty-five years of age. Interestingly, the BLS found that fewer than 10 percent of married men — no matter what their age — choose to put in fewer than thirty-five hours per week. Among single men, though, 35 percent choose part-time work, as do 14 percent of those men who are separated, divorced, or widowed.

---

7. See Carol Leon and Robert W. Bednarzik, "A Profile of Women on Part-time Schedules," *Monthly Labor Review* 101 (October 1978): 3–12.

YOUNG ADULTS AND TEENAGERS: ONE-FOURTH OF THE PART-TIME FORCE

Almost 27 percent of all part-time workers are young people under the age of twenty. Part-time work appeals almost equally to young men and young women, as the introduction to the first illustration in the chart on page 8 points out. Yet once these workers enter their twenties, there is a major change. Only about 35 percent of the males continue to work part-time, compared to 44 percent of the females.

Why Do They Work? To Pay the Bills

"Why do you work?" Ask any employed person, full- or part-time, and you'll undoubtedly get the reply: "Money."

Of course. With spiraling inflation an unfortunate fact of life throughout most of the past decade, almost every one of us knows what it means to be strapped for cash. According to The Conference Board, a prestigious New York business research firm, the consumer price level has risen an incredible 90 percent in the past decade. What's more, the firm concluded in a 1981 survey, a family of four had to earn $22,477 before taxes to match the spending power that a $10,000 pre-tax income provided in 1970.[8]

Given the grim reality of inflation that just won't quit, it's not surprising that women in so-called typical American families have entered the labor force in record numbers in recent years. After all, what family can't use help in meeting the monthly rent or mortgage payments? Who wouldn't like to be able to worry less about how to pay for food and clothing, heating oil or gas, electricity, medical and dental care, cars and auto maintenance, gasoline, insurance, education, and all the other expenses that take an ever-larger bite out of our annual incomes?

Considering the skyrocketing costs of the essentials, it's no wonder that for millions of American families, such extras as yearly vacations and occasional weekend trips, new cars every

---

8. The Conference Board, *The Two-Way Squeeze, 1981; Economic Road Maps Nos. 1900–1901,* April 1981.

Profiles of Part-Time Workers

Teenagers Working Part-Time

Number (1976): 4,000,000; equally divided between the sexes.

Typical reasons for working: To get work experience or to earn money for education or miscellaneous expenses.

Kinds of jobs: Most work in service jobs; teenagers amount to almost one-third of part-time cleaning workers and nearly one-half of part-time food service workers. Occupations tend to differ by sex. Men are typically employed as cleaning workers, dining-room attendants, cooks, operatives, laborers, and dishwashers. Women often work as waitresses, cashiers, sales clerks, and household and child-care workers.

20- to 54-Year-Olds Working Part-Time

Number (1976): 6,800,000; about 85 percent are women.

Typical reasons for working: To supplement household income.

Kinds of jobs: More than 25 percent of the women work in clerical jobs — as bookkeepers, receptionists, and teachers' aides, for example. Another quarter work in service jobs like child care or hairdressing. A somewhat smaller but still substantial percentage are professional and technical workers — primarily registered nurses and teachers. The teachers include preschool, kindergarten, music, dance, college, and university teachers. Women also make up more than half of the part-time bus drivers and real-estate agents.

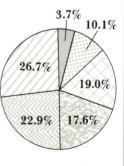

Men constitute nearly half of the part-time college and university teachers and three-quarters of the part-time musicians and composers. Many men work in service jobs as cleaning or food service workers.

Older Part-Time Workers
Number (1976): 2,200,000.

Typical reasons for working: To supplement household income.

Kinds of jobs: Women 55 years of age or older with a high-school education often work in clerical jobs, as bookkeepers or secretaries. Others are employed as household servants or nonfactory dressmakers.

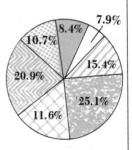

Many men over 55 work as school crossing guards and bridge tenders, constituting over half of all these workers. Some farm, and others work in food or cleaning service occupations.

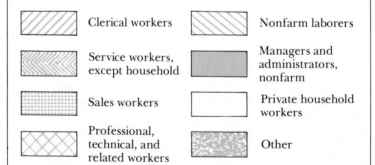

Clerical workers	Nonfarm laborers
Service workers, except household	Managers and administrators, nonfarm
Sales workers	Private household workers
Professional, technical, and related workers	Other

Source: U.S. Department of Labor, Bureau of Labor Statistics, *Occupational Outlook Quarterly* (Washington, D.C.: Government Printing Office, Summer 1979.)

few years, and even beef for dinner have rapidly become out-and-out luxuries. For countless families, the only way to obtain these now-elusive extravagances has been to find a source of additional income. And for most of these families, that has meant Mom goes out to get a paying job.

Yet it's certainly not only married people heading that increasingly atypical "typical American family" who find themselves in a financial bind. Single heads of households (usually unmarried or divorced women who receive little, if any, child support) are perpetually strapped. So are students — young people in their teens or early twenties who often must provide at least a portion of their support in addition to attending classes and studying at home. Older teenagers and young adults who plan to continue their formal education, for example, must contend with tuition, room and board payments, and the cost of books for classes. Even if a student has parents who are willing and able to pick up most of the tab or has found other sources of financial assistance, there is still the matter of everyday living expenses. Most of those aren't covered by financial grants. Younger teenagers, such as the sixteen-year-old who must buy his own clothes or the thirteen-year-old who must pay for her own record albums or roller skates, need to earn quite a bit of money, too.

Today's families and young students certainly are hard-pressed for money. Yet the group that unquestionably suffers most in periods of high inflation is senior citizens, particularly those living on fixed incomes. Clearly, yesterday's comfortable "nest egg for the future" barely covers today's food, rent, and utility payments — if, indeed, it covers all three. Consequently, more and more senior citizens are delaying their retirements, and growing numbers of men and women over fifty-five, and even over sixty-five, are looking for work.

Then Why Don't They Work Full-Time? For Many Reasons

With economic need squarely behind the trends to find work, get back to work, and stay at work longer, it would seem that most people in need of more cash (with the obvious exception of students) would seek full-time jobs — positions that offer them the greatest opportunity to increase their incomes. Yet as we have already seen, three times as many workers have opted for part-time as for full-time schedules. Why? The answer is twofold: (1) many *need* to work part-time rather than full-time, and (2) many *want* to work fewer than thirty-five hours per week.

Let's take yet another look at the largest group of part-timers, women, to see the wide range of reasons they may choose to work part-time.

As I indicated earlier, today's average female part-time worker is the mother of preschool or school-age children. Therefore, child raising takes up at least a portion of her day. If other family income is sufficient to meet regular expenses, she may wish to devote the bulk of her time to mothering and to spend only a few hours each day at a paying job.

On the other hand, the mother of a preschool child may find after a short while that she has had enough of full-time parenting. Having spent considerable time at home with a baby, or countless hours chasing after her own (and her friends') two- or three-year-olds, she may begin to view a few hours away from the house each day as the only way to preserve her sanity.

By contrast, the older mother (whose children are somewhat more self-sufficient) may find that a part-time job offers the best way to enter or re-enter the job market with a minimum of disruption to other family members. And for women of all ages with children of all ages, a part-time job provides a way to keep professional knowledge current or job skills sharp until it is feasible to resume full-time employment.

To find an example of a young mother who works part-time for several of these reasons, I needed to look no farther than next door, to my neighbor, Roberta Trachtman. For several years Roberta, thirty-one, had held a job teaching Spanish in the New York City public schools. As the city's fiscal problems became acute and teachers began to find pink slips in their mailboxes, Roberta recognized that she, too, could soon be laid off. One day she learned of an opportunity to teach English as a second language for one semester, at night, at Queens College. She decided to apply for the position.

"I didn't know how much longer I'd have my job," Roberta recalls, "and at least this was a way to make some money. What's more, I'd taken several courses in teaching English to foreign students during my master's degree program, so the opportunity to get some practical experience seemed ideal." Roberta got the job and for one difficult semester worked full-time during the day and then rushed off to teach the college course at night. It was hectic, she says, but worthwhile.

Two years later, she was again offered the teaching post at Queens College. But by this time Roberta had lost her full-time job and was expecting a child. Understandably, when the job offer came, she had mixed reactions about accepting it. "Going back to Queens meant starting just six weeks after the baby was born," she recalls. "But I realized that there weren't any other teaching jobs around, and that I'd probably be smart to take it."

Looking back on her decision, Roberta now realizes just how smart she was. Public school positions in the New York metropolitan area are still difficult to obtain, but Roberta has been working steadily for the last few years. She teaches two morning classes per week during the fall, spring, and summer semesters, and earns almost $7000 a year. "I guess I'd prefer to work full-time once Allison is in school for the whole day," she says. "But right now, my schedule works out well. I teach while she's in nursery school." Not only has Roberta been able to earn money while spending most of her time with her young daughter, but her part-time job has enabled her to keep both her teaching and her language skills sharp until she does resume full-time work.

Teri Conway, of Santa Monica, California, is another young woman whose switch to a part-time work schedule coincided with the assumption of a new role in her life. Teri, twenty-four, had been supporting herself for five years, working as a full-time secretary at UCLA (the University of California at Los Angeles). Then she decided to enroll as a student, so she applied for and got a part-time job as an insurance assistant at the school's student health insurance department. She takes eight credits' worth of courses each quarter and works twenty hours per week processing insurance applications and explaining policy regulations to students. Teri earns $5.50 an hour, which enables her to continue paying her own way while she attends school.

Unlike Roberta and Teri, who are working part-time during transitional periods in their lives, Elvira Oglesdy of Chicago once figured that her days of gainful employment were over for good. For fifteen years Elvira had worked as a mail analyst at Chicago's Bankers Life and Casualty Company. At the age of sixty-five, she retired. Six years later, and quite unexpectedly, she got a call from a retirement counselor at the bank. The woman asked Elvira if she would be interested in coming back to the bank to share the job of receptionist with two other women. Each of them, the counselor explained, would work one full week every three weeks.

Since Elvira had been just "taking it easy" since her retirement, the opportunity to get back to a stimulating work environment and to earn some extra cash appealed to her, she says. Today Elvira goes to the bank every three weeks. She answers the phone and opens mail for a busy executive. She says she likes the work and the opportunity it gives her to interact with other people. Moreover, she likes the $4.08 an hour that she earns — a wage that helps her meet today's living expenses.

Elvira Oglesdy originally stopped working because retiring at sixty-five seemed "the thing to do." Many older citizens, however, decide they *don't* want to give up their careers or jobs just because they turn sixty-five or seventy, even if they are fortunate enough to be able to afford to do so.

Silvia Gronich was sixty-three years old the last time she looked for work. Formerly the manager of a bookstore chain's art gallery, Silvia had lost her job as the result of company reorganization. Fortunately, her financial situation wasn't critical, so for a while Silvia was spending her time doing volunteer work that she enjoyed.

Then one day, she remembers, she was taking the bus home to her Upper East Side apartment in Manhattan when she looked out the window and noticed that a new art gallery was about to open in her neighborhood. "I thought to myself,

'That place is absolutely enormous. They *must* need help.' "
So as soon as she got home, Silvia picked up the phone and
called the gallery. "They told me they'd already talked to all
the people they planned to interview, but suggested that I
send in a résumé for future reference. I quickly replied, 'I
live so close, why don't I just come in right now?' " Silvia was
hired as a full-time salesperson that afternoon.

Several years later, when the gallery opened a branch in the
SoHo district of Manhattan, the management wanted Silvia to
switch to the downtown gallery. "I wasn't wild about the idea
of having to travel, so I told them that I would switch but that
I wanted to work part-time," she recalls. "They knew how old
I was, so they thought my request was a reasonable one. Besides, what could they say?" She chuckles. "I'm pretty good at
what I do."

Today, at age seventy, Silvia works three days a week at the
Circle Gallery in SoHo. She earns a commission of 10 percent
against a draw of $21 a day. ("No gallery pays much," she
notes with a sigh. "But I can't complain. The last few years,
I've really done quite well.") During her days off, she pursues
a number of different activities. One of them is studying nine-
teenth- and twentieth-century art at Hunter College. "I have
to keep up," she explains. "I've got to know what's happening
in the field." And how long does the energetic Silvia plan to
remain in the field and on the job? "Oh, I don't know." She
laughs, as though the thought of retiring had never entered
her mind. "I guess until I can't maneuver."

Like Silvia Gronich, many senior citizens choose to remain
actively employed indefinitely. Some would like to ease into
retirement. Still others, like Elvira Oglesdy, simply want to fill
their remaining years with stimulating, challenging, or otherwise satisfying activity. And some, of course, wouldn't slow
down at all if it were not for physical problems that prevent
them from working an eight-hour day or a five-day week.
Philip Kaplan, a retired vice-president of a Connecticut oil
company, falls into this category. After retiring, he took a
part-time job teaching business education at a Windsor Locks,
Connecticut, junior high school. The seventy-three-year-old
former executive would never have thought of giving up this

new career if worsening eye problems had not recently forced him to curtail many of his activities.

Physical limitations also shape the work schedules of still another group of Americans: the handicapped, people of all ages who frequently opt for part-time jobs. Clearly, discrimination and lack of access to public buildings and transportation are two of the biggest obstacles many handicapped people face in trying to find employment of any kind. However, because of disabilities caused by illness or injury, some men and women would be forced to forgo full-time work even if these obstacles were removed. For example, they might be unable to work more than several hours a day without suffering discomfort or fatigue; or their incapacities might make it difficult for them to travel during rush hours. And sometimes, of course, the need for ongoing medical treatment or therapy may limit their availability for full-time work.

S. Tapper Bragg, of Manhasset, New York, is one handicapped person who has found that part-time work fulfills many of his needs. Afflicted with cerebral palsy, thirty-four-year-old Tapper is confined to a wheelchair and has the use of only one arm. Yet this determined young man attended Hofstra University and earned not only a bachelor's degree in political science, but a law degree and a master's degree in social science as well.

Since 1977, Tapper has worked as the coeditor and principal writer of *Family Law Commentator,* a bimonthly newsletter for lawyers which deals with domestic relations law, developments pertaining to separation agreements and alimony, child custody, adoption, and related subjects. Tapper puts in from twenty to twenty-five hours a week researching and writing the newsletter. For each issue, he earns $150. The pay, he admits, is extremely low. But Tapper points out that he's glad to have the chance to do work that interests him. "Also," he adds, "there are other psychic rewards. In this job I feel I'm able to make a contribution." Fortunately, his experience and hard work are beginning to pay off monetarily as well. Tapper was recently hired to compile an exhaustive index of legal articles for a New York law firm. For the additional work, he is making $7 an hour.

Besides women, students, senior citizens, and handicapped people, there are others for whom part-time work is the best work. One group consists of the nation's gifted artists and performers — painters and sculptors, playwrights and other writers, musicians, actors, and dancers — people who aspire to careers in the fine or performing arts yet who recognize that until they do make it big, they must find a way to pay their bills.

In her "Careers" column in the March 15, 1978, *New York Times,* Elizabeth M. Fowler described many of these men and women.

> . . . thousands of young people right out of college who are aiming for careers in dance, the theater, art, music or novel writing are part-timers in more prosaic fields. The jobs offer variety and experience, along with the rent money. More than that, the limited hours give the artistic ones the time they need to audition, practice and generally keep themselves free to take advantage of the ever-hoped-for "big break."

One young woman who currently works part-time while dreaming of a career on the stage or screen is twenty-four-year-old Stephanie Taylor of Los Angeles. Since she was thirteen years old, Stephanie has worked as an actress, primarily in TV commercials. She still does commercials, but now she also performs in plays put on by All Right Productions, a new Los Angeles repertory company for black actors.

To support herself, Stephanie works as the assistant athletic academic coordinator at the University of Southern California, counseling college athletes who may be having scholastic or other difficulties. The position pays $600 a month for twenty to thirty hours a week. In addition to this job, Stephanie puts in a few hours each week doing secretarial work at her church, for which she receives $200 a month. And on Saturdays, she teaches ballet to a group of underprivileged children — boys and girls who otherwise might not have the opportunity to take dance lessons. There are some twenty kids in her classes each week; Stephanie charges them $1 per lesson. "That job," she says with a laugh, "is for gasoline money." Yet Stephanie is quick to point out that she, like Tapper Bragg and so many other part-timers, enjoys the feeling that her part-time work "makes a difference." Most of the aspiring actors and actresses that Stephanie knows aren't quite as lucky. Almost all of them, she says, are making ends meet by waiting on tables in Los Angeles restaurants.

> *"A theatrical producer, to many people, is a middle-aged man with manicured nails who rides around town in a chauffeured limousine with a gorgeous blonde on his arm. He is often rich to begin with, or if not, has made a pile of money since he started producing . . . And then there is Joan Stein. She is one of the producers of the hit Off-Broadway comedy, 'Table Settings,' at the Chelsea Theater Center. She is 27 years old, rides around town on the subway, and supports herself by working four nights a week as a waitress. She averages between $50 and $70 a night, including tips."*
> — JUDY KLEMESRUD, "A Broadway Producer Who Moonlights as a Waitress," *New York Times,* June 18, 1980.

The last group of people who regularly choose part-time work is certainly the smallest; yet thanks to support from women's organizations and from women themselves, this group should be expanding in the future. Who's in it? Fathers — men who want to participate actively in the raising of their children and who are willing and able to arrange their schedules to allow time for parenting.

Adam Schesch, thirty-seven, is one of the members of this small segment of the part-time work force. Adam is a social service planner for the Wisconsin Department of Health and Social Services. He is also a divorced father who has partial custody of his eight-year-old son, Aaron. In order to spend as much time as possible with Aaron and to pursue his studies at the University of Wisconsin, where he is a Ph.D. candidate, Adam works twenty hours a week: full days on Monday and

Tuesday and a half-day each Wednesday. He earns $11,000 a year.

Adam feels that working part-time is terrific, and believes that many men would benefit from adopting more flexible work schedules. "Men are way behind women in changing their roles," he says. "They simply haven't taken advantage of all the new opportunities that are open to them." Adam does admit, however, that the financial pressures of working part-time have been burdensome for him and that he may soon be forced to increase the number of hours he puts in each week. But his long-range plans are clear. "Eventually, I would like to teach," Adam says, "but I don't think I'd ever want to hold a full-time job."

Who works part-time? The answer is, all kinds of people: men and women; people in their teens, twenties, and seventies; single, married, divorced, and widowed people; parents and nonparents; students and future film stars.

What are their reasons for working part-time? Some have to. Most want to. For many, it's a little of both.

The Jobs They Hold

So far, we have met only a handful of part-time workers. As you can see, they hold diverse (and sometimes multiple) part-time jobs. Let's recapitulate for a moment. We've seen individuals teaching English to foreign students and dance to ghetto children, handling health insurance claims at a college, working as a receptionist at a bank, editing a legal magazine and compiling indexes for a New York law firm, counseling college athletes, acting in a repertory company and doing secretarial work for a church, selling prints and sculpture for a Manhattan art gallery, and devising social welfare programs for Wisconsin citizens who have developmental disabilities. That's quite a variety of jobs for seven people to be holding!

Now take a look at the table on pages 20–23 to see the wide spectrum of jobs that other part-timers hold. Of course, none of the occupations described in the last paragraph would be listed quite as specifically in the table. For example, Silvia Gronich's job, selling works by some of today's best-known artists in a top gallery in one of the most exciting art centers in the world, would probably fall under the heading "sales clerks, retail trade." Jobs in the legal field or in social welfare agencies, such as those held by Tapper Bragg and Adam Schesch, would be classified under that catchall heading, "other." (Interestingly, many of the well-paid part-timers you'll meet in the chapter "Today's Best Part-Time Jobs" would find their jobs lumped together under the "other" heading, too.) But at least the table does indicate that part-timers work in virtually every field, which is absolutely true. It also gives you an idea of the fields that are most and least hospitable to part-time workers.

Now look at the numbers. Those in the first column aren't all that exciting, but move over to columns two and three and it gets a bit more interesting. For instance, on the second line you can see that librarians make up only a tiny proportion of the nation's part-time work force (.3 percent). Yet 23.7 percent of all librarians work part-time, which gives you some insight into the likelihood of finding a part-time job if you happen to be or plan to become a librarian. Similarly, only .1 percent of the nation's part-timers work as dental hygienists. But of all the dental hygienists in the country, 41.2 percent work part-time, which indicates that opportunities probably abound.

At the same time that you're looking at the job titles and percentages, notice that an extremely high proportion of part-timers work at low-paying jobs. Taken all together, for example, the lucrative professional, technical, managerial, and craft occupations employ only 20.6 percent of all part-timers. But clerical workers alone account for 22.9 percent. Many of the jobs listed in this table seem to be the kinds of positions that people take only when they can't get other work. Few individuals, it seems safe to assume, aspire to careers as counter clerks, private household workers, or gas-station attendants.

This leads us to the last part of our overview of the part-time alternative: a realistic evaluation of the advantages and disadvantages of working part-time. In the next chapter, you'll see how part-time opportunities have developed over the past

Occupations of Part-Time Workers	Voluntary Part-Time Employment 1976	Voluntary Part-Time as Percent of Total Part-Time Employment	Voluntary Part-Time as Percent of Occupational Employment
TOTAL	13,508,543	100.0	15.2
Professional, technical	1,792,558	13.3	12.9
Librarians	43,460	.3	23.7
Registered nurses	264,576	2.0	23.9
Dental hygienists	13,609	.1	41.2
College teachers	115,812	.9	20.6
Elementary school teachers	174,820	1.3	12.1
Preschool and kindergarten teachers	85,689	.6	38.8
Secondary school teachers	109,268	.8	9.2
Other teachers, except college, not elsewhere classified*	135,409	1.0	56.7
Athletes	44,030	.3	41.1
Musicians and composers	82,786	.6	53.4
Other	723,099	5.4	8.4
Managers and administrators, except farm	513,691	3.8	5.3
Salesworkers	1,406,176	10.4	25.8
Demonstrators	62,773	.5	64.1
Peddlers	137,176	1.0	60.4
Newspaper carriers and vendors	81,679	.6	74.9
Real estate agents, brokers	83,914	.6	18.2

	Voluntary Part-Time Employment 1976	Voluntary Part-Time as Percent of Total Part-Time Employment	Voluntary Part-Time as Percent of Occupational Employment
Sales clerks, retail trade	850,932	6.3	39.3
Other	189,702	1.4	7.9
Clerical workers	3,076,812	22.8	19.7
Bookkeepers	422,483	3.1	26.1
Cashiers	569,984	4.2	41.2
Counter clerks, except food	77,687	.6	23.3
Library assistants and attendants	78,108	.6	54.6
Receptionists	139,710	1.0	26.9
Secretaries	566,309	4.2	17.2
Teacher aides	183,110	1.4	56.3
Typists	203,857	1.5	20.2
Other	835,564	6.2	11.9
Craft workers	474,606	3.5	4.1
Operatives, except transport	594,766	4.4	5.9
Dressmakers, except factory	54,780	.4	37.0
Garageworkers, gas station att.	134,352	1.0	30.7
Other	405,634	3.0	4.3
Transport equipment operatives	297,974	2.2	8.9
Bus drivers	119,936	.9	36.8
Delivery and route workers	64,003	.5	11.8
Other	114,035	.8	4.6

Occupations of Part-Time Workers	Voluntary Part-Time Employment 1976	Voluntary Part-Time as Percent of Total Part-Time Employment	Voluntary Part-Time as Percent of Occupational Employment
Laborers, except farm	789,867	5.9	18.4
Gardeners, groundskeepers	220,828	1.6	28.5
Stockhandlers	307,439	2.3	36.8
Other	261,600	1.9	9.7
Farmers and farm managers	161,093	1.2	10.0
Farm laborers, supervisors	380,931	2.8	27.9
Service workers†	3,354,017	24.8	30.3
Janitors and other cleaning service workers	561,929	4.2	24.3
Bartenders	67,959	.5	22.4
Dining room attendants	117,451	.9	52.9
Cooks†	349,149	2.6	32.3
Dishwashers	132,074	.9	47.4
Food counter, fountain workers	256,408	1.9	63.1
Waiters and waitresses	601,198	4.5	44.3
Dental assistants	39,157	.3	29.7
Attendants, recreation and amusement	84,852	.6	43.7
Child care workers†	146,677	1.1	36.0
Hairdressers and cosmetologists	169,473	1.3	34.1

	Voluntary Part-time Employment 1976	Voluntary Part-time as Percent of Total Part-time Employment	Voluntary Part-time as Percent of Occupational Employment
Crossing guards and bridge tenders	43,296	.3	69.8
Other	784,393	5.8	20.4
Private household workers	649,794	4.8	51.0
Child care workers	253,691	1.9	50.0
Housekeepers	47,621	.4	41.8
Servants	328,661	2.4	53.7
Other	19,821	.2	49.6

*Most workers in this category are music or dance teachers.
†Except private household workers.
Note: This table is based on the 1976 Survey of Income and Education; data tabulated by BLS.
Source: U.S. Department of Labor, Bureau of Labor Statistics, *Occupational Outlook Quarterly* (Washington, D.C.: Government Printing Office, Summer 1979).

few decades. You'll also see encouraging projections for their future growth. Right now, though, let's consider part-time work as it is today.

The Part-Time Pros and Cons

The Good Points . . .

What comes to mind when you think of the advantages of a part-time job? More free time? Flexibility? If so, you've hit on the primary attractions a part-time job offers. Such employment affords you more time to tend to your responsibilities as a wife or husband, daughter or son, mother or father, homemaker, student, or any combination of these. It lets you work while you earn your degree. It allows you to keep your job skills sharp while you enjoy watching your preschooler discover the world. It lets you maintain contact with coworkers while you relax and pursue leisure activities. It gives you the opportunity to work in community or other voluntary organizations. It lets you sign up for a weekly Tuesday morning tennis game, or a Wednesday afternoon cooking class, or perhaps Thursdays at the "Y" for an hour of swimming. It lets you spend time with family members and friends, people you otherwise might not get to see. It gives you some time for yourself — time to read, sew, take up photography, whatever.

Sure, people who work full-time handle their other responsibilities. But they live in a constant state of battle with the clock. Since weekdays are usually accounted for, such personal activities as pursuing an advanced degree, taking occasional adult education classes, or participating in a physical fitness program must be scheduled during evenings and weekends, after the kids, the cooking, the cleaning, and other household chores have been tended to. And of course we all want time to visit with friends and family, or just sit around and relax — "But not this Saturday, I'm afraid. I've got a dentist appointment in the morning, and then I have to pick up the clothes at the cleaners and take the kids shopping for sneakers. Besides, there's nothing in the refrigerator, the house is a mess, and Susie has a soccer game at three-thirty."

To say the least, full-timers live on incredibly tight schedules, particularly if they also happen to be mothers. Making choices is an ongoing necessity, a way of life. There is never enough time for everything you want to do.

No, there's no getting around it. Having a part-time job does let you do more things. Moreover, it lets you do those things while you still reap all of the job satisfactions that full-time workers say make working worthwhile — namely, the pleasure, fulfillment, and recognition that most jobs provide.[9]

---

9. See Morton Hunt, "Making a Living Versus Making a Home," *Redbook* 150 (April 1978): 70. One of the more interesting findings of this survey of married women was that two out of every three who worked, including those in low-paying jobs, said they would miss their jobs if they were to leave them for one reason or another.

It is little wonder, then, that when *Redbook* magazine surveyed married women on the importance that work has in their lives, more than 80 percent maintained that if money was no object and child care was not a problem, they would still choose to work, "though many of those who now work full time would prefer to work part time."[10]

Nor is it surprising that when the National Commission on Working Women surveyed so-called nonworking mothers in 1979, half of the women reported that they would take a job outside the home if it was part-time. Part-time work *does* have its benefits.

. . . and the Bad

Of course, there are two sides to the proverbial coin. Not everything about working part-time is sunshine and flowers. For many people putting in fewer than thirty-five hours per week at paying jobs, there are decided disadvantages. Most of the negative aspects of part-time work, as we'll soon see, center around money — or the lack thereof. First, however, it is appropriate to look at one of the more frequently voiced problems of many part-time workers. What is it? The answer may surprise you: lack of time!

THE SUPERWOMAN SYNDROME

As we have already seen, most women who work outside the home do so because they need money. Over 14.6 million women today are the sole support of their families. Other women contribute almost as much to the family income as their husbands do. And there are some, particularly part-time workers, whose "extra" income makes the difference between keeping up with the skyrocketing cost of living and falling a bit behind. Their income may or may not help pay the monthly bills, but it definitely does subsidize extra family purchases such as new appliances or vacations. Yet even today, despite the fact that 50 percent of American women work

---

10. Ibid.

outside the home, work within the home remains largely their responsibility, too.

"Now we get the jobs, all right, *all* the jobs — at home, with the kids and at work," complained Tina Oakland, director of the Women's Resource Center at UCLA, in a May 19, 1980, cover story in *Newsweek* magazine. As the *Newsweek* article pointed out and many experts agree, balancing work at the office with work at home is one of the critical problems faced by all working women today, and it promises to be one of the major social issues of the 1980s.

However, there is another aspect of the so-called Superwoman problem that bears directly on women who work part-time — those who have the seemingly ideal situation. It has to do with their husbands' attitudes about the work they do and about the work that must still be done at home.

Dr. Suzanne McCall, professor of marketing at East Texas State University, recently surveyed 216 husbands in the Dallas–Fort Worth area on their attitudes about their wives' earnings.[11] What she found was rather enlightening. The typical husband, it seems, is happy with his wife's job if she earns almost as much as, as much as, or even more than he does. However, if she earns substantially *less* than he does, he is not very pleased at all. The least satisfied husbands, Dr. McCall found, were those married to women who worked part-time and who earned only that "little extra."

When a wife works part-time, all of the inconveniences in the home, or at least many of them, still are there, but her income isn't enough to make them tolerable, Dr. McCall explained. Therefore, the husband feels little compulsion to help take care of either the house or the children. Even more

---

11. See Nancy Baker, "Does He Respect Your Paycheck?" *Working Woman* 5 (May 1980): 46.

interesting is that under similar circumstances, the wife agrees. The more she earns compared to her husband's salary, Dr. McCall found, the more she expects her husband's participation. On the other hand, if she earns very little (as is the case with too many part-time workers today), she feels she has no right to demand his help. "The wife still is operating under a cultural guilt complex," Dr. McCall discovered. "She says to herself, 'If I'm not justifying my working outside the home by making a lot of money, I'd better take care of the home, too.' "[12]

Again, it is not the amount of the wife's earnings that determines the man's or woman's attitudes about who assumes the domestic chores. Rather, it is the proportion of the total family income that a woman brings home. As a result, the "I should do everything" compulsion exists at all economic levels, Dr. McCall found.

Bonney Sheahan, a $12,000-a-year part-time assistant program director of the History and Philosophy of Science Program at the National Science Foundation in Washington, sums up the Superwoman crush as it pertains to her and to other part-timers: "Women who work full-time generally make some compromises. They hire housekeepers or babysitters or put their kids into day-care centers. They make a definite decision to cut certain things out of their lives. But for a mother working part-time, there's an equal and full commitment to do everything."

Extra time is the attraction named by most people when they explain why they would prefer a part- to a full-time schedule. However, for many mothers, taking a twenty- or thirty-hour-a-week job simply means having twenty or thirty fewer hours in which to do all of the household work they did before becoming income producers. And as Dr. McCall's survey indicates, redefining and renegotiating household tasks is infinitely harder if those twenty or thirty hours don't produce a significant proportion of the family income.

Therefore, the mother contemplating a switch from a full- to a part-time schedule, or the one planning to take a first

12. Ibid.

part-time job, is liable to face a problem before she talks to her boss or goes for her first job interview. If she doesn't establish appropriate work-division plans before she begins a part-time work schedule, she is likely to find herself in the "Mom still (or again) does everything" bind. Furthermore, lack of support from her husband and from other family members will leave her not with the extra time she had hoped for, but with a great deal of anger and a tremendous potential for family conflict.

Obviously, this particular set of circumstances doesn't pertain to all would-be part-timers. But it is a serious problem faced by many of those within the largest group of part-time job-holders: women. And though the problem of having as much or more to do but less time in which to do it isn't an inherent disadvantage of part-time work, it is a negative by-product of part-time work that countless women now endure.

LOWER EARNINGS
One problem faced almost universally by part-time workers of all ages, both sexes, and every marital situation is reduced earning power. Everyone knows that if you work less, odds are you earn less. Yet the discrepancy between full- and part-time earnings is more than just a matter of the total number of hours worked each year. For example, even among people who work full-time, that all-too-familiar disparity between the wages paid to men and those paid to women is evident. Women still earn less than sixty cents for every dollar earned by men. Today's average female college graduate still earns only as much as the average male eighth-grade graduate does. Yet as labor expert John Owen points out, it's not only women who earn less; it's all part-timers. Once you account for differences in education and experience, race, family status, and student status, male part-timers earn 30 percent less than their full-time counterparts, and female part-timers earn 17 percent less than women who put in a thirty-five-hour week.[13]

---

13. See John D. Owen, "Why Part-time Workers Tend to Be in Low-Wage Jobs," *Monthly Labor Review* 101 (June 1978): 11–14.

In 1979, part-timers of both sexes earned, on the average, 29 percent less than full-timers did.[14]

Why the disparity? Because most of the nation's 23 million part-time workers are concentrated in the lower-paying fields — clerical jobs, retail sales, private household work, and so on. Women (and some men) work in these fields either because they lack education, experience, or skills, or simply because they don't have the opportunity to get better jobs, regardless of their qualifications. Furthermore, employers have traditionally been able to get away with paying lower salaries to part-timers of both sexes because many of the workers have traditionally been willing to trade flexible work schedules for low pay.[15]

> *"I'm looking for a part-time job — one with evening hours so my husband can babysit . . . Oh, here's one: 'Retail Sales: Full or Part Time' at a department store . . . 'How,' my husband asks, 'can a girl with your education work for $3.25 an hour?' "*
>
> — CAMILLE BELOLAN, former teacher, "We're Broke on $25,000 a Year," *New York Times*, March 30, 1980.

We should note that it is not only women who have been willing to trade pay for flexibility. Students often make the same exchange, especially if the work offers not only flexibility but experience in their chosen field. As almost any college student can attest, the best on-campus jobs often pay little more than the minimum wage. The more sought-after internship programs, which enable students to work in their chosen fields in return for academic credit and/or salary, usually pay next to nothing, or nothing. For example, in 1980, Women in Communications, Inc., conducted a survey of college intern-

14. "Worktime: The Traditional Workweek and Its Alternatives," *1979 Employment and Training Report of the President,* p. 86.
15. Owen, "Low-Wage Jobs," pp. 11–14.

ship programs at newspapers, TV and radio stations, public relations firms, and advertising agencies around the country. The survey revealed that only 56 percent of the interns earned any salary at all. (Interestingly, the study revealed that some colleges actually prohibit students from earning both a salary and college credits.)

Therefore, because most part-timers are women, who earn less to begin with, and because most part-timers are employed in low-paying fields, it stands to reason that when the average wages of all the nation's part-time workers are calculated, they are going to be low. They are.

> *"Equal pay for equal work . . . turned out to fall short of helping women in the mostly female, non-unionized jobs of the pink-collar ghetto . . . What did 'equal pay' do for the waitress or secretary, for instance, who was getting the same low salary as the woman working next to her?"*
>
> — GLORIA STEINEM, "The Way We Were — And Will Be," *Ms.*, December 1979.

FEWER FRINGE BENEFITS

Part-time workers often face an economic hardship other than lower annual and hourly wages: fewer company-paid fringe benefits. Since benefits can account for as much as 35 percent of a worker's salary, the loss can be significant. Today, slightly more than half of all part-time workers receive fringe benefits of some sort. The rest get none. In fact, as Dr. Stanley Nollen and his fellow researchers at Georgetown University found out, some companies pointedly hire part-time workers so they won't have to provide a full package of benefits. Here is a list of who offers what:

> Among users of part-time employment, about 44 percent paid no fringe benefits to part-time workers. About 10 percent offered only prorated vacation and sick leave, while an additional 12 percent offered vacation and sick leave plus some form of

group life and health insurance. Roughly a third of all users made the full range of fringe benefits, including pension benefits, available to part-time workers.[16]

Some people feel that because working part-time is their only alternative, they must accept the attendant economic disadvantages philosophically. They reason that whatever pay and benefits they do receive are more than they would be getting if they didn't have a job in the first place. However, if full-time work is an option and someone chooses to work part-time, that individual must recognize that his or her choice could be an expensive one. Buying leisure time with forfeited income and benefits can be costly indeed.

LIMITED JOB OPENINGS AND PROMOTIONS

Then, of course, there is the matter of what types of jobs are available and whether they offer potential for advancement. Everyone knows that part-time jobs in the lowest-paying fields are always available, and that department stores and luncheonettes are constantly looking for help. However, many companies are not receptive to hiring part-time workers. Of those that are, many hire part-timers only at the very lowest levels in their companies — the least responsible jobs. What's more, even among companies that do hire part-time workers at higher levels, few offer possibilities for advancement. Their assumption, as Adam Schesch of the Wisconsin Department of Health and Social Services explains, is that part-timers simply aren't serious about building careers; if they were, they obviously wouldn't be working part-time.

In considering employees for promotion, managers take into account the degree of loyalty they feel the employees have to the company. As the Georgetown research team found, loyalty is simply not expected of part-time workers. Part-timers are viewed as "different" by their employers, even if they hold the same jobs that full-time workers hold. "This is why part-

16. Stanley D. Nollen, Brenda B. Eddy, and Virginia H. Martin, *Permanent Part-time Employment: The Manager's Perspective* (New York: Praeger, 1978), p. 42.

time employment is so rarely found among management positions," the authors reported. "Since part-time workers are perceived as uninterested in advancement, and not particularly loyal, it is unthinkable for them to hold management jobs, which usually result from promotion from within and which require unusual attachment to the enterprise."[17] As a rule, companies don't view part-timers as having much long-range promise. Employers see them as people whose motivation and commitment are questionable, whose loyalty is suspect, and who are likely to be around only for a while, anyway.[18]

Ironically, almost every study ever done on the subject of part-time workers has indicated that once part-timers are hired, managers find they perform as well as, and often *better* than, full-timers. Part-timers also exhibit more job satisfaction, less absenteeism and tardiness, and lower turnover than full-time workers do.[19] Yet employers continue to view part-time workers as being "different." Unfortunately, as a result, employment and promotion opportunities for part-timers are also "different" — which usually means worse.

Susan Tijada, who has worked for three years as a part-time editor and writer and one year as a part-time public information specialist with the Environmental Protection Agency in Washington, D.C., expresses the anti–part-timer bias she has felt throughout her career: "Mobility is limited. There are only a certain number of jobs you can apply for. And as you advance, the number of opportunities gets less and less. I feel I'm up against the wall in terms of promotion." Susan echoes the sentiments of many part-timers.

> *"Employers still perceive that the truly committed employee arrives at 7 A.M. and leaves at 7 P.M."*
> — LINDA PENNINGTON, vice-president for affirmative action at Citibank. Quoted in *Newsweek*, May 19, 1980.

17. Ibid., p. 35.
18. Ibid., pp. 25–37.
19. See Nollen, *New Patterns of Work*, p. 6.

FEW FIELDS WELCOME PART-TIMERS

If most companies and many employers are reluctant to hire and/or promote part-time workers, there are some industries that are virtually closed to those who would like to work fewer than thirty-five hours per week. All the blue-collar fields are examples, particularly mining, manufacturing, and rail transportation. As the *1979 Employment and Training Report of the President* indicates, "Most employers insist that their expensive plants and equipment can be fully and smoothly operated only by full-time workers. Employers," the report continues, "have been generally unwilling to establish morning or afternoon shifts for part-time workers," or even to hire part-timers for extra or so-called minishifts (after a full day's operation), even though such shifts "would actually increase capital utilization."[20]

Besides feeling that part-timers won't use equipment to its best advantage, many employers, in all industries, believe that hiring part-timers will probably end up costing them more than using only full-timers (despite the evidence that part-timers are paid less and get fewer fringe benefits!). Again, actual surveys of employers of part-time workers show that extra expenses related to recruitment, training, or record keeping are at most insignificant, and that any additional costs are more than made up for by the benefits we mentioned previously.[21]

Many employers continue to have erroneous or exaggerated ideas about part-time workers and the costs of hiring, training, and promoting them. Yet, unfounded or not, these opinions are largely responsible for the ongoing lack of good jobs and advancement opportunities that part-timers face today.

The following table, based on BLS statistics, shows the industries in which most male and female part-timers were

---

20. "Worktime: The Traditional Workweek and Its Alternatives," *1979 Employment and Training Report of the President,* p. 87.
21. See Nollen, Eddy, and Martin, *Permanent Part-time Employment,* p. 40; Nollen, *New Patterns of Work,* p. 6.

employed in 1977.[22] In the next chapter, you'll find a more detailed examination of current and future opportunities in the goods-producing versus the service-producing sector. For now, though, simply be aware that opportunities for part-time work are concentrated in only a few fields.

Part-Time Workers by Industry, 1980

Industry	Percent of Employees Working Part-Time
Construction	4.9
Manufacturing	3.2
Transportation and public utilities	6.0
Wholesale and retail trade	24.9
Finance, insurance, and real estate	10.4
Service	20.7
Public administration	6.0

Source: U.S. Department of Labor, Bureau of Labor Statistics, "Employment and Unemployment: A Report on 1980," Special Labor Force Report 244 (Washington, D.C.: Government Printing Office, 1981), p. A-32.

Those, then, are the drawbacks of part-time work as it exists in America today. There are many. Yet despite the grim realities of the present, there are indications that circumstances will improve in the future. Why? Because many forces are currently at work to make matters better day by day. Let's take a look at how things got the way they are and why they should be improving. Then we'll begin to consider how you can best ensure that your part-time job will be a good one.

---

22. For an analysis of the industries receptive to part-time workers, see Deutermann and Brown, "Voluntary Part-time Workers," pp. 3–10. Also, for information on the industries that employ female part-timers, see Leon and Bednarzik, "A Profile of Women on Part-time Schedules," pp. 5–6.

The Way
It Was
and Will Be

EARLY IN the first chapter, we noted that the part-time work force has become the fastest-growing segment of the entire labor force. In 1960, one of every ten workers was a part-timer. By 1970, the figure had jumped to one of every eight. Now, it's one of every five. Why such enormous growth? There are several key reasons.

Shift to a Shorter Work Week

The trend toward less time on and more time off the job has been progressing steadily throughout our history. During the eighteenth and nineteenth centuries, the average American put in a twelve-hour day and worked six days a week. Then the total dropped from twelve to ten hours per day, at the beginning of this century. The sixty-hour week remained the norm until the New Deal, when the forty-hour week was established by law. That week officially remains today, unless certain bills that would alter the official work week to five days and thirty-five hours have been passed by Congress since this book went to press.

Today there is considerable pressure to decrease further the number of hours most workers put in. Some labor officials argue that a shortened work week would help alleviate chronic unemployment. Dropping the official forty-hour week to thirty-five hours, they claim, would add an additional five million jobs to the American economy and would help it absorb the ever-increasing numbers of women seeking paid employment. John Owen, labor expert and professor of economics at Wayne State University, maintains that not only might we soon see the thirty-five-hour week become law, but under certain conditions the United States could eventually adopt an even shorter work week: we could move to the four-day, thirty-two-hour schedule.[1]

The Influx of Women to the Labor Force

At the start of the 1960s, one-third of all adult women were in the work force. Today, it's one-half. By the end of the 1980s, almost 60 percent of all women over the age of sixteen will be working outside the home. The movement of women into the labor market, which started as a moderate trend in the early sixties, became by the mid-seventies a phenomenon termed "extraordinary" by Alan Greenspan, chairman of the President's Council of Economic Advisers during the Ford administration.

The importance of the exodus from the kitchen to the office can't be stressed enough. The "working woman," as she has come to be called, has changed the nature of the workplace, the home, and the way we as a nation live. Eli Ginzburg, the Columbia University economist and human resources expert who headed the National Commission for Manpower Policy, has called the growth of the female work force "the single most outstanding phenomenon of our century. It will affect women, men and children, and the cumulative consequences of that will only be revealed in the twenty-first and twenty-second centuries."[2]

The reasons for the incredible rise in the number of female workers have been well documented: (1) the advent of effec-

1. Work in America Institute, Inc., *World of Work Report* (July 1977): 79.
2. Quoted in Robert Lindsey, "Women Entering Job Market at an 'Extraordinary' Pace," *New York Times,* September 12, 1976, pp. 1, 49.

tive birth control and the resulting drop in the number of children born each year; (2) the growing number of female college graduates who have sought careers, postponed marriage, and put off child bearing in the immediate or even near future; (3) the rise in the divorce rate; (4) the startling increase in the number of households headed and supported by women; (5) efforts by women's groups to increase and improve opportunities for female workers; and (6) the overriding and familiar economic imperative — the need to keep up with a cost of living that has more than doubled in the last decade alone. It is largely this last reason that accounts for the fact that four-fifths of all employed women work full-time, even though many indicate that they would prefer to work at part-time jobs.[3]

The relationship of part-time work to the increase in the number of women in the work force is also well documented. Women wishing to combine wage earning with child rearing have always looked for part-time work. Similarly, for those mothers of school-age children who lack suitable child-care alternatives, the part-time schedule has been a necessity. And for older women whose child-rearing responsibilities are behind them, the return to the job market has often been coupled with a desire to pursue the educational or leisure activities that they previously were forced to curtail or forgo altogether.

For many reasons, the number of women in the work force has increased dramatically during the past decade. Yet for those women who hold or seek part-time jobs, the reasons tend to be the same as they always have been.

Shift from a Goods- to a Service-Producing Economy

Hand in hand with the gradual decline in the length of the work week and the remarkable influx of women to the work force has been a slow, steady, yet profound change in the

---

3. See Morton Hunt, "Making a Living Versus Making a Home," *Redbook* 150 (April 1978): 70.

nature of our economy. That change has been a shift from an economic structure that requires most workers to make the *products* we consume to a structure that requires men and women to provide the *services* we need. It has been going on for four decades, and has recently begun to accelerate. It will certainly continue in the future, as automation and improved technology make it possible to turn out more products in less time, with fewer workers actually involved in the manufacturing process.

Where, then, have Americans increasingly found employment? Mostly in the so-called service-producing industries — among them transportation; public utilities; wholesale and retail trade; finance, insurance, and real estate; business and personal services; entertainment and recreation; health care and professional services; and public administration.

The chart on page 39 shows the relative growth of the goods- and the service-producing segments of the economy. As you can see, the trend of the future is quite clear.

What does all of this mean for part-timers? Plenty. But in order to see how it affects those who work part-time, you should first recognize the relationship between the service-producing industries and women. Historically, it has been the service-producing industries rather than the goods-producing fields that have offered the warmest welcome to women. What's more, industries with the largest concentration of women employees have always been the ones most likely to offer good prospects for part-time work.[4] They still are.

Growth of Service Jobs

We've already seen that the service-producing sector includes (among other fields) transportation, government, and wholesale and retail trade. In addition, within this enormous group is a subdivision that stands out as the *single largest growth area* for the 1980s. That subdivision is called, rather confusingly, service jobs. (That's right, "service" jobs within the "service-

---

4. Carol Leon and Robert W. Bednarzik, "A Profile of Women on Part-time Schedules," *Monthly Labor Review* 101 (October 1978): 4–5.

Growth of the Service-Producing Industries

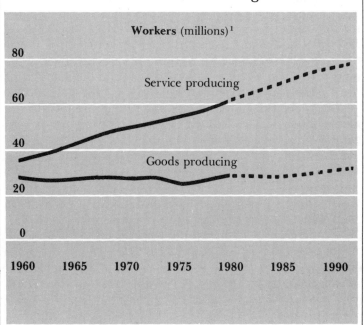

Workers (millions)[1]

Service producing

Goods producing

1960 1965 1970 1975 1980 1985 1990

Service producing:
Transportation
  and public utilities
Trade
Finance, insurance,
  and real estate
Services
Government

Goods producing:
Agriculture
Mining
Contract
  construction
Manufacturing

[1] Wage and salary workers, except for agriculture, which includes self-employed and unpaid family workers.

Source: U.S. Department of Labor, Bureau of Labor Statistics, *Occupational Outlook Handbook,* 1980–81 ed. (Washington, D.C.: Government Printing Office, 1980), p. 19.

producing" sector.) To see exactly what the service fields are and to recognize the familiar activities that are actually classified as services, take a look at the following:

Where Most Part-Time Jobs Will Be: The Services

As women continue to march off to work, as senior citizens stay on the job longer, and as young men and women study and train in order to seek employment, there will be no shortage of work for them. Why? Says Caroline Bird in *The Two-Paycheck Marriage* (New York: Rawson, Wade, 1979), "They will make work for each other."

Consider the services that *you* already use and need. Then think about all of these other job-holders and job-hunters. The Bureau of Labor Statistics predicts that there will be an additional 20 million Americans in the labor market by 1990. Consider all of the business or personal services that *they* will require. But don't stop there. In addition to more Americans in the work force, some 17 million babies and over 4 million immigrants will add to our population during the coming decade. And don't forget about the 20 percent projected growth in the number of Americans over the age of sixty-five. If you think about all of these groups and individuals for a moment, it's fairly easy to predict where many of tomorrow's jobs will be.

That service industries will continue to flourish is an assumption based on the needs of all Americans — rich or poor, old or young, working or unemployed, born here or recently arrived. By 1990, there will be almost 244 million of us. That's a lot of people, with a lot of need for a lot of services.

Here are the major service fields — those, incidentally, that happen to employ the greatest number of part-time workers.

♦ Health care — direct patient care, plus medical, dental, technical, and administrative support.

- Education — for adults as well as for children, and particularly for those with physical or learning disabilities or other special needs.
- Day care — preschool and after-school programs for children of working parents.
- Home services — household maintenance, home repair and improvement, painting, decorating, and so forth.
- Social services — counseling and therapy, public assistance support, services for the elderly and handicapped, and related services.
- Business support services — clerical, legal, advertising and public relations, information and financial services, equipment maintenance and repair, commercial cleaning, and so on.
- Leisure services — travel, sports, recreation and entertainment, and vacations.
- Personal services — beauty and grooming, repair of household appliances, automobile maintenance, care of clothing and personal belongings, and other services related to individual needs.

It's really not critical for you to understand the distinctions that the government makes in categorizing all of these industries. What *is* useful is for you to recognize that according to the Bureau of Labor Statistics, the number of service jobs grew by a whopping 77 percent between 1965 and 1978. By 1990, this group is expected to increase by another 53 percent. In fact, the service subsection is expected to grow *twice as fast* as the rest of the larger service-producing group.[5]

The chart on page 42 will give you a visual indication of just how fast the service group is expected to grow. By 1990, some 8.4 million new service jobs will exist.

---

5. See the *Occupational Outlook Handbook* 1980–81 edition, prepared by the U.S. Department of Labor, Bureau of Labor Statistics (Washington, D.C.: Government Printing Office, 1980), particularly pp. 16–23, for a complete analysis of projected growth of all the various industries.

Why am I dwelling on this particular subsection, when I've already said that part-timers are most likely to find jobs in the larger service-producing sector? Because, as the chart indicates, the greatest sources of potential job openings for people who seek part-time work are within this particular subsection. As you continue reading, you'll see that most of your best opportunities for landing a good part-time job will result from preparing to enter one of the service fields.

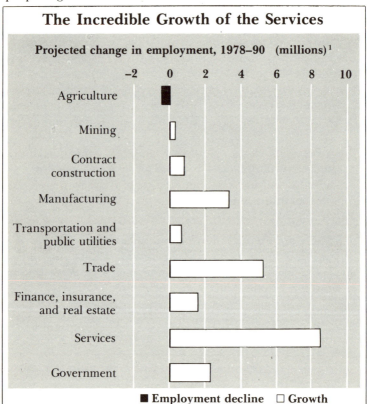

The Incredible Growth of the Services

Projected change in employment, 1978–90   (millions)[1]

■ **Employment decline**   □ **Growth**

[1] Wage and salary workers, except for agriculture, which includes self-employed and unpaid family workers.
Source: U.S. Department of Labor, Bureau of Labor Statistics, *Occupational Outlook Handbook,* 1980–81 ed. (Washington, D.C.: Government Printing Office, 1980), p. 19.

But Will Tomorrow's Part-Timers Get a Better Deal?

There is no question that the number of part-time jobs, particularly in the service industries, will increase dramatically during the coming decade. But will they be better jobs than those offered in the past? Will they pay more? Will they offer established career paths to people who want to advance in their fields? Will part-timers no longer be considered peripheral workers, as they too often are now, but rather be thought of as men and women able to do whatever job needs to be done and willing to give it their best?

An effort to predict whether part-time workers will do better in the future is, of course, based on a number of considerations. Many of the clues offer great encouragement. Some don't.

The Role of Unions

The organization of men and women into labor unions has probably been the single most important factor in raising the standard of living and improving working conditions for most of America's workers. Where it exists, union membership plays a tremendous part in securing better pay and working conditions for part-timers, too.[6]

Consider, for instance, the relationship of women to unions. Today, some 22 percent of female full-timers belong to unions, compared with only 10 percent of female part-timers. The unionized full-timers earn 40 percent more than their nonunionized counterparts. Among part-timers, women who belong to unions earn roughly 50 percent more than those not covered by union contracts, particularly in such fields as retail sales.[7]

Why then is the number of part-timers who belong to unions so low? One reason is that few unions want them. In the chapter "Who Is Hiring and Who Isn't," we will consider

6. Leon and Bednarzik, "A Profile of Women," p. 10.
7. Ibid., pp. 10–11.

in greater detail the reluctance of unions to incorporate more part-timers into their ranks or to welcome the inclusion of part-timers, unionized or not, into the work force at large. For now, simply recognize three of the most often cited objections of union leaders to part-time workers, so you can get an idea of why so much negativity toward part-timers has existed in organized labor.

First, many union leaders believe that the use of part-time workers is likely to cost full-time workers benefits they have already won in previous contracts — for instance, payment of overtime. Second, union leaders fear that part-time work will erode the seniority system, which is at the very heart of the union structure. For example, during recessions and economic downturns, companies (or municipalities) may be forced to lay off workers. Except in extreme cases, such as when an entire plant must be shut down, the last workers hired are the first ones let go; that means that the jobs of senior workers are usually protected. However, if management adopts a work-sharing plan, under which all employees might work on reduced schedules until things got better, senior workers would be in the same position as everyone else. Third, as union leader Patsy Fryman of the Communications Workers of America recently put it, unions fear that the evolution of part-time work would mean "permanent part-time for the full-timer." In other words, all of us might eventually be forced to work part-time schedules, whether we want to or not.

In some cases union fears have been well founded; in other cases they have not. Nevertheless, union opposition to part-time work remains prevalent in our country. Some locals, particularly those representing government employees and retail sales workers, have fought hard for the part-timers in their ranks. In the future, other unions may be willing to pay more attention to the needs of part-timers, especially since unions have lost some of their membership base through declining enlistment. Any courting of part-timers by union officials, however, remains to be seen.

Clearly, union advocacy of the rights of America's 23 million part-time workers has been slow in coming. But in some segments of the work force, it is becoming evident. As more groups, particularly those at the low end of the pay and status scales (clerical workers and household employees, for example), begin to organize themselves, they will undoubtedly be able to secure better pay and working conditions for their members, whether those members work full- or part-time.

A Boost from the Government

Some of the most progressive programs for hiring and promoting part-time workers have emanated from the federal government, and also from a number of state governments. (All of these are examined in the chapter "Who Is Hiring and Who Isn't.") Many of these government programs started out as one- or two-year experiments. Almost all of the pilot programs have been successful and have been continued or expanded. The U.S. government now employs over fifty thousand part-time workers. Moreover, as new studies of these programs are conducted and data are released, word of the advantages found by government managers who have hired part-timers will undoubtedly spread to the private sector.[8]

Uncle Sam has also helped part-timers in ways other than by offering them more and better jobs and compiling data about workers and employers. Laws establishing and sponsor-

---

8. One of the most important examinations of employer attitudes and experiences with part-time workers was sponsored by the Employment and Training Administration of the U.S. Department of Labor. The 1977 report *Permanent Part-time Employment: The Manager's Perspective,* by Stanley D. Nollen, Brenda B. Eddy, and Virginia Martin of the Georgetown University School of Business Administration, examined attitudes of managers in the private sector. The researchers, as mentioned in the first chapter, found that those who do not employ part-timers often expect part-time workers to exhibit low productivity, high absenteeism, and high turnover. However, those hiring part-time workers have usually found that there are benefits rather than liabilities in all three areas.

In its "Policy Recommendations" section, the study also concluded that "almost any job can be successfully scheduled on a part-time basis," and that both the difficulties and minor costs that may be incurred by hiring part-timers are "usually small and relatively easy to manage, or . . . are outweighed by concurrent economic advantages."

ing work-study programs have enabled thousands of college students to help finance their educations by working during and after school hours. Changes in the Social Security law, which now allows senior citizens to earn $6000 a year (instead of $5500) before forfeiting part of their monthly pensions, make part-time work a possibility for many more men and women over the age of sixty-five.

By offering jobs, conducting studies, and passing new legislation, the executive and legislative branches of the U.S. government have done much to improve the lot of part-time workers today and to provide more opportunities for them in the future. Many states have done likewise.

Efforts by Women's Groups

Throughout the country, women's groups, and specifically organizations concerned with better job opportunities for part-timers, labor tirelessly in an attempt to convince local business and government leaders to hire more part-time workers. These groups also conduct studies of part-timers, their employers, and their experiences. They send representatives to local managers to persuade them to fill one job with two people or to try other innovative work-scheduling patterns.

For example, one organization, FOCUS, Inc. (formerly called Focus on Part-time Careers), in Seattle, Washington, recently located a number of professionals working on a part-time basis throughout the Seattle area. The group published a booklet highlighting the part-timers and their jobs, the benefits they receive, and even comments by their supervisors, all for the purpose of proving that high-level jobs can be successfully held on a part-time basis. The booklet also includes a hypothetical conversation with a skeptical employer, in which most of the common questions about hiring part-timers are answered and the misconceptions are cleared up.[9]

Another organization, Catalyst, which is a major national resource center for women and women's groups, also put out

---

9. "Employing Professionals Part-time" is published by FOCUS, Inc., 509 Tenth Avenue East, Seattle, WA 98102; cost: $2.

a booklet designed to help employers overcome real or imagined difficulties in hiring part-time workers. For example, one of the most commonly mentioned reservations about hiring part-timers that employers have is that prorated fringe benefits would be very expensive. So in 1975, the New York–based organization published a booklet entitled "Constructing an Employee Benefit Package for Part-time Workers: How to Calculate an Equitable Benefit Package at No Extra Cost to the Employer."[10]

During the past ten years or so, groups such as these (see "Organizations That Help Part-Timers," page 361) have worked to create many of the top part-time job opportunities that exist today. With their continuing efforts, they are helping pave the way for more and still better part-time jobs in a growing number of U.S. cities.

Wanted: A Change in Attitude

Overcoming the ungrounded fears of certain union leaders that part-timers threaten the jobs and job security of full-time workers is a slow and arduous task. Getting the message to employers that part-timers can be valuable and cost-effective additions to their staffs is a never-ending job, and one that is being done well by government agencies and women's groups. Yet even if these efforts were more successful than they have already been, they still wouldn't be enough to ensure that part-time workers would be more highly regarded, better utilized, or even better paid in the future.

The fact is, the future status of part-time workers is still tied inextricably to the general status of women. Most parttime jobs are held by women. Most fields that offer part-time jobs to anyone are those that already employ women in large numbers. And the sad truth is that in our society, the work women do is simply not valued as highly as that performed by men. Consequently, women continue to earn substantially

10. Available from Catalyst, Inc., 14 East 60th Street, New York, NY 10022; cost: $1.25.

less than their male counterparts.[11] When those same women also happen to be part-timers, they are frequently paid even more poorly. In many fields and in most companies, they remain at the bottom of the organizational heap in low-paying, dead-end jobs.

Two major developments would greatly improve the pay and prospects for all women, and by extension for part-timers. The first is placing a higher value on all of the jobs that have come to be lumped together under the usually disparaging heading "women's work." That, of course, means work in the teaching and caring professions, work that involves nurturing and support, human contact and concern, the maintenance of order and continuity. The second is for women to forgo the "women's fields" and concentrate on entering the better-paying "men's fields" — for example, business, science, and the skilled crafts: the nontraditional fields. These two ideas may seem contradictory; they really are not.

"WOMEN'S WORK"

As author Caroline Bird points out in *The Two-Paycheck Marriage,* "Women have always wanted meaningful work helping people." Economist Helen Axel of The Conference Board, the New York–based business research firm, refers to the prizes women traditionally seek in their work as "psychic rewards." Surveys continue to indicate that most women place family responsibilities above their own ambitions; many have willingly accepted lower pay in exchange for the opportunity to care for their children and their homes. Furthermore, as Bird notes, many women now earn money for performing the same caring and helping activities that women have always done without pay. Therefore, receiving compensation for work that they naturally enjoy doing is viewed by many women almost as an extra benefit. For all of these reasons,

---

11. Nationally, women earn 59 percent of what men earn. In managerial and administrative positions, the figure is 60 percent; in professional and technical jobs, it's 70 percent. For an analysis of why women continue to earn so much less than men, see Froma Joselow, "Salary Survey 1980," *Working Woman* 5 (February 1980): 31–34, 80.

women — and particularly those who want to work part-time — have been extremely easy to exploit.

However, if women expect to continue working in the "women's fields" and also to gain the other work-related benefits — namely money, power, and prestige — they will have to lobby actively for a better attitude about the work they do. By supporting the equal-pay-for-comparable-work idea, for example, they may help bring such "women's occupations" as house cleaning, organizing and filing, and teaching up to the pay levels of jobs that require similar skills but are done by men (janitorial and custodial work, warehouse loading, supervising work shifts). They may also help nurses earn as much as garbage collectors.

Another concrete step toward improving the status of "women's work" would be to encourage more men to enter the fields now associated with females. Invariably, whenever men have become teachers, nurses, or even hairdressers, the salary and prestige attached to those jobs have increased. As feminist leader Gloria Steinem has pointed out, when several women become airline pilots, that's a change for the better. But far more women benefit from the addition of young men to the ranks of flight attendants.

A change in attitude about the value of work traditionally done by women is a positive goal for the future. Unfortunately, however, a sudden mass movement toward recognizing the immense contribution that women as workers make to our society is unlikely. So, keeping that in mind, many employment counselors are now advising career-oriented women to try yet another strategy in their pursuit of well-paying jobs — to forgo the undervalued and grossly underpaid "female-intensive" career areas altogether. (You know the argument: If you can't beat 'em . . .)

"MEN'S WORK"
Today, many counselors advise women to opt for careers in "men's fields": to break into such high-paying male bastions as economics, mathematics, engineering, business, and the physical sciences. And for those women with neither the desire nor the wherewithal to spend prolonged years in college

and/or graduate school, obtaining jobs in the construction trades and other so-called nontraditional areas should be the top priority, they contend.

But aren't women already doing this? You may well ask. After all, we pick up women's magazines and newspapers and see photos of women in hard hats perched high above the street fixing telephone cables. We see pictures of female police officers in the driver's seats of patrol cars. We turn on the TV and see commercials in which the young doctor fresh out of medical school and now in need of the services of Chase Manhattan Bank to manage a burgeoning income is a young woman. Women, we're told, are breaking the sex barrier on a daily basis and on a large scale.

The truth is, it ain't so.

"We tend to focus on the exceptional women as role models, but this obscures the fact that most women are not moving into traditionally male fields rapidly," said Pearl M. Kamer, chief economist for the Long Island Regional Planning Board, in a recent interview in the *New York Times*.[12]

---

12. See Frances Cerra, "Study Finds College Women Still Aim for Traditional Jobs," *New York Times,* May 11, 1980.

Kamer has conducted a study to determine which fields to-day's young women are planning to enter in the future. The results of her survey are astonishing: By 1987, some 71 percent of all doctorate degrees awarded to women will be in those six low-paying fields labeled by the Census Bureau as traditionally female: education, English and journalism, fine and applied arts, foreign languages and literature, nursing, and library science.

Recent government statistics bear out Kamer's projections. Between 1970 and 1979, these six fields plus the social sciences, psychology, and the other health professions accounted for over 60 percent of all undergraduate degrees awarded to women. And incredibly, despite the generally dismal prospects for getting a full-time job in kindergarten, elementary, or secondary schools (prior to the middle of the 1980s), some 30 percent of all college women still major in education, according to the National Center for Education Statistics.

Dr. Lois Shaw, an economist with the Center for Human Resources in Columbus, Ohio, recently began a study that will track some ten thousand young and mature women for fifteen years in order to survey their career attitudes and experiences. She, too, has already found that most American women still aspire to be teachers, nurses, office workers, and now technicians.

> *"For every woman who becomes the first welder or meat cutter, there remain hundreds working on a line in a garment factory or in a steno pool."*
> — LOUISE OTT, "'Equal pay for work of comparable value': A Story of Dollars and Sense," *Matrix,* spring 1980.

To prepare young women for the hard realities of the working world that most of them will enter as adults, employment consultant Kay McVey of Columbus, Ohio, recommends that employment counseling begin in the ninth grade. "I had no idea you worked after college," she recalls. "And it's still like that. An adviser asks a girl, 'What do you like to do?

Write poetry? Fine. Be an English major!' "[13] Obviously, given today's job market, such counseling is ill-advised unless the young girl is also informed that she is apt to have an awfully tough time finding work in her chosen field.

The benefits to be gained by more women from entering currently male-dominated fields go far beyond the obvious ones: more jobs, better pay, and more prestige (even though most women would gladly settle for those three!). For one thing, laws would change. For example, it was only because women entered the work force in such large numbers that pressure arose for the Pregnancy Discrimination Act of 1978, which banned discrimination because of pregnancy or childbirth.

Another likelihood is that the needs of women would be recognized (and sometimes even met) by employers who never realized that by accommodating their female employees, their company stands to benefit in the long run. On-site day-care facilities run by Control Data and Connecticut General Life Insurance are just two examples of progressive programs begun in recent years, as more women have entered the work force.

> *"We need programmers, and we figure people will be more productive if we can help solve their problems."*
>
> — JAMES STATHOPOULOUS, manager of corporate staffing for Control Data Corporation, Minneapolis, Minnesota. Quoted in *Newsweek,* May 19, 1980.

If more women were working in an even wider range of jobs and companies, they would be able to begin lobbying for the same humanization that already exists in the so-called women's fields. Unquestionably, flexible workdays and alternative work schedules would be among the demands of the new workers as they became more entrenched in their jobs and more valuable to their employers. Part-time jobs would

---

13. Quoted in Rosemary Armao, "Career's Goal? Outthink Men," *City News,* September 17, 1978.

begin to open up at even higher levels and in more job categories as part-timers became eligible for promotion. Part-timers would come to be considered career-oriented rather than uncommitted as more and more had the chance to prove themselves.

With an influx of women to all occupations and companies, men could also benefit from an overall improvement in their work lives and their personal lives. With a greater acceptance of part-time work, men as well as women could opt for reduced work weeks. They could take advantage of the opportunity to pursue outside interests, whether educational, recreational, or parental. And we would be much closer to realizing one of the principal goals reiterated by feminist leaders at the turn of this decade: more sharing by men and women of all of the responsibilities and the rewards of both career and family.

The Best Hope for the Future

What if *all* industries, not just government agencies and service-oriented fields, were receptive to the idea of career-oriented part-time work? Wouldn't it be nice if more unions suddenly took up the plight of underpaid part-timers? What if women's groups existed in *all* cities, and were able to show local employers how easy and how advantageous it can be to hire highly qualified and motivated people who simply aren't able to work nine to five, five days a week? Wouldn't it be nice if "women's occupations" were finally given their long-overdue recognition and brought up to the pay and prestige levels of "men's fields"? What if women and men worked side by side in *every* field, as a matter of course? Wouldn't it be nice if such distinctions as "his" career and "her" family responsibilities finally became relics of the unenlightened past?

All of these "what if's" and "wouldn't it be nice's" are the stuff of impassioned public speeches. They fill the daydreams of feminists and of groups working for a better quality of life for all people, men and women. Most of us already look forward to the establishment of some sort of new order in which equality in the workplace and in the home is more a reality than a rallying point. However, changes such as these, desirable though they are, take more than wishful thinking to achieve. They take re-education. They take a willingness to depart from the familiar. They take money. They take time.

For the person without years to wait, it seems that there must be ways to attain at least some of these desirable goals in the short run. Indeed, there are. If you're a woman or a man seeking good part-time employment, you would be well advised to formulate your career plans by taking into account the time-honored and familiar law of supply and demand. *Think of the demands of the job market and how you can fill them to your best advantage.*

The reality of the 1980s is that highly skilled and trained workers are becoming increasingly rare throughout all levels of society and in all regions of the country. The reasons: (1) Young people in high schools and colleges aren't acquiring the necessary training to cope with increasingly technical occupations, and (2) because of rapid population shifts during the past decade, critical shortages of certain kinds of workers have cropped up almost everywhere. For example, in the Sun Belt, the rapid growth in population has already created a shortage of trained health professionals. In California, the microelectronics companies in the "Silicon Valley" area are desperate for engineers and other technically trained workers. Insurance companies and banks in the Hartford, Connecticut, area have found themselves so short of trained and highly skilled office workers that they have held "job fairs" to attract potential employees. And consider the following item from the June 17, 1980, *Wall Street Journal:*

> Incentives abound for scarce, skilled technical help, despite the recession.
>
> To retain or attract such people, still-booming industries try many gimmicks. Some oil-and-gas exploration companies share oil-well ownership with everyone from secretaries to geologists, a Dallas management consultant says. At two other Texas energy concerns, new engineers win an extra month's salary up front . . .
>
> Elsewhere, workers land bonuses for helping to fill slots — if recruits stay a month or more. Connecticut General Life Insur-

ance Co. employees receive $200 and a $750 videotape re-
corder for referring data processors, $1000 for actuaries. A
Northrup Corp. defense plant hires 40 percent of its professional and factory workers through "bounties" of from $100 to
$3000.

Shortages of well-trained workers will become even more
acute in the future. That's what all the experts say. Therefore,
those people who offer top skills and experience, whether
they are men or women and whether their fields are "men's"
or "women's" fields, will be in high demand everywhere. They
are the people who will be in the best position to negotiate the
pay and benefits they need as well as the work schedules they
want.

It's really not that complicated: If you have the solid skills
and proven abilities an employer badly needs, that employer
is going to try to get you on his or her team, even if that
means having to accommodate your need for an under-thirty-
five-hour work week. On the other hand, if you're already a
valuable member of the team, the employer is going to try to
keep you, even if that means letting you cut back from a full-
time schedule. That's what the law of supply and demand is
all about. And as you'll see over and over again in examples
throughout this book, using that law to their own advantage
is exactly what enabled many of today's most successful part-
timers to land the well-paying jobs they now hold.

For the reasons outlined earlier in this chapter (particularly
efforts by government agencies and women's groups), more
and better part-time jobs will be available in the future. However, if you plan to wait around until top-flight opportunities
appear in the help-wanted ads each Sunday, you have quite a
long wait ahead of you. On the other hand, if you decide to
go out and make that old law of supply and demand work for
you, there's a good chance that you can land a better part-
time job than you ever dreamed possible.

3

Your
Options

─────────◆─────────

BY THIS POINT you should have a pretty good idea of what *part time* means. You know who works on a reduced schedule, why they do, and what kinds of jobs they hold. You're aware of the principal problems faced by many part-timers today, and you have an idea of what's going to be needed to help alleviate those problems in the future. Most important, though, you now know what it's going to take for *you* to land a top-flight part-time job: (1) You're going to have to be skilled, and (2) you're going to have to focus your job hunt on employers in fields likely to be receptive to alternative work scheduling, and particularly employers that really need the skills you have to offer. (But more of that appears in the chapter "Landing a Good Part-Time Job.")

Let's take a look at some of the more common options that are open to you. Of course, your other responsibilities, needs, and desires will greatly influence your choice of work schedule. So will the needs of your employer. But odds are that the job(s) you eventually take will fall within one or more of these categories: permanent (year-round) part-time employment, free-lancing, temporary work, and — perhaps the most promising part-time innovation to come along yet — job sharing. (Job sharing is actually a form of permanent part-time employment, but it's a very special one which I believe deserves separate discussion.)

Permanent Part-Time Work

If you had to guess which is the most common schedule on which permanent part-timers work, what would your guess be?

No idea? O.K., here are some choices:

    (a) two or three full days each week
    (b) a certain number of hours each workday
    (c) evenings and weekends only
    (d) one full week every three or four weeks.

If you answered (b), you're right. The part-day schedule is by far the most prevalent.[1]

Various studies have revealed the obvious preference of mothers for working while their children are in school; hence the popularity of so-called mothers' hours, usually from 9 A.M. or 10 A.M. to 2 P.M. or thereabouts. Senior citizens tend to enjoy working entire days on a part-week schedule; and students, after school and on weekends. Most moonlighters, of course, work night shifts and weekend jobs; some, however, such as teachers, may be free to take late-afternoon jobs as well. By and large, the preferred work schedules of most part-timers are fairly predictable. So is their principal reason for choosing permanent part-time work over the other part-time options: the work is steady and year-round, and so is the pay.

On the negative side, however, year-round work can present problems, particularly for mothers of schoolchildren. Day care may not be a problem for mothers working part-time during the fall, winter, or spring. But come summer, it can be a major hassle. School holidays can also be difficult: some women are forced to take a leave of absence without pay every time there is a school vacation.

For students in college, maintaining a permanent part-time

---

1. In a survey of 391 users of permanent part-time employees, Dr. Stanley Nollen and his associate, Virginia Martin, found that 75 percent employed part-timers on a part-day schedule and 49 percent employed them on a full-day but part-week or part-month schedule (some employers used both). Minishifts were used by 23 percent of firms, and 22 percent hired job sharers. The results of the study are contained in Stanley D. Nollen and Virginia Martin, *Alternative Work Schedules, Part 2: Permanent Part-time Employment* (New York: AMACOM [a division of American Management Associations], 1978).

job may mean renegotiating schedules as often as every semester, or even every quarter. Class hours change, and invariably some required course is offered only at the worst possible time for the job-holder. Flexibility is essential for both the student and his or her boss if a permanent part-time job is going to suit both.

For people unencumbered by child-care worries or school schedules, the difficulties of holding a year-round part-time job are less acute. But even though the idea of a regular paycheck may be attractive, taking a job that offers one might mean giving up something that is even more important — your day-to-day freedom.

Part-Time Versus Free-lance: A Choice to Consider

To some people, going to the same office, sitting at the same desk, doing the same work, and having lunch with the same people every day provides a feeling of stability and security. It gives them a sense of solidity that makes the office seem almost like a second home. Without the feeling of being part of a team or of a work "family," they wouldn't enjoy the time they spend on the job. They like a set routine; they don't like change.

To other individuals, however, the thought of showing up at the same time and place each day, doing the same job day in and day out, and looking across the desk at the same faces each morning represents only one thing: unbearable boredom. And to some people, the ideal work situation provides some degree of constancy along with the potential for a change of scenery and the opportunity to work with new people now and then.

Elizabeth Nagler, of Valley Stream, New York, is someone who enjoys the best of both worlds — the security of steady work and familiar faces plus the diversity of constantly changing free-lance assignments. Elizabeth, fifty-five, calls herself a "free-lance professional interpreter for the deaf." The hearing daughter of deaf parents, she learned her skill literally from birth. She has been working professionally for thirty-five years and holds two part-time jobs in addition to handling assorted free-lance assignments. Elizabeth works at Nassau Community College, accompanying deaf students to class and translating lectures for them. She also teaches sign language twice a week at Catholic Charities offices on Long Island.

Elizabeth's free-lance assignments have included working for doctors, lawyers and judges, even for President Gerald Ford. Jobs bring in between $10 and $50 per hour, depending on the work she must do, how much traveling time is involved, and the length of the assignment. When she works for the courts, for instance, Elizabeth gets a fixed amount: $44.37 per "commitment" — which, she explains, means a job lasting "anywhere from two minutes to several hours."

The divorced mother of two teenagers, Elizabeth enjoys the financial cushion that two part-time jobs offer as well as the opportunity to get out and do other work. "Most people in my field work full-time," she says, "but I've always preferred free-lancing. The work is so much more varied."

As Elizabeth Nagler and other successful free-lancers know, major trade-offs are involved in deciding whether to work for one boss or one company or to be your own boss and hire yourself out to various people or companies during the course of the year. Temperament plays a large part in determining the decision.

Think about your own preferences for a moment. Do you like a set routine and a structured environment? Or do you prefer constant change? Are you more comfortable working in a place that has a Christmas party each December and a company picnic on Memorial Day weekend? Or do you like the idea of a "nice meeting you, let's have lunch sometime" arrangement?

> *"It's a good job. I'm my own boss. I come and go when I please, and even if life gets a little crazy at times, it's worth it for the independence I have."*
>
> — TIMOTHY ROBINSON, free-lance piano tuner. Quoted in "Tuning a Piano: When It's Out, It's In," by Fred Ferretti, *New York Times*, June 25, 1980.

The following list indicates some of the major differences between working permanent part-time and working freelance. Some are obvious advantages and disadvantages. Others may be considered either pluses or minuses, depending on how you see them.

PERMANENT PART-TIME

♦ Most part-time jobs are still in low-paying fields; potential earnings are somewhat limited. However, jobs are available in a number of different industries in almost all locations.

♦ Income is predetermined.

♦ Prorated fringe benefits are offered by 50 percent of all firms that hire part-timers.

♦ Protection in the form of unemployment insurance, workmen's compensation, and disability insurance is paid by the employer.

♦ Income taxes are withheld from your paycheck.

♦ Employer absorbs job-related expenses (materials, supplies, use of phone, and so on).

♦ More opportunities exist for people first entering the job market or those with limited skills and experience.

FREE-LANCE

♦ Most free-lance jobs are in fields that pay well. However, very few fields do use free-lancers, and of those companies that do, most are in large cities.

♦ No guaranteed income.

♦ No benefits, which can equal up to 35 percent of salary.

♦ No protection in case of loss of work.

♦ No withholding; you must pay your own taxes and Social Security.

♦ Job-related expenses may all be yours, unless you make other arrangements in advance.

♦ Most successful free-lancers are both talented and experienced; many have successfully held salaried jobs and simply feel they can do better on their own. It is often hard for newcomers to break in.

◆ Once you're hired, the selling is over; you've got the job.

◆ You have set job responsibilities, predictable raises and promotions; however, at high-level positions, promotion opportunities may be limited.

◆ Your schedule is predetermined; it allows you to make plans in advance.

◆ You have continuing contact with the same people at work.

◆ No job security; you must constantly sell yourself and your abilities.

◆ You must always negotiate both work and pay agreements, which may vary from place to place and job to job.

◆ You sometimes work more than thirty-five hours per week; sometimes you don't work at all. Schedules may vary each day, forcing you to change plans you have already made. On the other hand, you're free to turn down work when you need or want to do so.

◆ You often work with different people, sometimes alone. You may or may not develop personal relationships on the job.

Is permanent part-time work comfortable, or confining? Is working as a free-lancer stimulating, or ulcer-producing? It all depends on how you view it.

Of course, there is a certain notion of glamour that many people attach to the concept of free-lance work. Perhaps that's because many free-lancers work in the so-called glamour fields, among them magazine writing and editing, fashion illustration and photography, theater and music, interior design, book publishing, motion pictures and TV, and public relations. Then there are the consultants who work in various fields. Say the word *consultant* and many people conjure up the image of an expensively dressed man or woman sitting with a corporate bigwig or government official in some fancy French restaurant, casually discussing a multimillion-dollar project over a lunch of poached salmon and Pouilly Fuissé.

Free-lancing, consulting — it all seems so . . . well, exciting. What people may not realize, however, is that making it in any free-lance business requires incredible persistence and discipline. If you're not busy working, you're busy soliciting work. And there is never any job security; you're only as good as what you did last.

> *"The best way to make it as a free-lancer is to become indispensable at what you do. That way, you're free to say you can't come in next Monday, or next week. They'll take you whenever they can get you."*
>
> — ANNA MARIE DOHERTY, women's service editor, *Family Circle* magazine.

Among successful free-lancers of all types, motivation is high. It has to be, because although it may be nice to have the freedom to work only when you want and for whom you want, those monthly bills have a way of coming in with maddening regularity, whether you're earning money or not. Deciding to work free-lance is a little like playing the stock market. The potential rewards are high. So are the risks — which is probably why only 7 percent of all Americans choose to work for themselves.

> *"I spent six weeks on a piece for Harper's and got $350 for it. I realized I was not going to make it as a magazine writer."*
>
> — ANDY ROONEY, TV commentator ("60 Minutes") and syndicated columnist. Quoted in *Time*, July 21, 1980.

If free-lance work does appeal to you, keep in mind that it's not only those who work in the "glamour" fields who can succeed as free-lancers. As you'll see in forthcoming examples, engineers can, food technologists can, microbiologists can. And people with unusual abilities, such as Elizabeth Nagler, will find no shortage of opportunities to supplement steady work with numerous and varied free-lance jobs.

Temporary Work

If part-time work means work done in fewer than thirty-five hours a week, as the Labor Department says, then some temporary jobs are indeed part-time. Most, however, probably aren't. More likely than not, temporary work is performed for a full thirty-five or even forty hours per week but only for several weeks or months at a time. Then, for the temporary worker, or "temp," it's back to another job, or perhaps back to school, or back to being blissfully unemployed.

"Some [women] return to nursing from time to time . . . and are what we call an 'appliance nurse,' which means she goes to work when she needs a new refrigerator."

— MARGRETTA STYLES, dean of the School of Nursing at the University of California Medical Center in San Francisco. Quoted in Maryann Bird, "Nurses' Duties Are Expanding — and So Are Their Demands," *New York Times*, March 25, 1980.

Who Works as a Temp?

Roughly three million Americans each year — often, a different three million from the year before. Why? Because the turnover rate among temporary workers tends to be extremely high. Temporary workers' need for extra money may be isolated as opposed to ongoing, or such employees may only have a certain block of time available for thirty-five or forty hours per week on the job. Therefore, people who are working as temps right now aren't necessarily the same ones who will be seeking temporary jobs in another year.

Like permanent part-time workers, temps usually decide on their work schedules because of other roles and responsibilities that affect their availability for work. Students are probably the single largest group of temporary workers for all the obvious reasons. However, other groups of people decide to work on a temporary basis for some very good reasons, too. Women in particular tend to use temporary work as a gradual way to re-enter the work force. Temporary jobs offer them a good opportunity to brush up on rusty skills. Retirees of both sexes may also want to work once in a while but don't wish to make a commitment to one job or employer.

Other people who regularly work as temporaries are actors and actresses, models, painters and sculptors, musicians, artists, writers, and craftspeople — all of whom work in their chosen fields when they can, but who may find that between, say, on-stage appearances or modeling assignments, they have to put in a week or two or even a few months at a job that can tide them over for a while. For such individuals, the flexibility of temporary work is its main attraction. They have the freedom to determine not only the hours they work, but also the days and weeks. Then, when an audition or an exhibit or perhaps a two-week singing engagement at a local club comes up, they are free to spend their time preparing for it.

The last group of temps is also one that uses temporary employment as a stopgap measure, not on an "as-needed" basis, as musicians or artists do, but rather for one time only. This group includes people who have been laid off or who are otherwise between jobs. It also includes people who have just settled in a new city and want to check out local job opportunities. Many of these men and women use temporary positions to scout for prospective full-time jobs. None plans to remain a temp for long; few plan to work as temps ever again.

One of the major differences between temporary and permanent part-time workers, then, is their long-range commitment to their jobs. Permanent part-timers, particularly those who have managed to find good jobs, may plan to hold on to those jobs indefinitely. Temporary workers see not only the beginning but the probable end to their stints as "temps."

The Give-and-Take

Working on a temporary basis may seem like the ideal setup. It offers the security of a regular paycheck plus all the diversity of free-lance work. Nevertheless, there are certain factors to consider before you sign on with one of the many agencies that send temps to corporate clients.

The first is that work may not be available in your field at the exact moment that you're ready to take a job. For example, let's say you're a college student planning to work as a temporary secretary during the summer. You have told the agency's placement counselor that you only want to work in stock brokerage companies, since you think you would like to enter the brokerage business after graduation and you want to gain experience in the field. You may find that on the day you're ready to begin, the only companies that have requested a secretary with your skills and at your pay level are Acme Textile Manufacturing and XYZ Construction. Or if a job is available at, say, E. F. Hutton, the request may be for a clerk to work in the mailroom, not a secretary to work on the floor with the account executives and customers. Therefore, you have to decide whether to take the job at E. F. Hutton at a lower pay rate, or head for Acme or XYZ for $3 more per hour.

Then there's the matter of salaries. Sometimes temps earn substantially less than people working at similar full-time jobs do. (It should be pointed out that in some of the higher-level temporary jobs, workers may earn substantially *more* than those on the staff. This is particularly true of accountants, drafters, and engineers.) Temporary agencies tend to report that their pay scales are "commensurate with those of private industry." Depending on the agency and its location, that may or may not be true. Fringe benefits, when offered at all, are usually provided only after the temp has put in one thousand hours for the agency. Even then, the benefits may be far fewer than those offered to full-time workers or permanent part-timers.

One aspect that *is* appealing about temporary work is that an agency is always glad to hear you're available. Unlike placement people at employment agencies, who may cringe at the sight of hard-to-place job-seekers looking for permanent part-time positions, those handling temps are delighted to see you at any time. And if you offer solid clerical skills, you can be on the job in less than a day.

Hourly Earnings of Temporary Office Workers

Salaries for temporary workers tend to be competitive with those of workers in private firms within the same geographical area. Here's a roundup of typical hourly wages paid to the most widely employed temps in 1980:

Clerks: $2.65–$3.50
Receptionists: $2.75–$4.00
Typists: $3.00–$4.75
Secretaries (without
    steno): $3.00–$5.00

Statistical typists: $3.25–$5.00
Secretaries (with
    steno): $4.00–$6.00
Stenographers: $4.50–$6.00
Word processors: $6.00–$9.50

The Peak Job Periods

Although jobs are available year round, summer is the prime time for temporary work. From the beginning of June through mid-September, people are needed to fill in for regular employees who are away on vacation. Needless to say, this is a happy coincidence for most students, since summer is precisely when they are available for full-week work. Christmas and Easter are other peak times, again because of vacations but also because of stepped-up business in stores, banks, and other establishments that find themselves in the midst of a holiday crush. Short-term or special projects can prompt employers to seek temporary workers. Conventions may generate a few or even several hundred temporary jobs at one time, as can a company headquarters' move to a new location. The principal moving time? June.

Today's Temporary Jobs
Like many positions available to permanent part-time workers, the majority of temporary jobs are for typists, secretaries,
receptionists, and bookkeepers, to name a few. Roughly, two-
thirds of all temporary positions are in fact clerical jobs. However, many of the larger temporary agencies also maintain industrial, marketing, and technical divisions. They can fill re-
quests from client corporations for warehouse loading
personnel, shopping-mall Santas and Easter bunnies, convention hosts and hostesses, and engineers to work on outer-
space communications projects. In all, about one hundred different occupations are now listed among those filled by part-
year employees.

Some temporary agencies specialize in one field, such as engineering or accounting. Agencies employing health-care
workers are among the fastest-growing of all, particularly in
the Sun Belt.

Karen Anhorn, twenty-four, of Pinellas Park, Florida, is a
health-care professional who recently had a firsthand look at
the boom in temporary work in her field. A registered nurse,
she took a full-time hospital job shortly after moving to Florida from New York. After one year, she decided to sign on
with a temporary agency "to see if I could find a better situation." For six months, Karen worked as a temp. What she saw
at that time were agency tactics she describes as "cutthroat."
Karen explains: "The agencies tend to be extremely aggressive. There are people from agencies roaming around the
hospital all the time. They come up to you and say, 'Why
don't you drop by and see us? We'll work out a deal.'"

In any area where large numbers of older citizens live, similar situations exist. Karen points out that the agencies in Florida are so desperate to get qualified people that they constantly try to steal them away from hospitals and from other
agencies. To lure health-care professionals, the agencies offer
totally flexible schedules, good benefits (including the essential malpractice insurance), and sometimes even same-day
pay. They also offer either competitive or higher-than-usual
hourly wages. Nurses with certain specialties, for example,
can make as much as $9 or $10 an hour. Knowing this, Karen

obtained cardiac-care-unit accreditation before she signed up with a temporary agency.

Many young women like Karen have taken the temporary route and have thereby taken advantage of the incredible demand for their skills. "Working on a temporary basis is especially useful for nurses who have just moved to a new location," Karen says. "It allows them to assess the hospitals in their area."

Interestingly, Karen recently decided to return to the hospital position she left prior to becoming a temp. Because of the aggressive recruiting efforts of the agencies, she says, local hospitals were forced to give huge raises to staff nurses. Therefore, money was no longer a consideration. Rather, Karen maintains, she returned to the hospital because during her six months as a temporary worker, she found she badly missed the ongoing professional and social relationships that a "regular" job can provide.

For Karen, as for many other people, working as a temporary had served its purpose. She had made good money, she had seen what was going on in her new community, and she had scouted opportunities at other hospitals. But in the end, Karen made the decision that most temps eventually make; she decided to leave the temporary work force and move on to something more permanent.

As Karen Anhorn's experience indicates, pay scales at temporary agencies have improved in the past few years. Most companies, particularly the huge national temporary agencies, do pay the going rates in the cities in which they have offices. Competition for qualified workers has created more attractive pay and benefit scales.

Yet for the person considering the temporary route, there are still other advantages to keep in mind. Temporary work offers an excellent earn-while-you-learn situation. Having the chance to practice operating sophisticated new office equipment or to upgrade skills you already possess makes temporary work one of the best training opportunities around. Working at different companies or in various fields can give you broad experience and exposure to many kinds of businesses. For example, if you find the day-to-day activities in the retailing field boring, you can always switch jobs next week and see if advertising is more to your liking. (Don't forget, along the way you may run into offers of permanent jobs that you would never find on your own!)

Temporary work, long a standby for young actors and artists, has much to offer the job-seeker. It may not be for everyone. However, for the college student, the woman planning to re-enter the work force after a long absence, the person recently arrived in a new town, the man or woman out of work for the time being, or the retiree just looking for now-and-then employment, temporary work may be just the ticket.

Job Sharing

"The Remarkable Miss Neef"

Thomas van Beek lives in Amsterdam. In 1961 Tom was a 25-year-old executive in need of a private secretary. After a procession of unpromising applicants, a bright, charming young lady came to Tom's office. She was Miss Neef. Her references were impressive, her typing and shorthand more than adequate. Beyond her obvious secretarial talent, there was the aura of personal stability Tom had been looking for. Miss Neef was hired on the spot.

She was an executive's dream. She was tireless. At the end of a long day, when even her young employer was exhausted, Miss Neef was as prepared to cope with her responsibilities as she had been before she went out for her brief lunch break.

The weeks became months and the months, years. During the seasons of heavy business, Miss Neef did the work of two — a one-woman miracle.

Then, in 1973, came the day Tom dreaded: Miss Neef wished to retire. As he thought about the splendid job she had done — really more than anyone could have asked of one person — Tom was determined that his remarkable Miss Neef should have the most lavish retirement party he could arrange.

It was at that celebration that the mystery of Miss Neef's boundless energy stopped being a mystery. For shortly after the guest of honor had arrived, the guest of honor arrived. For 12 years, Tom had been convinced his one secretary was doing the work of two. Instead, two secretaries were doing the work of one. Two sisters, sharing the same job, worked half time and split the paycheck.

They were identical twins.

— From *More of Paul Harvey's The Rest of the Story* by Paul Aurandt (New York: William Morrow, 1980).

Numerous terms have been used to describe the fairly recent phenomenon of two people sharing one job. *Split-level job*, *job pairing*, and *job twinning* are among those you still see now and then. All of these terms represent attempts to distinguish between jobs that are split according to responsibilities and those that are divided on the basis of how much time each worker puts in.

Nevertheless, in recent months *job sharing* has emerged as the most popular and most widely accepted term. *Job sharing* simply describes any situation in which two people voluntarily split a job formerly held by one full-time worker. The sharers may divide their job into projects during the course of the year; or they may tackle assigned work together, splitting their tasks according to each one's strengths or areas of expertise; or both may do the same work at different times of the day, days of the week, or months of the year.

Besides the various ways of handling tasks and time, there are differences in terms of pay. Job sharers don't necessarily get paid an equal amount of money. Since job-sharing arrangements can be and sometimes are established between one highly trained and experienced worker and one just starting out, it stands to reason that the levels of compensation can differ. They frequently do.[2] Benefits are also generally pro-

2. See Gretl S. Meier, *Job Sharing* (Kalamazoo, Mich.: W. E. Upjohn Institute for Employment Research, 1979). According to the author, who has con-

vided, and usually prorated, although not all job sharers do receive benefits.

Unlike Other Part-Time Situations

Job sharing is different from other permanent part-time situations in that it represents a *deliberate conversion* of a single full-time job to one done by two people. Regular part-time work needn't involve such a conversion; the job may always have been part-time. Also, although all job sharers are part-timers, the reverse, of course, isn't necessarily true.

It is also worth noting the difference between job sharing and an arrangement known as work sharing. The latter represents a usually involuntary reduction of working hours, with accompanying pay cuts, during periods of economic downturn. Work sharing is most widely used by employers as an antirecessionary tool that is an alternative to layoffs.[3] Usually, it is a temporary arrangement. Once economic conditions improve, workers resume their full-time schedules.[4]

Job sharing, then, is a unique arrangement among the part-time alternatives. And as far as many job sharers are concerned, the benefits of this particular type of arrangement make it the most attractive of all part-time options.

"There never seem to be enough high-level part-time jobs to go around. But job sharing offers people good,

ducted the most extensive survey to date on job sharers and their employers, most job sharers earn between $8500 and $16,500 a year. Only slightly more than half are paid at the same rate as their partners.

3. For an analysis of work sharing as it is practiced in the United States today, see Robert W. Bednarzik, "Worksharing in the U.S.: Its Prevalence and Duration," *Monthly Labor Review* 103 (July 1980): 3–12.

4. Interestingly, in 1976–77, when financial problems forced Santa Clara County, California, to propose a work-sharing arrangement as an alternative to widespread layoffs, some 1500 of a total of 10,000 employees accepted work and pay cuts while maintaining fringe benefits and seniority. The following year, when the partial work-reduction schedules were no longer necessary, 700 employees applied for continuation of their reduced work schedules; 675 of the applications were approved.

> *career-oriented part-time work, which becomes avail-*
> *able simply by restructuring a full-time position."*
>   — BARNEY OLMSTED, codirector, New Ways to Work,
>   San Francisco, California.

Chief among the pluses is the range of jobs open to job sharers — usually positions at much higher levels than those traditionally open to other permanent part-timers. Shared jobs "are apt to offer higher pay and a better quality of work than most part-time jobs," concluded the *1979 Employment and Training Report of the President.* Indeed, many positions now shared by two people are at the professional and top technical levels in both private industry and government.[5]

Among the fields in which job-sharing arrangements can be found today are:

Medicine. Shared residencies in primary-care specialties were authorized by the 1976 Health Professions Educational Assistance Act. For several years, Harvard Medical School has published *Institutions Offering Reduced Schedule Training,* which is based on a survey of approximately 1700 hospitals with residency training programs approved by the American Medical Association. Shared research, training, and hospital staff jobs are also found at institutions and medical schools throughout the country.

Education. Particularly at small liberal arts schools, professorships are increasingly available to two people (often married couples). The two may share lecturing, administrative, and research responsibilities. (See the education section in "Today's Best Part-Time Jobs." According to job-sharing expert Gretl S. Meier, who studied such arrangements in 1978, roughly sixty shared appointments existed in U.S. colleges in that year.) At the elementary-school level, job sharing or

---

5. See Project JOIN (Job Options and Innovations) Quarterly Progress Report (April 1, 1978–June 30, 1978), "A Demonstration Project to Develop and Test a Job Sharing Service" (Madison, Wis.: Wisconsin Department of Employment Relations, Division of Human Resource Services, Federal Manpower Program Section, 1978).

"partnership teaching" situations are growing in number. This is particularly true on the West Coast, where organizations are actively lobbying for more and better part-time opportunities for people already in or re-entering the job market.

Administration. Codirectorships are becoming more widespread in many women's groups as two and sometimes three women share all of the responsibilities of running vocational counseling or other women's assistance programs. At the Capitol Hill Community Service Office in the state of Washington, for example, social workers Jean Berman and Carol Haines jointly hold the position of community resource coordinator. For several years they have worked with volunteers and have helped to place both students and recent parolees in jobs. Also in Washington, Phyllis Elgin and Ann Lau together run the office of Secretary of State Norma Paulus. The two women share virtually all administrative tasks (see "State and Local Governments" in the chapter "Who Is Hiring and Who Isn't"). In Hampstead, New York, Gail Schwartz and Sheila Sarett jointly coordinate special events and publicity for the huge Abraham & Straus department store. Administrative tasks of all kinds are split successfully by these and other job sharers everywhere.

Personnel. This is a field that lends itself particularly well to job sharing, and it's one in which job sharers are well represented. Let's take an in-depth look at one such arrangement.

Carolyn Gorin, thirty-three, and Kathleen Kuba, twenty-nine, both of Portland, Oregon, share the title "office specialist" at Western Bancorp, the holding company for the First National Bank of Oregon and several other banks in the Pacific Northwest. Carolyn, who had previously worked full-time as an office manager for eight years, held this particular position for two years. At first she worked part-time, but gradually the job responsibilities grew to such an extent that it became apparent that hers was not a part-time but rather a full-time job. Carolyn went to her boss, Michael House, an assistant vice-president and manager of personnel, and suggested job sharing. He was all in favor of the idea, particularly since his wife shares a job at another company.

Carolyn interviewed a number of applicants and eventually hired Kathleen. "It's important for you to spend time together, to get to know your proposed partner and to establish rapport," Carolyn says. "For example, besides job qualifications, I knew I needed someone who would be flexible about filling in if one of my two kids got sick or just needed me at home for some reason."

Kathleen was also interested in flexibility. Formerly an editor of an employee benefits publication, Kathleen had stopped working prior to the birth of her daughter. Several months later, she decided she wanted to resume working but only on a part-time basis. So when Carolyn interviewed Kathleen for the shared position, they discussed the matter of flexibility in great detail. Kathleen said that filling in wouldn't be a problem for her. (She is quick to point out that she is lucky to have a very reliable and flexible babysitter, who in turn allows Kathleen to be flexible.)

At the office, the women split their job according to both time and function. Carolyn works from nine to noon. She conducts interviews and coordinates the hiring of clerical employees. She greets job applicants, administers the various typing and shorthand tests, reviews applications, and checks references. Once an applicant is hired, Carolyn helps to set up his or her benefit program.

Kathleen works from 12:30 to 4:30. She handles the payroll for the office's 150 employees. In addition, she helps establish and maintain benefit programs and does some of the secretarial work that the position generates.

As far as pay is concerned, since Carolyn's experience and present responsibilities are greater, so is her salary. She earns $7.00 an hour, compared with Kathleen's $5.50. Kathleen has no objections: both her level of responsibility and her pay scale suit her just fine. "The position is very busy and very stressful," she says. "It would be extremely hard for me to carry out all of the responsibilities for forty hours each week. Besides," she adds, "the job gives me exposure to all aspects of personnel work, and there's a greater career orientation in this job than in most other part-time jobs I might have found."

Carolyn and Kathleen have found their arrangement virtually perfect. The two women have worked out a notekeeping system to keep each other informed. Furthermore, they try to overlap their schedules by five to fifteen minutes each day so they can fill each other in on what's happening. When there is a particularly complex situation or a problem they have to solve, one calls the other at home.

The only problem that does arise every so often involves communication — despite the notes, talks, and phone calls. "When problems do arise," Kathleen points out, "you have to be really honest with your partner. We both have to be ready to admit what went wrong." Katheen also mentions the need to communicate well with coworkers. In their case, it works out "because there's always someone here," she says.

Constant coverage is one of the chief advantages job sharing offers employers, as Michael House has come to appreciate. The other advantages he mentions are frequently cited by other employers as well: "You have the benefit of two minds instead of one. It's much more productive and creative. It's immensely helpful for me to have two points of view," he says.

There is still another benefit that Michael has recognized during the year that Carolyn and Katheen have shared their job. "Managers usually don't understand the job-sharing concept," he maintains. "They only see potential liabilities, and they fear that job sharers won't be committed to their jobs. The fact is, job sharers are *especially* committed to doing well. They know they're in a situation they can't get at every company. Therefore, because they're given great flexibility and because they know they have only four hours in which to do the job, they actually spend those four hours working. It's not like the eight-hour-a-day employee who really only spends five to six hours working," Michael points out.

Higher productivity does indeed seem to be one of the primary benefits realized by employers of job sharers, regardless of what jobs are shared.[6] Gerard E. McCaffrey, a vice-

6. A perfect example of the kinds of productivity benefits realized by employers is contained in the now-classic study conducted by Catalyst and the

president at the New York Life Insurance Company, recently commented on his firm's experiences with 240 people who fill 120 clerical jobs: "It's worked out very well. They've proven to be a good source of qualified and conscientious employees. Overall, our turnover experience has been favorable and their level of performance has been as good as our full-time employees."[7]

A larger labor pool containing better-qualified job applicants. Lower absenteeism and less sick leave. Higher employee morale. Lower turnover. Better use of existing workdays. Higher productivity. These are the benefits that employers have realized by hiring part-timers in general and job sharers in particular.

> *"At first, employers thought job sharing was off the wall. 'People can't share a good job,' they said. Some even laughed when they heard the idea."*
> — BARNEY OLMSTED, codirector, New Ways to Work, San Francisco, California.

True, some problems must be dealt with. Carolyn Gorin and Katheen Kuba mentioned two of them, the need for ongoing flexibility and the difficulties that may arise because of poor communications. For employers, there are others. For example, dividing salary and benefits can be troublesome in certain organizations. Then there is the question of whether to hire only people who apply for a job together, or to hire one worker and then find a partner for him or her, or perhaps to let an existing employee make the selection.[8]

Massachusetts Department of Public Welfare in 1973. The study revealed that social workers who shared jobs and who worked half-time were able to handle 89 percent of the caseload managed by full-time workers. See Catalyst, "Part-time Social Workers in Public Welfare," New York, 1973.

7. Quoted in Carey Winfrey, "Job Sharing — a Working Alternative," *New York Times,* January 8, 1980.

8. According to Gretl S. Meier, firms that already employ part-time workers are more likely to favor the introduction of job-sharing arrangements. More-

Other problems that employers must deal with are potentially higher initial training costs and the possibility that Social Security contributions could be elevated if the sharers earn above the base salary covered by Social Security (which is unlikely, as Meier points out). Should employees be evaluated separately or as a team? What about promotions and seniority? And, of course, which jobs can be opened to job sharing in the first place is an important question. As Gretl Meier mentions, establishing a job-sharing arrangement is always easier when time and tasks are clearly defined and easily divided. It is not always possible to make such clear-cut distinctions.

Job sharing is relatively new in this country. Not all employers are familiar with the concept. Among those that are, many remain skeptical. Unions, too, are suspicious; they fear that previous contracts will be undermined or that job sharing, like other part-time alternatives, could turn out to be involuntary for workers and costly for those who have earned seniority and top fringe benefits. Job sharers themselves often want assurances that if they change their minds once they enter a job-sharing arrangement, they will be free to resume full-time work.

Clearly, studies and demonstration projects are helping to familiarize potential employers and employees with the benefits of job sharing. The problems do remain to be solved, but sincere efforts by companies and job-seekers are doing much to alleviate groundless fears and to point toward positive solutions.

Interestingly, many of the most prominent groups working for better part-time opportunities in Seattle, San Francisco, Chicago, Washington, D.C., and other cities across the country are now beginning to focus more of their efforts on the job-sharing alternative. The reason is that job sharing clearly does offer the best hope for would-be part-timers who seek

---

over, she maintains, organizations are "more likely to permit sharing when one or, more often, both applicants" already work for the firm (see *Job Sharing*, p. 152). In most cases, she found, job sharers were hired separately (ibid., p. 48).

well-paying and career-oriented part-time jobs. What's more, the groups are finding that employers tend to be more receptive to part-time scheduling if it still provides full-time coverage in the office. As more attention is focused on this new and exciting work alternative, the goal expressed by Gretl Meier is becoming more and more a reality: job sharing is already increasing not only "the number but also the quality of part-time opportunities."

For the Different Times of Your Life

Not only are a number of different options available to any would-be worker, but seemingly there are as many possible combinations of work schedules as there are people holding jobs. A few examples:

♦ Elizabeth Nagler, the free-lance interpreter for the deaf, relies on two permanent part-time jobs for steady income and does some free-lancing on the side.

♦ Bob Bresler of Watertown, Massachusetts, thirty-two, supports himself by doing free-lance engineering design and consulting work. When times get tough and electronics firms have little money available for research and development projects, Bob signs on with a temporary agency and takes assignments that pay him $25 an hour. So far, Bob has never considered taking a full-time job.

♦ After working full-time for thirty-two years, Adam C. Eivich retired from his post office job and now shares the position of mail clerk at First Federal of Broward County, a bank in Fort Lauderdale, Florida. Adam comes in three days a week and thinks of his new job as play.

♦ Holly Bergen of West Hartford, Connecticut, hadn't held a paying job since before her seven-year-old twin sons were born. Now she is teaching high-school chemistry and English on a temporary basis, waiting for a full-time position to open up.

♦ Richard Rapp, a Huntington Beach, California, father of two, works full-time ten months a year as a fourth-grade teacher. After school, on weekends, and during school vacations, Richard moonlights as a savings counselor for a local bank. He calls on community residents at home and tries to get them to come into the bank; he is also trained as a teller and can open new accounts. Richard has held the two jobs for over nine years.

As you can see, today's part-time (and full-time) possibilities are almost limitless. Furthermore, the schedule that makes sense for you today might be impossible tomorrow. It all depends on your particular circumstances. Some sort of permanent part-time, temporary, or free-lance work might best suit your needs right now. Or perhaps your ideal situation would include a combination of part-time options, as it does for Elizabeth Nagler and Bob Bresler. Then there is always the possibility of taking a full-time job — or a full-time job plus some free-lancing, or even an extra part-time job, for a while.

The point is this: Choose the work schedule that makes the most sense for you right now. But recognize that if it doesn't work out, or if your needs and circumstances change, there's always another possibility . . . and another . . . and another . . .

4

The Jobs of the Future

THE MAJOR GROWTH during the 1980s, the Bureau of Labor Statistics indicates, will be in white-collar areas — for example, clerical and related fields, transportation, energy and the environment, computers, and sales. Blue-collar occupations will grow more slowly, with work increasingly available for highly skilled craft workers. Unskilled laborers will find it harder and harder to land a job. The services, as we have already seen, will employ millions more Americans as our need for health care, education, and office support systems, among others, continues to grow.[1]

Before we look at occupations within the various fields, and particularly at the best jobs of the coming decade, let's take a minute to consider two numbers that definitely bear noting. The first: By 1990, there will be some 67 million job openings that didn't exist at the start of the decade. Second: Of that total, roughly 20 million will be brand-new jobs; the other 47 million will be positions created as workers die, retire, or leave their jobs for other reasons.

What that means is that in *all* fields — even those that are expected to grow slowly, or even to decline — *work will be available*. Job openings may not always appear in the Sunday

---

1. For an interesting analysis of the BLS projections for this decade, see Jeremy Main, "The Right Stuff for Careers in the Eighties," *Money* 9 (May 1980): 68–72.

papers in every U.S. city at exactly the moment you happen to be looking for a particular position. Of course, some jobs (such as acting or modeling) will be difficult to obtain under the very best circumstances. But by and large, work will be available in virtually every field in which people currently spend their working hours.

Will the 67 million jobs be *good* ones? That depends on who's defining the word *good*. For example, there will be work for barely skilled warehouse loaders, as high turnover creates a steady stream of openings. There will be plenty of jobs for semiskilled office clerks and for inexperienced salespeople, as both offices and retail outlets continue to grow in number. There will be work on assembly lines and behind cash registers, jobs waiting on tables and washing dirty dishes. Though working at these jobs is certainly honorable, to many people such work is unappealing. The reasons are obvious. Most of these jobs (which together will employ some 27 million Americans by the year 1990) offer little promise of good pay and even less opportunity for advancement. Moreover, the work is often boring, repetitious, or both.

The "better" jobs — interesting positions that offer good money and a bright future — will increasingly go to the men and women who enter the job market with skills and/or training. There's no question about it. The future belongs to those who are well equipped to grow and adapt with it. Therefore, the best advice for any would-be worker is quite simple: If you don't already have marketable skills or training, get them.

Needless to say, preparing for a good job doesn't necessarily mean you need a graduate or even a college degree. Today it is possible to obtain training (and certification, if necessary) for any number of well-paying jobs in a year or two, sometimes less. There are adult education courses, apprenticeship programs, and countless vocational training opportunities in the

United States today. What's important is that you *prepare* to enter the field of your choice. Select your occupation not only for the number of anticipated job openings, but also according to your own interests and native abilities, your background or experience. Use the skills you possess, or will obtain, to wrap all of the other components into a neat and highly marketable package — namely, you!

Richard Nelson Bolles, author of *What Color Is Your Parachute?* and director of the National Career Development Project in Walnut Creek, California, sums up the present and future realities of the job market in the United States: "The higher a skill level you can legitimately claim, the more likely you are to find a job."[2] For full-time workers, coming into the job market with solid skills is the key to finding a good job. For the part-timer, it's essential.

Which Are the Best Jobs?

Your choice of jobs will, of course, be partially determined by your aptitudes and your work or life experience. But you should be aware of those occupations in which a high demand is expected, for even though there will be job opportunities in low-growth occupations, competition for the best positions will be tremendous. Put another way, if there are more qualified applicants than there are jobs to fill, the employer has the advantage. And for the part-timer in particular, an overabundance of qualified job-seekers spells trouble. Why? If there is a huge labor pool from which the employer can draw, he or she won't be forced to make any concessions in terms of salary or benefits, much less some form of alternative work schedule.

On the other hand, if you possess skills that are in great demand, you are in a much better bargaining position. If you prepare yourself to enter, say, the fast-growing computer science field, or any of the burgeoning medical or technical specialties, you may just find that you can have it all: good, chal-

---

2. Richard Nelson Bolles, *What Color Is Your Parachute?* (Berkeley: Ten Speed Press, 1979), p. 79.

lenging, well-paying work with the potential for advancement, plus a greater likelihood that you can immediately or eventually negotiate a work schedule that suits your personal needs. Once again, it's that familiar law of supply and demand: If the company needs what you offer, that company will do what it can to get you and keep you.

A selected list of some of the best (and, for comparison, some of the worst) job prospects of the 1980s begins on page 84. The information is based on data from the U.S. Department of Labor, and particularly the National Industry–Occupation Matrices, compiled in 1980.

The number immediately to the right of each occupation is the percentage of projected growth. A minus sign indicates anticipated decline. Pay particular attention to those occupations with a projected growth rate of over 20 percent — for example, those in the familiar health, scientific-technical, and data-processing fields. Many of these are jobs that will offer the greatest opportunities for the part-time as well as the full-time worker.

Also note the projected number of annual openings, included whenever available and based on figures published by the U.S. Labor Department in the spring 1980 *Occupational Outlook Quarterly* (available at your local library or at regional offices of the Bureau of Labor Statistics). These are listed within parentheses. They will help indicate the jobs that will be most widely available, whether in fast-growing fields or not. For instance, consider that although the need for actuaries will jump by over 32 percent, there will be only about five hundred openings between 1980 and 1990. On the other hand, the demand for accountants will rise by a slightly lower 25 percent, but there will be 61,000 openings each year. In which field would a qualified job-seeker be more likely to find a good job?

Projected Growth and Decline Through 1990
PROFESSIONAL, TECHNICAL, AND KINDRED

	Percentage of Growth or Decline	Annual Openings
Engineers	22.5	
Aero-astronautic	20.7	(1900)
Chemical	20.0	(1800)
Civil	22.8	(7800)
Electrical	21.5	(10,500)
Industrial	26.0	(8000)
Mechanical	19.1	(7500)
Metallurgical	29.0	(750)
Mining	58.3	(600)
Petroleum	37.7	(900)
Life and Physical Scientists	24.7	
Agricultural	32.0	
Atmospheric, space	12.0	
Biological	27.0	
Chemists	23.5	(6100)
Geologists	41.3	(1700)
Marine	21.1	(150)
Physicists and astronomers	6.0	(1000)
Mathematics Specialists	28.1	
Actuaries	32.2	(500)
Mathematicians	8.7	(1000)
Statisticians	35.2	(1500)
Science Technicians	28.3	
Agricultural, biological (except health)	24.2	
Chemical	25.4	
Drafters	32.8	(11,000)
Electrical, electronic	29.2	
Industrial engineering	29.3	
Mathematical	58.3	
Mechanical engineering	31.8	
Surveyors	17.9	(2300)
Engineering, science	26.6	(23,000)

	Percentage of Growth or Decline	Annual Openings
Medical Workers		
Chiropractors	17.2	(1500)
Dentists	30.0	(5500)
Dietitians	42.9	(3300)
Optometrists	25.9	(1600)
Pharmacists	37.0	(7800)
Physicians, M.D.'s, osteopaths	34.2	(19,000)
Podiatrists	53.1	(600)
Registered nurses	45.3	(85,000)
Licensed practical nurses	62.4	(60,000)
Therapists	39.9	*
*(occupational 2500; physical 2700)		
Veterinarians	34.5	(1700)
Clinical laboratory technologists	21.7	(14,800)
Dental laboratory technicians	55.6	(2800)
Dental hygienists	85.7	(6000)
Health record technicians	26.8	(4900)
Radiologic (x-ray) technologists	34.9	(9000)
Therapy assistants	37.0	*
*(occupational 1100; physical 400)		
Other health technologists, technicians	30.8	
Technicians (except health)		
Airplane pilots	38.6	(3800)
Air traffic controllers	22.1	(700)
Flight engineers	28.9	
Radio operators	27.9	
Computer Specialists	30.8	
Computer programmers	29.6	(9200)
Computer systems analysts	37.6	(7900)
Other (including operators)	6.1	(12,500)
Social Scientists	36.1	
Economists	38.8	(7800)
Political scientists	65.4	(500)
Psychologists	34.5	(6700)
Sociologists	59.1	(600)
Urban and regional planners	29.4	(800)

	Percentage of Growth or Decline	Annual Openings
Teachers	−3.2	
Adult education teachers	13.0	
College and university	−14.3	(11,000)
Elementary school	16.6	(86,000)
Secondary school	−26.5	(7200)
Entertainers and Other Artists		
Actors	34.3	(850)
Athletes and kindred workers	8.1	
Authors	15.2	
Dancers	37.5	(550)
Designers	10.1	
Editors and reporters	25.7	(2400)
Musicians and composers	34.6	(8900)
Painters and sculptors	6.5	
Photographers	15.1	(3800)
Public relations specialists	24.4	(7500)
Radio and TV announcers	24.1	(850)
Writers, artists, entertainers	3.0	
Other Professional, Technical		
Accountants	25.1	(61,000)
Architects	59.2	(4000)
Archivists and curators	15.4	
Clergy	5.4	
Other religious	25.0	
Foresters, conservationists	16.3	
Judges	8.7	
Lawyers	23.2	(37,000)
Librarians	8.6	(8000)
Personnel, labor relations	12.5	(17,000)
Recreation workers	26.4	
Social workers	18.9	(22,000)
Vocational, educational counselors	9.3	(1400)
MANAGERS, OFFICIALS, AND PROPRIETORS	20.8	
Buyers, Sales, Loan Managers	43.2	
Bank, financial managers	51.5	(28,000)

	Percentage of Growth or Decline	Annual Openings
Buyers, wholesale, retail	19.6	(7400)
Sales managers, retail trade	54.0	
Administrators, Inspectors	18.8	
Construction inspectors	50.5	(2200)
Health administrators	53.7	(18,000)
Inspectors (except construction)	24.5	(5800)
Officials, administrators, public	10.1	
Postmasters, mail supervisors	31.6	
College administrators	6.6	
Elementary and secondary school administrators	3.6	
Other Managers, Officials	16.0	
Funeral directors	0.0	(2200)
Office managers	36.8	
Restaurant, café, bar managers	10.3	
SALES WORKERS	27.7	
Advertising agents, sales workers	42.4	
Auctioneers	5.7	
Demonstrators	13.9	
Hucksters and peddlers	2.7	
Insurance agents, brokers	20.0	(30,000)
Newspaper carriers and vendors	8.0	
Real-estate agents, brokers	20.7	
Stock and bond sales agents	10.1	(5500)
Other sales workers	31.5	*
*(retail 226,000; wholesale 40,000)		
CLERICAL WORKERS	28.4	
Secretarial	33.3	(305,000)
Secretaries, legal	43.5	
Secretaries, medical	117.2	
Secretaries, other	45.8	
Stenographers	−27.7	
Typists	19.4	(59,000)
Office Machine Operators	5.0	
Bookkeeping, billing operators	56.9	
Calculating machine operators	24.3	

	Percentage of Growth or Decline	Annual Openings
Office Machine Operators, cont.		
Computer, peripheral equipment	18.3	(12,500)
Duplicating machine operators	32.5	
Keypunch operators	−26.7	
Tabulating machine operators	−39.9	
Other Clerical	25.5	(241,000)
Bank tellers	13.6	(17,000)
Billing clerks	59.9	
Bookkeepers	11.8	(96,000)
Cashiers	49.7	(119,000)
Clerical supervisors	25.6	
Collectors, bill and account	21.8	(4600)
Enumerators and interviewers	−7.3	
File clerks	22.7	(16,500)
Insurance adjustors, examiners	40.5	(10,250)
Library attendants, assistants	13.4	(7700)
Mail carriers, post office	6.1	(7000)
Mail handlers (except post office)	23.1	
Messengers, office helpers	−3.0	
Meter readers, utilities	8.6	
Payroll, time-keeping clerks	12.7	
Postal clerks	−19.2	(2000)
Proofreaders	35.8	
Real-estate appraisers	27.2	
Receptionists	27.9	(41,000)
Shipping, receiving clerks	23.0	(22,000)
Statistical clerks	26.0	(23,500)
Stock clerks, storekeepers	18.3	(23,000)
Teacher aides	51.8	(26,000)
Telegraph messengers	−72.0	
Telegraph operators	−44.5	
Telephone operators	−6.8	(9900)
Ticket agents	10.5	
CRAFTS AND KINDRED WORKERS	20.0	
Construction Crafts Workers	19.2	
Carpenters and apprentices	10.9	(58,000)
Brick and stonemasons, apprentices	7.8	(6200)

	Percentage of Growth or Decline	Annual Openings
Bulldozer operators	57.0	*
*(operating engineers 36,000)		
Cement and concrete finishers	34.1	(4400)
Electricians and apprentices	24.6	(12,900)
Excavating, grading machine operators	35.2	*
*(operating engineers 36,000)		
Painters and apprentices	20.7	(26,000)
Paperhangers	10	(1500)
Plumbers, pipefitters, and apprentices	19.9	(20,000)
Roofer and slaters	22.8	(4500)
Tilesetters	36.4	(1800)
Metalworking Craft Workers	21.8	
Blacksmiths	−36.4	(300)
Machinists and apprentices	20.7	(22,500)
Sheetmetal workers and apprentices	27.5	(3500)
Tool and diemakers, apprentices	23.5	(8600)
Mechanics, Repairers, Installers	29.7	
Air conditioning, heating, and refrigeration mechanics	16.7	(8200)
Aircraft mechanics	10.1	(3500)
Auto body repairers	27.0	(7800)
Auto mechanics and apprentices	23.4	(37,000)
Farm equipment mechanics	24.2	(3500)
Heavy equipment mechanics	47.4	(58,000)
Household appliance mechanics	24.2	(6900)
Office machine repairers	56.0	(4200)
Radio, TV repairers	26.7	(6100)
Printing Trades Workers	2.5	
Bookbinders	21.9	(2600)
Compositors and typesetters	−12.8	(3900)
Photoengravers, lithographers	45.8	*
*(photoengravers 150; lithographers 2300)		
Press operators and apprentices	8.9	(5000)

	Percentage of Growth or Decline	Annual Openings
Other Crafts, Kindred Workers	16	
Bakers	−7.1	
Cabinetmakers	7.0	
Floor covering installers	32.4	(3200)
Decorators, window dressers	35.2	
Glaziers	38.9	(1000)
Jewelers and watchmakers	29.4	
Motion-picture projectionists	−4.6	(750)
Opticians, lens grinders, polishers	28.4	(1200)
Piano and organ tuners, repairers	10	(700)
Shoe repairers	−4.6	(1600)
Tailors	2.9	
Upholsterers	21.2	(1100)
OPERATIVES	15.3	
Operatives (except transport)	15	
Semiskilled metalworking	19.3	
Lathe, milling machine	12.3	
Solderers	−36.5	
Welders and flame cutters	33.6	(35,000)
Semiskilled Textile Workers	−7.6	
Semiskilled Packing, Inspecting	22.7	
Asbestos, insulation workers	27.5	(2600)
Assemblers	42.8	(77,000)
Dressmakers (except factory)	−18.3	
Garage workers, gas station attendants	−13.5	(5200)
Laundry, dry-cleaning operators	52.1	
Meatcutters, butchers	16.8	(5200)
Mine operatives	21.0	
Photographic process workers	19.8	(2700)
Sewers and stitchers	29.2	
Transport Operatives	16.2	
Bus drivers	3.0	*
*(local 3100; intercity 500)		
Conductors and operators, urban railroads	23.6	(1700)

	Percentage of Growth or Decline	Annual Openings
Delivery and route workers	11.2	
Fork lift, tow motor operatives	26.2	
Parking attendants	13.6	(3200)
Taxicab drivers, chauffeurs	−9.8	(4300)
Truck drivers	21.5	*
*(local 64,000; long distance 21,500)		
SERVICE WORKERS	29.9	
Cleaning Service Workers	24.5	
Building interior cleaners	41.1	
Janitors and sextons	10.0	*
*(all building custodians 180,000)		
Lodging quarters cleaners	55.0	
Food Service Workers	33.1	
Bartenders	30.9	(21,600)
Busboys/girls	61.9	*
*(37,000, including dishwashers)		
Cooks and chefs (except private)	31.9	(86,000)
Dishwashers	63.8	
(See busboys/girls)		
Food counter, fountain workers	40.0	(34,000)
Waiters/waitresses	18.2	(70,000)
Health Service Workers	60.0	
Dental assistants	50.0	(11,000)
Health aides, homemakers (except nursing)	101.8	(36,000)
Lay midwives	0	
Nurses' aides, orderlies	51.5	(94,000)
Personal Service Workers	28.7	
Flight attendants	69.7	(4800)
Attendants, recreation and amusement	55.0	
Baggage porters and bellhops	17.2	(600)
Barbers	15.7	(9700)
Boarding, lodging housekeeper	50.8	(2000)
Bootblacks	−61.6	
Child-care workers (except private)	44.1	

	Percentage of Growth or Decline	Annual Openings
Personal Service Workers, cont.		
Elevator operators	−35.7	
Hairdressers, cosmetologists	15.1	(28,500)
Housekeepers (except private)	43.0	
School monitors	20.1	
Ushers	15.4	
Social service aides	20.9	(7500)
Protective and Service Workers	33.5	
Crossing guards, bridge tenders	14.9	
Firefighters	22.7	(7500)
Guards	49.7	(13,000)
Police and detectives	23.2	*
*(18,300, including state police officers)		
Private Household Workers		(45,000)
Child-care workers	−31.0	
Cooks, private	20.0	
Housekeepers, private	−46.8	
Private household cleaners, servants	−12.2	
Laborers (except farm)	8.1	
Animal caretakers	34.5	
Carpenters' helpers	−2.6	
Construction laborers	12.5	(49,000)
Garbage collectors	63.7	
Stock handlers	12.8	(23,000)
Warehouse laborers	−3.1	
FARM WORKERS	−15.9	
Farmers and Farm Managers	−13.1	
Farmers (owners and tenants)	−15.1	
Farm managers	67.1	
Farm Labor Supervisors	−19.0	
Laborers, wage workers	−18.2	
Laborers, unpaid family	−27.9	
Laborers, self-employed	130	

And Now the Condensed Version

The *Occupational Outlook Quarterly* published by the Bureau of Labor Statistics in the spring of 1980 contains two job outlook summaries: one, of the fastest-growing jobs between 1978 and 1990; the other, of those occupations that will have the greatest number of annual openings during the same period. The accompanying tables provide a look at BLS's "Top 26" in each category. Notice how many good jobs in the first table are traditionally open to part-time workers. (Indeed, growth in an industry is always encouraging to part-timers.) On the other hand, note how many dead-end jobs are listed in the second table. As you can see, no-future positions are also available simply *because* they offer no future. No one wants to stay in a dead-end job longer than absolutely necessary.

Fastest-Growing Jobs, 1978–90*

Occupation	Annual Openings
Bank clerks	45,000
Bank officers and financial managers	28,000
Business machine repairers	4200
City managers	350
Computer service technicians	5400
Construction inspectors	2200
Dental assistants	11,000
Dental hygienists	6000
Dining-room attendants and dishwashers	37,000
Flight attendants	4800
Guards	70,000
Health service administrators	18,000
Homemakers and home health aides	36,000
Industrial machinery repairers	58,000
Landscape architects	1100
Licensed practical nurses	60,000
Lithographers	2300
Nursing aides, orderlies, and attendants	94,000
Occupational therapists	2500

continued next page

*Employment in 1990 is projected to be at least 50 percent higher than it was in 1978.

Occupation	Annual Openings
Occupational therapy assistants	1100
Physical therapists	2700
Podiatrists	600
Respiratory therapy workers	5000
Speech pathologists and audiologists	3900
Teacher aides	26,000
Travel agents	1900

* * *

Jobs with the Most Openings, 1978–90

Occupation	Annual Openings
Secretaries and stenographers	305,000
Retail sales workers	226,000
Building custodians	180,000
Cashiers	119,000
Bookkeepers	96,000
Nursing aides, orderlies, and attendants	94,000
Cooks and chefs	86,000
Kindergarten and elementary teachers	86,000
Registered nurses	85,000
Assemblers	77,000
Waiters and waitresses	70,000
Guards	70,000
Blue-collar worker supervisors	69,000
Local truck drivers	64,000
Accountants	61,000
Licensed practical nurses	60,000
Typists	59,000
Carpenters	58,000
Industrial machinery repairers	58,000
Real-estate agents and brokers	50,000
Construction laborers	49,000
Engineers	46,500
Bank clerks	45,000
Private household workers	45,000
Receptionists	41,000
Wholesale trade sales workers	40,000

Where You Work Counts, Too

Knowing the occupations that will be in greatest demand is helpful in determining future career plans. However, it's also a good idea to note *where* jobs will be available. For example, people seeking teaching positions will be more likely to find them in, say, San Diego — a rapidly growing area — than in the New York metropolitan area. But what about those who would like to find work as marine biologists? Undoubtedly, the Denver papers would have few ads listed.

On a larger scale, the demand for, say, registered nurses will grow by over 45 percent during the next decade. What's more, there will be some 85,000 annual openings, as we saw in the preceding table. Yet the U.S. Labor Department points out that while nurses will find particularly good opportunities in some southern states and in inner-city areas, they "may find competition for higher-paying jobs and for jobs in some urban areas with large training facilities." The "where" does indeed matter.

The Fastest-Growing States

The government predicts that by 1985, some nineteen states plus the District of Columbia will realize an increase in job openings of between 10 percent and almost 27 percent. The top four, all of which are expected to grow by over 20 percent, are Alaska, Wyoming, Utah, and Nevada. Coming up behind them (from west to east) are Hawaii, Idaho, Arizona, Colorado, New Mexico, Texas, Kansas, Minnesota, Wisconsin, Florida, South Carolina, Maryland, Delaware, the District of Columbia, Vermont, and New Hampshire.

The other thirty-one states should grow by 2 percent to about 10 percent. Again, that doesn't mean that jobs won't be available in these states. It only points to the fact that present job-seekers might have an easier time in some places than in others. The government figures indicate which pastures are currently greenest. As we will see in the following section, areas of the country do experience growth, decline, and other resurgence. Therefore, although the states mentioned above may have the edge right now, they won't necessarily have it for long. And they certainly don't have *all* of the top jobs.

The Cities of Tomorrow

" 'Seventy-five percent of all additional jobs created will be in the South and West, and the high point of concentration will be in the small cities,' says George Sternlief, director of the Center for Urban Policy at Rutgers University. Many of these jobs will be the highly skilled, highly paid and highly portable ones associated with advanced-technology fields . . . Most urbanologists think the largest [cities] will retain their roles as the center of finance, management, corporate law and specialized medicine."

— CARRIE TUHY, "Big Futures in Small Cities," *Money,* October 1980.

"The typical small town is free of the city's unruly ambience but not of its nagging problems . . . Downtown decay is common in small-town America, as are shortages of housing, medical service, diversions for the young and suitable settings for the lonely aged . . . The hyperkinetic metropolis, by sheer energy and the density of its cultural and economic shadow, will continue to dominate American consciousness and style."

— FRANK TRIPPETT, "Small Town, U.S.A.: Growing and Groaning," *Time,* September 1, 1980.

During the past several years, we have all read about the incredible growth of the Sun Belt area. Indeed, many of the states just cited as having the greatest anticipated growth are located in that stretch of America that lies between Virginia and California. Recently, the "desirable" regions of the country seem to have been defined as much by climate as by geography, as vast numbers of business owners and city dwellers abandoned the cold and congestion of the North and Midwest and headed for the warmer, more spacious environs of the South and West.

But as corporations made their well-publicized way southward and westward and some 4 million people headed toward the Sun Belt to seek a better life for themselves and their families, something interesting began to happen. Many of the problems the migrants had left behind them — such as crowding, pollution, crime, and unemployment — suddenly began to emerge in their new communities. The result? Kenneth Goldstein, an economist with The Conference Board, explains: "The final figures aren't in yet, but we're likely to see that the rapid growth in the Sun Belt has already begun to slow."

Even more interesting, he points out, is that some of the boom areas of the coming decade could turn out to be the cities the migrants left behind — cities pronounced dead in the 1960s and 1970s. Goldstein explains: "There's a popular theory around today that cities, like people, experience life cycles. First, there's the 'young' period of a city, which is characterized by vigorous growth and heavy construction; businesses and people rush in to conquer the virgin territory." That's what we have seen happening in the Sun Belt. After a while, Goldstein continues, growth slows and the new area becomes settled; the economy of the region stabilizes. "That's when some of the old, familiar urban problems begin to become evident. Gradually, after the city has reached its peak, it begins to fall into decline. People and companies begin to pack up and move elsewhere." Where? Often back to the once-abandoned cities, which may now offer brand-new opportunities for growth and expansion. The old cities are in effect rejuvenated.

Of course, none of this happens overnight. "The entire cycle can take as long as thirty to forty years to complete," says Goldstein, who works in The Conference Board's business conditions analysis department. "But a good example of the entire process can be seen in New England. In the 1930s, most of the textile companies that had flourished in the Northeast moved out of New England, prompting a long, slow period of decline. But now new industry and different

businesses have come in." For example, New England has become a major center of the electronics industry and of the
insurance business, among others. "Now the growth that's taking place in the Northeast is tremendous. It's similar to what's
been happening in the Sun Belt," he says.

Among the other cities Goldstein points to as examples of
those undergoing revitalization are Pittsburgh, Baltimore, Detroit, and New York City. "In addition," he says, "during the
1960s and 1970s, firms in Cincinnati and Newark chose to
relocate rather than build new plants in dreary, decaying
areas. But now companies have begun to realize that they
can't keep moving south and west forever. So with the help of
government rezoning and tax abatements, plus the willingness
of banks to put more resources into inner cities and rundown
urban areas, these cities too are beginning to show signs of
renewed growth."

What does all of this mean to you as a prospective job-
hunter? It means that you shouldn't assume you have to run
to the Sun Belt if you expect to find a good job. In some cases,
the movement southward *has* created critical shortages of
trained personnel, as in the health field. But on the other
hand, Goldstein points out, so many people have already
moved to certain parts of the Sun Belt that in certain fields,
there are more workers than jobs for them to fill. Construction is a prime example.

If economists like Kenneth Goldstein are correct, there will
be renewed growth in many cities throughout the United
States. That means industry, housing, *and* employment. So
stay tuned to developments in your own area. Read the newspapers. Take note, for example, of talks about corporate expansion, of plans for new hotels or sports complexes or hospitals or convention centers, of any influx of small businesses
to nearby communities. Keep abreast of what's happening in
the immediate and near future. That way, you will have a
better chance of anticipating tomorrow's job market and of
preparing yourself to fill one of the openings that may become available. Or you will be better able to identify opportunities to serve newcomers in your community by starting a
profitable business of your own.

The Highest-Paying Areas

According to Labor Department data published in 1979, the areas of the country in which salaries were highest during 1976 were the North Central and Western regions. The top-paying cities are typically large ones with huge labor markets. Lower-paying areas were often smaller cities, typically located in the South.

A 1980 survey by the Robert Half organization of starting salaries for all types of workers in the huge finance and data-processing fields bears out the government's conclusions. The study, which includes the pay of everyone from bookkeepers and computer operators to systems analysts and chief financial officers, indicates that salaries can vary considerably depending on where you work.

The table on page 100 is a state-by-state listing, with salary variances indicated by percentage above and below the national average. As Robert Half specifies, salaries above the $50,000 level aren't necessarily covered by these variances. Furthermore, for salaries under $50,000, figure on an additional 5 percent if the job is located in a city with a population of 1 million or more.

Finally, the U.S. Labor Department analyses of salaries for office workers, including clerical and data-processing personnel, and of maintenance and unskilled plant workers are summarized in the table on page 101. Once again, note the higher salaries in larger cities, and the lowest earnings in the South.

NEW ENGLAND	Percent	SOUTHEAST	Percent
Connecticut	+5	Alabama	−7
Maine	−10	Arkansas	−8
Massachusetts	+3	Florida	−9
New Hampshire	−1	Georgia	−4
Rhode Island	0	Kentucky	−4
Vermont	−6	Louisiana	−8
		Mississippi	−10
MIDEAST		North Carolina	−8
Delaware	0	South Carolina	−8
District of		Tennessee	−9
Columbia	+1	Virginia	0
Maryland	+1	West Virginia	−9
New Jersey	+2		
New York	+3	**SOUTHWEST**	
Pennsylvania	0	Arizona	−3
		New Mexico	−9
GREAT LAKES		Oklahoma	−7
Illinois	+5	Texas	+1
Indiana	0		
Michigan	+5	**ROCKY**	
Ohio	+1	**MOUNTAIN**	
Wisconsin	+1	Colorado	−1
		Idaho	−7
PLAINS		Montana	−9
Iowa	−3	Utah	−2
Kansas	−1	Wyoming	0
Minnesota	+1		
Missouri	0	**FAR WEST**	
Nebraska	−3	Alaska	+18
North Dakota	−4	California	+5
South Dakota	−5	Hawaii	+12
		Nevada	+5
		Oregon	−2
		Washington	+2

Source: "Financial and Data Processing Prevailing Starting Salaries, 1980,"
copyright © 1980, Robert Half of New York, Inc. Used by permission.

Office Workers (includes clerical and data-processing personnel)

High-paying areas	Low-paying areas
Anaheim–Santa Ana–Garden Grove	Chattanooga
Atlanta	Greenville–Spartanburg
Chicago	Jackson (Miss.)
Detroit	Memphis
Los Angeles–Long Beach	New Orleans
Newark	Oklahoma City
New York	Richmond
San Francisco–Oakland	San Antonio
San Jose	
Seattle–Everett	
Washington, D.C.	

Maintenance and Unskilled Plant Workers

High-paying areas	Low-paying areas
Buffalo	Greenville–Spartanburg
Chicago	Huntsville
Cleveland	Jackson (Miss.)
Davenport–Rock Island–Moline	Miami
Dayton	Norfolk–Virginia Beach–Portsmouth
Detroit	Oklahoma City
Kansas City	Providence–Warwick–Pawtucket
Minneapolis–St. Paul	
Portland (Ore., Wash.)	
Sacramento	
San Francisco	
San Jose	
Seattle–Everett	
Toledo	

Source: U.S. Department of Labor, Bureau of Labor Statistics, *Profiles of Occupational Pay*, Bulletin 2037, 1979.

⚜ 5 ⚜

Today's Best
Part-Time Jobs

◆━━━━◆━━━━◆

THE PURPOSE of this chapter is not to try to give you a complete description of every single job imaginable, with details about what personal characteristics you need to do the job or information about what people do during their workdays. There are plenty of excellent books around that do just that. (See "Career Guides" in the "Resources" section, page 367.) Nor is it my intention to imply that the jobs mentioned here are the only jobs that can or should be done on a part-time basis. On the contrary. I heartily agree with such experts as Georgetown University's Dr. Stanley Nollen, Brenda B. Eddy, and Virginia H. Martin that almost any job can be done successfully on a part-time basis.

Rather, this chapter is designed to help you focus on those fields and the jobs in them that currently offer the best opportunities for would-be part-timers. Sure, you can pound on doors of manufacturing firms looking for a part-time job as a tool- and die-maker, but odds are you'll wear out your knuckles long before you find anyone willing to talk with you. Look for a job as a physical therapist, however, and you'll find any number of employers eager to set up an interview. This chapter reflects the fact that the best opportunities still remain in white-collar areas, and in the service fields in particular. We all hope that in the future, as news of the benefits of hiring part-timers spreads, more and more employers in all industries will realize that it is in their best interest to add part-time workers to the payroll. For now, however, the occupations described here are among the top choices.

Each of the fields mentioned in the coming pages begins with a section called "General Information/Part-time Prospects." The purpose of this section is to highlight, among other features, the types of organizations that hire part-timers, or perhaps the parts of the country in which part-time jobs are most widespread. Opportunities for student jobs or the availability of free-lance work are also included where applicable. If related occupations within the field are likely to offer good part-time opportunities, these are mentioned, too.

After the general introduction, you will find details about several of the jobs within that field that probably offer good part-time opportunities. Again, not every single job within the field is listed. (The *Occupational Outlook Handbook* in your library can give you the specifics about almost every job that exists.) Rather, those occupations that seem to offer some of the best bets for part-timers are described in terms of earning potential, the education and training required to get a good job, and the most likely paths to advancement. (Earnings for the occupation in general are listed in terms of full-time employment. If you are able to work only twenty hours per week, obviously you must figure on a salary of about half that listed; for a thirty-hour-per-week schedule, roughly 75 percent of the salary stated.)

For almost every one of the fields mentioned, you will read at least one example of someone who holds a good part-time job. Sometimes several different people are presented. These successful part-timers, as they are called, offer details about what they do, how much they earn as part-timers, and how they got their present jobs. They also frequently mention some of the advantages or drawbacks they have encountered as part-timers. Some, for instance, have found it easy to adjust and love their jobs; others are disappointed that their careers seem to be bogged down, or that coworkers don't take them seriously. All of them have been generous with their time and honest in their responses. Their insights should be most helpful to people seeking similar jobs.

In some of the fields included in this chapter, individuals

working at the highest-level jobs on a part-time basis are few and far between. Only a tiny proportion of lawyers work part-time, for instance, but a top-level part-time attorney is included in the law section. The purpose of the example isn't to suggest that getting such a job is a snap, but to indicate that if such individuals have been able to land good part-time jobs at enviable salaries, there is no reason why — with proper training, a well-directed job hunt, and persistence — you can't also.

A word about sources: In addition to using the *Occupational Outlook Handbook* and numerous full-length career guides, I relied on information provided by professional and trade associations, periodicals and newspapers of all descriptions, government studies, research by private groups, comments from experts in numerous fields, and countless interviews with employers and employees to develop this chapter.

Use the chapter as an overall guide to help you identify the fields most likely to welcome part-timers and the best-bet jobs in each field. Get further information about specific careers from the career guides mentioned in the "Resources" section at the back of the book. Then send for additional details from the organizations and groups associated with each profession. When you write, ask about general career information and specifically for publication lists or booklets the organizations send out free.

One note: Even though most organizations and associations don't have specific information on part-time opportunities in their respective fields — many don't even know how many people are working in the field on a part-time basis! — be sure to mention that you are interested in working part-time. That way, even though you may not get all of the details you would like, you will at least alert the organizations to the fact that there are people looking for part-time work in their industry. Once word starts to get around that people are inquiring about part-time opportunities, the groups may begin addressing themselves to the question of how would-be part-timers *can* find work. Furthermore, companies that belong to the various trade and professional associations may become more familiar with and amenable to the idea of hiring part-timers. Then we'll be that much closer to achieving the goal of helping every woman or man who wants a good part-time job to find one.

The Highest-Paid Part-Timers

If you have exceptional ability in sports or breathtakingly good looks, you don't need this book to tell you how to get a high-paying part-time job. Undoubtedly coaches, agents, teachers, or family and friends have already steered you to the people who can help you make the most of your natural abilities or gifts in the least amount of time.

In all fairness, of course, we should point out that it takes more than a strong pitching arm, a beautiful face, or a golden voice to make it into the income stratosphere. When opera star Luciano Pavarotti performs for forty-five minutes or so and receives upward of $15,000, many years of voice coaching and countless hours of rehearsal have gone into that singular performance. Similarly, when tennis ace Chris Evert walks onto a tennis court, demolishes still another tournament finalist in less than an hour, and walks away with a check for $50,000, we should remember that the skill that enabled her to get to the top of her profession was perfected with lessons, practice, more lessons, and ever more practice.

Nevertheless, it is always nice to dream about being, say, former lightweight and welterweight champion Roberto Duran and walking into the ring to fight challenger Sugar Ray Leonard for an estimated $10 million. Just for fun, here are ten of today's top-paid part-timers, people who often work less than thirty-five hours a week and who earn a whole heap of money.

- Paul McCartney, singer and composer, 1979:
  $2 million per album, plus 22 percent of the royalties
- Bjorn Borg, tennis player, 1979 and 1980:
  $1,008,742 winnings for 1979; $3 million in 1980 for endorsing almost sixty different products
- Cheryl Tiegs, model, 1980:
  $1.5 million, including modeling and TV commercials
- Johnny Carson, TV and nightclub personality, 1980:
  Reportedly, $5 million from NBC, plus an estimated $250,000 per week for nightclub performances
- Tracy Austin, tennis player, 1979–80:
  Over $1 million in eighteen months, after turning pro at the age of fifteen
- Burt Reynolds, actor, 1980:
  $5 million plus an undisclosed percentage of the profits for *The Best Little Whorehouse in Texas*
- Mel Allen, sportscaster, 1980:
  $750 per hour
- Nancy Lopez, golfer, 1979:
  $197,489 winnings, Ladies' Professional Golf Association (LPGA) tour
- Elizabeth Taylor, actress, 1978:
  $100,000 for nonspeaking role in *Winter Kills*
- Dave Winfield, New York Yankees outfielder, 1981–91 contract:
  Between $13 million and $25 million in salary and bonuses, depending on which account you read; endorsements extra

Accounting

GENERAL INFORMATION/PART-TIME PROSPECTS

Accounting is one of the fields that offer the greatest opportunities to those wishing to work part-time. "Almost every accountant who has his own business once put in time working several days a week for someone else," says Milton Sherman, a successful New York accountant and lawyer who has worked part-time on numerous occasions throughout his career. Per diem accounting work is always available, particularly during tax season. So is temporary work: assignments can range from a few days to six weeks or more. Temporary employment agencies specializing in accountants and the major tax services are logical sources of employment.

Students should find no shortage of part-time work throughout the year, through either the school placement office or ads in local papers. Permanent part-time positions may also be available, although most openings will probably be in smaller companies.

Private practice is another logical route to lucrative part-time work, and for CPAs (certified public accountants) in particular, local elective offices such as receiver of taxes can pay a tidy $12,000 to $16,000 a year for a twenty-hour week.

EARNINGS

$12,500 to $50,000, depending on experience and the size of the accounting firm. CPAs earn an additional 10 percent. Those with less than a four-year bachelor's degree can earn from $11,000 to $20,000. The per diem rate for accountants is usually about $75. Temporary assignments pay $6 to $8 an hour and up to $10 an hour during tax season.

TRAINING

A bachelor's degree with a major in accounting is usually the prerequisite for a good accounting job; some firms, though, will accept those who have majored in business administration or economics. Junior and community colleges award associate degrees, which will also qualify applicants for accounting positions; however, salaries and advancement opportunities will be more limited.

ADVANCEMENT

Advancement comes with experience, and particularly with certification, which can be obtained by passing an examination prepared by the American Institute of Certified Public Accountants. Most states require CPA candidates to be college graduates; nearly all insist on at least two years of public accounting experience. For many accountants, the ultimate career goal is to establish their own firms. Those who do so successfully can earn upward of $100,000 a year.

SUCCESSFUL PART-TIMER

Marva Dawson, of Brooklyn, New York, holds an associate degree in accounting from Brooklyn College. In years past, she worked full-time as an assistant accountant and as an economic developer for an antipoverty program in New York City. Now, the forty-year-old accountant free-lances for $75 a day. She also works as a temporary for the Robert Half agency, and says that the advantage of working as a temp is that she can be choosy about her assignments. Since Marva recently underwent surgery, working when and where she wants has proved to be a decided advantage.

FOR MORE INFORMATION

National Association of
   Accountants
919 Third Avenue
New York, NY 10022

American Women's Society
   of Certified Public
   Accountants
Box 389
Marysville, OH 43040

Art

GENERAL INFORMATION/PART-TIME PROSPECTS

Part time, particularly in the world of commercial art, usually means free-lance — with the obvious potential for making whatever schedule one chooses. Permanent part-time positions for layout designers or those who can do paste-ups and mechanicals may be available at firms that put out local classified advertising directories, supermarket circulars, or department store catalogues and other brochures. Teaching is another logical part-time possibility. With these few exceptions, however, people looking for positions in the art world will find very little in the way of permanent part-time work. Free-lancing is the norm.

Temporary positions at magazines may be available to a small number of talented artists, associate-level art directors, or paste-up and mechanical specialists. For example, when a major magazine puts out a special or a double issue, or even an extremely large issue — say, at Christmas — a harried art director might decide to pick up the phone to call a couple of free-lancers who can come in and help out for a few weeks or even months.

Because the field is so diverse, potential employers of free-lancers are everywhere: magazines and newspapers, publishing companies, greeting card firms, printing and lithography businesses, photo studios, theaters, retail stores, fashion houses, advertising companies, product manufacturers, and TV stations, to name some of the more obvious ones.

EARNINGS
Income can range from next to nothing to $50,000 a year or more for successful free-lance photographers, art directors, or established illustrators.

TRAINING
Formal training in the art field isn't as important as talent is, although a degree from one of the more respected art schools in the country can be an important credential, particularly in cities such as New York or Chicago, where most magazine and advertising businesses are located.

ADVANCEMENT
Again, talent is the key. Contacts and word-of-mouth recommendations help, of course. But in the end, it's your portfolio that sells you.

Some examples of people who have achieved success in the art world on fewer than thirty-five hours a week follow. Note the diversity of the jobs they hold.

SUCCESSFUL PART-TIMERS

Technical illustrator — Elaine Gamp, forty-seven, has free-lanced for the past sixteen years doing illustrations for scientific, technical, and medical publications. A former airline hostess for TWA, Elaine received her training in a most unconventional way. Recuperating in the hospital from a severe auto accident, she was told she would never walk again. At that point, a friend who taught technical drawing at the Massachusetts Institute of Technology (MIT) began to tutor Elaine.

The lessons continued throughout her hospital stay and later at home. While the friend helped Elaine get her first free-lance assignments, Elaine was soon receiving referrals of her own. "At first, I sort of bluffed my way through jobs because I was really inexperienced." She laughs. "I found that if I just said, 'Yes, I can do that,' I could learn how to do it on my own." Within a short time, not only had Elaine proven her doctors wrong, but she had built up her new free-lance business to such an extent that she had five other free-lancers working for her in her home studio.

"In all the years I've worked as an illustrator, I think I solicited only one job," she says proudly. "Everything was on referral." But she is quick to add that membership in a professional society has helped tremendously. Today Elaine charges either $15 an hour or a flat rate on large jobs, "which works out to about $10 an hour." Occasionally, she works through a temporary agency in Boston for about $65 a day.

Paste-up artist — Amy Seidman, a fifty-one-year-old mother of three grown children, learned to do paste-ups and mechanicals during a two-year stint at a New Jersey weekly paper. She recently listed her name in a New York City publication that is sent to prospective employers of free-lancers in the art field. *Freelancers in the Graphic Arts* charges Amy $6 a month for her listing; she now gets $10 an hour doing paste-ups. "Free-lance work is ideal for me at this stage of my life," says Amy. "It frees me to pursue my major interest, which is writing and illustrating children's books."

Museum curator — Pat Chieffo, forty-three, actually holds two part-time jobs, both of which are fascinating. She puts in twenty hours a week as associate curator of Georgetown University's art collection and another twenty hours at the Smithsonian Institution, where she works with colleges and universities to train students in museum work. As part of her responsibilities, Pat coordinates both one-year and summer internships at the Smithsonian. The mother of two, she holds a degree in education, attended the Corcoran School of Art for two years, and began working in 1959. Since then, she has only worked part-time. "I was offered full-time positions," she recalls, "but I just talked them into giving me the jobs on a part-time basis." Promotions, she laments, have not been forthcoming, but her salaries are excellent: she holds a high Government Service position (GS-12) at the Smithsonian, and earns $12,000 a year at Georgetown University. "But I get more than just monetary compensation," she is quick to point out. "My work is very stimulating — it's never boring."

Typesetter — Fern Mitchell, thirty, works as a free-lancer for both advertising and publishing companies. In addition to typesetting on Compugraphic equipment, she does page make-up and proofreading work. Fern received a degree in art from Brooklyn College in 1980 and also holds an associate's degree in graphics. At first she worked only as a paste-up artist; later, while working for the Manhattan Yellow Pages, she was trained on typesetting equipment. Today word-of-mouth recommendations, classified ads, and professional listings get her more work than she can handle, plus earnings of $10 to $12 an hour. "There's as much work out there as anybody wants," she says. Many of the people who do similar work are former secretaries, Fern has discovered over the past eight years. "They do it because the money is so good," she says.

Painter/teacher — "My first love is my painting, and I work at it every single day," says Margit Beck, a Great Neck, New York, painter who was recently named in an article in *Working Woman* magazine as one of the top twenty-five female artists in the country. Like most successful artists, Margit struggled for many years before she achieved prominence. Today her oil paintings command as much as $10,000; her drawings, $1000 or more. Margit, the mother of two grown children, holds major exhibits every two years; she spends much of her time preparing for the shows. However, for the past thirteen years she has also taught drawing at New York University, and in her spare time she counsels private students who bring their works in progress to her at-home studio. "The going rate for private art instruction is $15 an hour," says Margit, "but I've always charged less than that. So far, I've produced a half-dozen professional painters, and that's what I consider the most gratifying part of my teaching."

Photographer/art director/art gallery salesperson — Photography is twenty-eight-year-old Arnie Svenson's real passion, and he spends as much time doing it as he possibly can — sometimes forty to fifty hours a week. Yet when he was supporting himself solely by his photography, Arnie was unhappy: "I didn't like much of the work I was doing; I felt I was compromising myself." What he wanted to do was fashion photography and, even more than that, noncommercial work. But noncommercial work does not pay the rent. As Arnie recalls, "One day, I decided to get a part-time job so that I could do only the shooting I wanted to do."

Almost as a lark, he applied for a job as a stock boy at the Circle Art Gallery in Manhattan's SoHo district. "I'd never swept floors or done really mindless work before." He laughs. "I thought it might be fun for a while." The job only lasted two weeks, however. When a salesperson at the gallery left, the manager offered Arnie the vacant selling job; he took it.

Today, Arnie works twenty-six hours per week, earning a 10 percent commission against a draw of about $21 a day. "Occasionally," he admits, "working at the gallery can be tense, as it is at any job where there's no set income. For days I might sell nothing, and then all of a sudden, over $10,000 worth of prints, and then nothing again for a while."

Despite the erratic income, he enjoys the job because it has given him the freedom to pursue an even more successful photography career. Recently a film director saw Arnie's portfolio and hired him to do all of the exterior shots and color work for the film *Union City*, which was released by a small production company in several U.S. cities. Arnie is also now doing more fashion photography and recently did some promotion pieces for rock 'n' roll groups.

The money he earns as a photographer varies tremendously. "It depends on who you're working for and what the arrangement is — for example, whether you retain rights to your photos or you sell them outright," he says. It is not unusual for successful free-lance photographers to make $100 to $300 an hour or more; some free-lancers, Arnie claims, make well over $100,000 a year. He doesn't know if he'll ever make it that big, but he does know that, for the time being, he has worked out a perfect arrangement: "I do only what I want to do, and I love it."

FOR FURTHER INFORMATION

National Art Education
  Association
National Education
  Association
1916 Association Drive
Reston, VA 22091

American Institute of
  Graphic Arts
1059 Third Avenue
New York, NY 10021

American Association of
  Museums
2333 Wisconsin Avenue,
  N.W.
Washington, DC 20007

Council of American Artist
  Societies
112 East 19th Street
New York, NY 10003

Banking

GENERAL INFORMATION/PART-TIME PROSPECTS

Banking is a field that is particularly hospitable to women. In 1978, over 30 percent of all bank officers and managers were female. For part-timers, though, opportunities still tend to be clustered at the low end of the pay scale. However, some platform assistants — people who aid managers, assist customers, and occasionally supervise tellers — do work part-time. Likewise, customer service representatives, loan managers, and other mid-level personnel are increasingly being considered for part-time positions. As an article in the April 1978 issue of *Savings & Loan News* states, "There are indications that supervisory, professional and even managerial tasks can be staffed by part-time employees."

As more and more banks increase their weekday hours and stay open on weekends, more part-time jobs will become available. Similarly, part-time jobs will also be available in such related businesses as credit card and finance companies, loan agencies, and retail-store credit departments.

If you want a bank job in particular, however, don't expect to see want ads or signs in the window. Many banks don't advertise. In fact, one industry trade magazine recently advised that want ads or window signs could attract "spur-of-the moment" applicants and people who may perform "shoddy and careless" work.[1] The author's assumption is that people who answer help-wanted ads for part-time jobs really want to work full-time; therefore, they have little commitment to their employers.

Instead, sources within the industry advise banks to check with employment offices of local colleges and universities or consult their own back records to find retirees who might be willing to work part-time. Local "Y's" are another recommended source of potential employees. *American Banker* magazine adds trade schools, church organizations, retiree groups, and skill centers to the where-to-look list. If those are the places where the banks look for part-time workers, they are where you should be well known.

Bank Officer or Manager

EARNINGS

$12,000 to $15,000 for management trainees; several thousand dollars more for those with MBA degrees. Department managers make from $16,000 to $20,000 a year; bank managers, $40,000 or more.

TRAINING

A bachelor's degree is the minimum requirement for new em-

---

1. Bess Ritter May, "In Search of Part-time Workers," *Burroughs Clearing House* (February 1980), p. 19.

ployees selected for in-house training. Sometimes it is possible for outstanding bank clerks or tellers to enter management training programs. Usually these are not college graduates but individuals who have demonstrated initiative and dedication by studying finance and related subjects at community colleges, or who have taken part in programs offered by the American Institute of Banking or the American Bankers Association. (Tuition reimbursement is often provided.) Training programs last from six months to a year or more; trainees serve in all departments to gain broad experience.

ADVANCEMENT
With additional experience or education, or both, a bank officer should advance with ease.

SUCCESSFUL PART-TIMER
Catherine Ryan, a forty-year-old mother of two, works as a trust officer at the Continental Illinois National Bank and Trust Company in Chicago. She handles foundations and trusts, overseeing their investments and grant-making operations, their tax returns, and their government obligations. Catherine received her college degree in economics and French and attended law school for one year. Then she went to work at the bank, where she was employed full-time as an officer. That lasted four and a half years. After the birth of her first child and a six-month leave of absence, Catherine attempted to resume full-time work. "That lasted two months," she recalls. "I was having babysitter problems and my family life was crumbling. I was going to quit. But the bank suggested that I continue part-time." That was in 1974. Since then, Catherine has received regular reviews and raises and now earns about $270 for a three-day week. "A lot of people didn't think part-timing would work," says Catherine, "but I made up my mind that I'd do my best to *make* it work, and it has."

"No employer can discriminate because of sex . . . [or] age. Yet if you want a young lady to work as a

*part-time teller, and your applicant is a male senior
citizen, can it be possible to transfer the pretty girl
who now works part-time in the bank's bookkeeping
department to the teller's cage, and offer the senior
citizen the job she is leaving?"*

— BESS RITTER MAY, "In Search of Part-time Workers," *Burroughs Clearing House*, February 1980.

Bank Teller

EARNINGS

Beginners (full- and part-timers) earn from $4 to $5 an hour;
those with more experience, $6 an hour. Supervisors make
from $6 to $7 an hour.

TRAINING

High-school graduates are preferred, particularly those with
some experience in typing, working with office machines, or
other office-related skills. Strong character references are a
must, since tellers are bonded. On-the-job training is provided
by employers.

ADVANCEMENT

Tellers are sometimes promoted to supervisor, sometimes to
customer service representative, although college graduates
are often hired (at $6 to $7 an hour) to open new accounts.
In general, though, promotions are given to those who work
full-time; later, full-timers may be able to negotiate part-time
schedules.

FOR FURTHER INFORMATION

American Bankers
    Association
Bank Personnel Division
1120 Connecticut Ave.,
    N.W.
Washington, DC 20036

National Association of
    Bank Women
111 East Wacker Drive
Chicago, IL 60601

Communications

GENERAL INFORMATION/PART-TIME PROSPECTS

The communications field encompasses numerous occupations. Under the heading of communications falls everything from TV and radio broadcasting to advertising and public relations, newspaper reporting, publishing, feature or short-story writing for magazines, and turning out full-length screenplays and novels.

In each of these separate fields, working part-time usually means working free-lance. Temporary assignments do exist. So do internships for college students, although only about half are paid positions, according to a 1980 survey by Women in Communications, Inc. Permanent part-time positions — salaried jobs that require fewer than thirty-five hours of work per week — are less prevalent than free-lance or occasional temporary opportunities are.

Even so, not all employers within the broad communications field regularly use free-lancers or part-timers. "In the advertising agency business, most part-time workers are clerical personnel," says Robert Purcell, vice-president of public affairs for the American Association of Advertising Agencies. "There are some people who do free-lance copy or artwork, but these people are used in a supplementary sense; it's a word-of-mouth kind of system."

For would-be free-lancers and other part-timers in the public relations field, the best opportunities are in small companies, particularly in nonprofit organizations. In such firms, the budget usually determines how many people are hired and how many hours they work.

In broadcasting, some radio announcers or reporters put in four- or five-hour shifts, as do part-time technicians (such as people who begin feature films or start video cartridges). Most of the part-time jobs are available at local radio and small TV stations, whether UHF, network affiliate, or cable. The major networks hire summer-replacement cameramen and -women and other trained operators to take over for vacationing regulars. College stations are the best bet for students seeking broadcasting experience, on or off the air.

Newspapers in small towns may use part-time or free-lance reporters. The large news magazines and wire services use "stringers" for their local coverage. Hired by local bureau chiefs rather than by the central personnel office, stringers aren't on salary; they are paid only when their stories make it into print. Needless to say, stringers' paychecks are small, few, and very far between.

In book publishing, steady part-time work is unusual. But free-lance copy-editing or book-designing jobs are often available. "To get a job as a free-lance copy editor, one must usually show related experience and then pass a copy-editing test," says Ruth Hapgood, an editor at Houghton Mifflin in Boston. Another free-lance possibility she mentions is working as an acquisitions editor. The editor brings in various proposed books; if one of the books is published, the editor earns a flat fee or a percentage of the book's profits. "Usually," Ruth maintains, "people who make such arrangements are former staff editors. About the only other part-timers you see in publishing firms are company librarians, plus perhaps one or two summer interns each year."

For free-lance writers, the number of potential markets is awesome. Yet the number of writers able to earn a living free-lancing is minuscule. Successful free-lance Murray Teigh Bloom, who has written over six hundred magazine articles, six books, and a play, recently estimated that only about three hundred writers earn enough to support themselves solely by writing. Nevertheless, the future for free-lancers should be bright, Bloom predicts. "No more than a decade from now, any individual who can write a decent declarative sentence will possess a specialized skill easily convertible to cash."[2]

One person who has parlayed the ability to write clearly, a bit of experience as a newspaper reporter, and five years of work in the real-estate business into a successful free-lance writing venture is fifty-four-year-old Edith Lank of Rochester, New York. Edith, the mother of three grown children, recently began syndicating her column on real estate, called

2. Quoted in Leslie Hanscom, "The Free-Lancer as Master of a Vanishing Skill," *Newsday*, December 18, 1977, p. 22.

"House Calls." "At first, I sold it to my local paper for $25 a week. Then I decided to try selling it elsewhere," she recalls. An initial mailing of five hundred brought no responses; undaunted, Edith continued her efforts. Today, she claims, the column appears in twenty newspapers nationwide. Edith also works as a part-time college instructor and is presently writing a book. All of her work, she contends, amounts to only two full days a week but nets her $800 a month. About part-time work, she says: "I wouldn't have it any other way. I haven't set an alarm clock in eight years."

If you would like to learn more about free-lance writing, head for the library and consult *Writer's Market* (published annually by Writer's Digest Books, Cincinnati, Ohio) and *Literary Market Place* (published annually by R. R. Bowker, New York, New York). Another excellent guide, one that contains an invaluable resource list for would-be writers, is *How to Get Happily Published,* by Judith Appelbaum and Nancy Evans (New York: Harper and Row, 1978; $9.95).

Technical writers can hook up with specialty publishing houses or temporary agencies and land an ongoing succession of assignments, particularly if they live in areas in which there are many drug, chemical, automobile, engineering, computer, or electronics firms. In addition, technical writers may obtain assignments on a word-of-mouth basis from members of professional organizations and people within firms they have already worked for. A top-flight technical writer can earn over $30,000 a year. For further information about technical writing, contact Society for Technical Communication, Inc., 1010 Vermont Avenue, N.W., Suite 421, Washington, DC 20005. For further information about the communications field in general, ask for "Careers in Communications," a comprehensive thirty-page booklet available free from Women in Communications, Inc., Box 9561, Austin, TX 78766.

Editor

EARNINGS

$12,000 to $14,000 at small publishing companies; $15,000 to $30,000 for experienced editors at larger firms; upward of

$50,000 for top editors at major publishing houses or national magazines.

TRAINING
A college degree is usually required for entry-level secretarial jobs. Typing, shorthand, and other office skills are also essential. Technical publications usually require appropriate education or experience.

ADVANCEMENT
Experience leads to promotion.

SUCCESSFUL PART-TIMER
In 1941, Ruth Hapgood, bright, enthusiastic, and armed with Phi Beta Kappa honors, graduated from college. "Like all girls looking for work at that time, I headed straight for secretarial school," she says. Her first full-time job was as secretary in the juvenile department of the William Morrow publishing company. She soon transferred into the advertising department and was promoted to manager.

Some time later, Ruth and her family (which by then included two small children) moved to Boston. Ruth thought she would stay home for a while, then took a school job on a part-time basis. But she began to realize that she missed publishing. "I decided to try to get some work as a free-lance copy editor," Ruth recalls. "I wrote about two hundred letters advertising myself and my qualifications." Shortly thereafter, Ruth was working for three different publishing companies, of which Houghton Mifflin was one. "I worked on an hourly basis, but soon they asked me to come in one day a week to work as a manuscript reader," she recounts. "I was still paid on an hourly basis, though."

Gradually, the one day a week became two, then three. Ruth was eventually promoted to the position of acquisitions editor in the firm's trade division. She brings in new titles and sees them through to publication.

During the two weekdays she was away from the office, Ruth did some free-lance writing, helping various medical doctors with their books and other writing projects. But word-of-mouth recommendations soon brought her more work than she could handle. Ruth decided to give up the medical writing altogether and work four days a week at Houghton Mifflin. "Now I'm off every Wednesday," she says, "and I use that time to read, go to the library, or just talk to authors. Sure, the company benefits from my 'free' time," she adds, laughing, "but I guess my work really is what I enjoy doing most."

Reporter

EARNINGS

Most newspaper and radio reporters start at between $9000 and $13,000 a year; network TV reporters earn considerably more. Top newspaper reporters can make over $40,000 a year, and network TV correspondents, more than $100,000 a year.

TRAINING

Most large newspapers will hire only applicants with a bachelor's degree; many prefer a major or even a graduate degree in journalism. Most successful job candidates also have experience working on college newspapers or small-town publications. Usually, radio and TV reporters work their way up to the top local and network shows by moving from one station to another, gaining broad experience and exposure along the way.

ADVANCEMENT

Advancement comes with experience. Occasionally, some reporters decide to switch to work in books or magazines, advertising, or public relations, where they may be able to earn more money.

SUCCESSFUL PART-TIMER

Sue Maushart, twenty-three, is the bright and extremely capable young woman who worked as a research associate on this book. Currently enrolled in a master's degree program in media ecology at New York University, Sue hasn't yet decided which area of the enormous communications field appeals to her most. So she has taken several different part-time jobs in order to gain broad-based experience. In addition to doing interviewing and other research for me, Sue has been working as a part-time reporter for Cablevision, a newly established cable TV station on Long Island. Among her assignments: an interview with U.S. Senator Jacob Javits prior to the 1980 New York State primary election, and a report on the trial in the local Island Trees school district book-banning suit. The pay Sue receives as a novice reporter is low, only $4 an hour. But Sue recognizes that the experience she is gaining now, while she is still in school, will hold her in good stead regardless of the career she eventually chooses.

FOR FURTHER INFORMATION

American Council on
 Education for Journalism
School of Journalism
University of Missouri
Columbia, MO 65201

American Newspaper
 Publishers Association
 Foundation
P.O. Box 17407
Dulles International Airport
Washington, DC 20041

The Newspaper Guild
Research and Information
 Department
1125 15th Street, N.W.
Washington, DC 20005

Public Relations Worker

EARNINGS

Starting salaries range from about $10,300 to about $15,000; experienced workers can earn between $25,000 and $40,000. Some successful publicists who free-lance can make as much as $600 or $700 a day, plus expenses.

TRAINING

A bachelor's degree — usually in journalism, communications, or public relations — is often required, as is some media or journalism experience. For those dealing with technical subjects, appropriate education is generally necessary.

ADVANCEMENT
Experience is the key. The Public Relations Society of America accredits people who have worked for at least five years in the field and who have passed an examination. Accreditation can be a useful credential in some areas.

SUCCESSFUL PART-TIMER
Susan Tijada, thirty-four, works as a public information specialist working for the Environmental Protection Agency in Washington. Her Government Service ranking is GS-12, just below the highest group of federal civil service jobs. The division she works for is concerned with air, noise, and radiation pollution; Susan assists one of the directors of the public affairs office. Her job is diverse. She helps coordinate such media projects as public service announcements, films, press releases, and press briefings. Besides an intriguing job, Susan also has an interesting work schedule. She puts in three days one week and four the next, and spends her free time with her four-year-old son. This young mother earns a good salary — $17,000 a year for her average twenty-eight-hour week — but she has felt limitations on her promotion prospects. "You just have to accept those disadvantages," Susan says philosophically, "because working part-time is worth it in the long run."

FOR FURTHER INFORMATION
Public Relations Society of
    America, Inc.
Career Information
145 Third Avenue
New York, NY 10022

Service Department
Public Relations News
127 East 80th Street
New York, NY 10021

Counseling

GENERAL INFORMATION/PART-TIME PROSPECTS

Webster defines *counselor* simply as "a person who counsels; adviser." We know that under the heading "counseling" falls an enormous range of professions dedicated to helping people in need of guidance, emotional support, or help with myriad problems, ranging from alcohol and drug abuse to child abuse, family violence, and educational difficulties stemming from learning disabilities. There can also be problems related to getting or finding a job, making it through a tough transitional period (such as after divorce or the death of a spouse), or discovering a way to overcome physical or emotional disabilities and become more self-sufficient. Counseling takes them all in — and then some.

Wherever people seek help with their problems, there are good jobs for those capable of helping. Among the facilities that employ such professionals as clinical and counseling psychologists and social workers are hospitals, mental health clinics, nursing homes, public and private schools, geriatric centers, prisons, public and private social service agencies, mental hospitals, child guidance centers, drug and alcohol abuse programs. For those involved in vocational guidance or rehabilitation, there are vocational guidance centers, secondary schools and colleges, schools for disabled persons, women's employment services, and halfway houses and other residential facilities.

As in most other fields, full-time work is the norm in counseling. However, part-time jobs exist or can be arranged in almost all of these settings, particularly those hampered by funding restrictions and budgetary considerations that may limit the amount of money available for hiring staff. Surprisingly, in some areas of the country there are actually more part-time than full-time opportunities. "Many social workers juggle part-time jobs in order to make a full-time salary," says Barbara Gastwirth, a social worker from Plainview, New York.

Private practice is another possibility; in fact, it is the goal of many psychologists and social workers. Those social workers with a master's degree (MSW) may seek temporary full- or part-time clinical positions to gain experience while they continue their schooling and otherwise prepare for the day they can hang out their own shingles.

Clinical or Counseling Psychologist

EARNINGS

Starting salaries for those with a master's degree and one year of experience range from $12,000 to $16,000; men and women with Ph.D. degrees can begin at $20,000 a year. The average salary for psychologists in the federal government in 1978 was $28,200. Those in private practice can earn considerably more.

TRAINING

A master's degree is the absolute minimum required for any good assistant's job in psychology; usually a Ph.D. or Psy.D. is a must for professional recognition. All states require psychologists who wish to practice independently to be licensed — in general a person needs a Ph.D., two years of professional experience, and must pass an examination to obtain a license to practice.

ADVANCEMENT

As the level of education rises, so do responsibilities and earnings. Master's-degree holders may administer and interpret psychological tests and otherwise assist psychologists with research, teaching, and administrative duties. They may be permitted to teach at two-year colleges in some states, or to work in public and private schools as counselors. With a doctoral degree, a psychologist can choose among positions in private industry, the government, universities, and top-level clinical settings.

FOR FURTHER INFORMATION

American Psychological
    Association
Educational Affairs Office
1200 17th Street, N.W.
Washington, DC 20036

American Personnel and
    Guidance Association
2 Skyline Place, Suite 400
5203 Leesburg Pike
Falls Church, VA 22041

National Association of
    School Psychologists
1140 Connecticut Avenue,
    N.W., Suite 401
Washington, DC 20036
    *Request information about
        their placement services.*

National Health Council
1740 Broadway
New York, NY 10019

Social Worker

EARNINGS
Starting salaries range from $11,000 to $13,000; experienced
social workers can earn as much as $20,000 a year.

TRAINING
For most jobs, the master's degree in social work (MSW) is the
minimum requirement, although some casework jobs are
open to those with only a bachelor's degree in social work
(BSW). Two years of postgraduate study plus some field instruction are usually required in order to earn an MSW.

ADVANCEMENT
Almost all advancement opportunities in the field of social
work require that you obtain an MSW. Some social workers
can become high-level administrators, running comprehensive counseling programs that offer diversified services. Others open their own practices and conduct individual and
group therapy sessions.

SUCCESSFUL PART-TIMER
Barbara Gastwirth, thirty-two, received her MSW degree
from the State University of New York at Stony Brook in
1978, shortly before her first child was born. She didn't work

for about a year. Then one day a friend, also a social worker, told Barbara of an opening for a part-time social worker in the criminal division of the Legal Aid Society. Since Barbara had once worked as a secretary to a lawyer, her experience gave her the edge over other job applicants. She got the job and worked at Legal Aid for just over a year, putting in three days a week. Later Barbara was offered a job at a Long Island mental health center, where she now works two nights a week. In her work as a psychotherapist Barbara deals with a wide range of problems. She counsels families, couples, children, and individuals; she does not do group therapy.

Barbara talks about the opportunities for part-time work in mental health clinics and about the fact that salaries are quite low: "MSWs earn only from about $7.50 to $11 or $12 an hour, but most social workers are happy to get jobs at mental health clinics." Why? She explains: "You do your time. They're willing to accept you while you're still pretty green. Meanwhile, you're getting training and supervision. It's a trade-off. Working at a clinic is a great way to gain experience. Despite the low salary, it's really been good for me. I'd hate to have to give it up."

FOR FURTHER INFORMATION

National Association of
  Social Workers
1425 H Street, N.W., Suite
  600
Southern Building
Washington, DC 20005

Family Service Association
  of America
44 East 23rd Street
New York, NY 10010

Council on Social Work
  Education
345 East 46th Street
New York, NY 10017

Child Welfare League of
  America
67 Irving Place
New York, NY 10003

United Way of America
801 North Fairfax Street
Alexandria, VA 22314

Also, consult your local telephone directory to see if a chapter of the National Association of Social Workers is in your area. Local chapters can offer both job information and referral services.

Vocational Counselor

EARNINGS

Starting salaries range from $9000 to about $12,000; experienced career counselors average about $15,000. Individuals with a background in rehabilitation counseling can earn more, as can those in private practice.

TRAINING

Usually a bachelor's degree with a major in counseling or psychology is the minimum requirement for entering the field. More often, however, a master's degree in vocational counseling, personnel administration, or some related field is preferred.

ADVANCEMENT

Advancement depends on experience and/or education. Those with experience in counseling, interviewing, and job placement may advance to supervisory or administrative positions. Higher education is usually required for top jobs in public and private agencies or at colleges.

SUCCESSFUL PART-TIMERS:

Phyllis Monoson of Woodbridge, Connecticut, works as a vocational counselor for learning-disabled adults. She holds a bachelor's degree in elementary education and a master's degree in special education and worked full-time in the San Antonio school system as a special education supervisor before she moved to Connecticut. Phyllis, a thirty-four-year-old mother of two, is one of four part-time counselors at Chapel Haven, a facility for adults in New Haven. "We try to assess an individual's abilities in the vocational area. Our goal is to have the learning-disabled employed full- or part-time." Much of Phyllis's work involves job placement with businesses in the community. She earns $470 a month for working twenty hours per week. "The job was offered on a part-time basis. I didn't make a conscious decision to work part-time," Phyllis maintains. "But I must say I have found working part-time much easier in terms of meeting my family responsibilities."

Susan Ogle, thirty-three, also works in New Haven, Connecticut. She is one of three codirectors of the Career–Life Alternative Counseling Center there. All of the codirectors are part-timers. Before helping set up the center, Susan worked as a counselor at a high school under a two-year internship program that was part of her graduate study in counselor education and human relations at the University of Bridgeport. Her two partners, Anita Perlman, fifty-two, of Woodbridge and Margaret Steere, thirty-seven, of North Branford, also hold degrees in counseling. They previously worked part-time for a New Haven center that has since closed. Today each of the women puts in about two days at the office plus time at home. "The center is not a placement agency," Susan explains. "What we offer are workshops, individual counseling, and vocational testing. We charge $25 an hour for the first visit and $20 thereafter. Four three-hour workshop sessions are $95." Although Susan admits that the money they are earning right now is "very minimal," the women plan to expand their two-year-old firm by securing business and government contracts; they have already landed a good contract with the Veterans Administration.

FOR FURTHER INFORMATION

American Personnel and
  Guidance Association
2 Skyline Place, Suite 400
5203 Leesburg Pike
Falls Church, VA 22041

National Rehabilitation
  Counseling Association
1522 K Street, N.W.
Washington, DC 20005

The College Placement
  Council, Inc.
P.O. Box 2263
Bethlehem, PA 18001
  *Ask for information on
  positions in career
  planning and placement*

Data Processing

GENERAL INFORMATION/PART-TIME PROSPECTS

People trained in the operation and maintenance of computers should be able to write their own ticket in today's job market — and in tomorrow's. For some of the highest-demand occupations, minimal training will guarantee maximum financial rewards.

> *"We have a wealth of technology, but we do not have a wealth of people who know how to use it."*
> — LYNN D. SALVAGE, president of the Katharine Gibbs School. Quoted in the *New York Times*, August 10, 1980.

To land a job as a programmer or a systems analyst requires two years, often more, of post–high-school training. Word-processing machine operators, however, who often learn their jobs when new equipment comes into the office, can quickly master the skills they need and find jobs that pay them as much as $10 an hour. Part-time possibilities in the data-processing field include temporary work and, for those who have established business contacts and a good reputation, free-lancing. In addition, as more corporations install computer or word-processing centers that run around the clock, there will undoubtedly be evening and weekend work on a steady basis.

Computer Programmer

EARNINGS

Beginners can earn from $10,500 to $14,000. With experience, programmers average around $20,000 in major cities. They can earn as much as $37,000 or more. Those with graduate degrees can count on an additional 10 percent.

TRAINING

Although there are no universally accepted standards, in almost all cases post–secondary-school training is necessary.

Most two-year colleges and business schools offer certificate programs that take about thirteen weeks to complete full-time and as much as forty weeks part-time. In addition, there are one- and two-year programs that lead to an associate's degree, and of course four-year colleges often have computer science departments. On-the-job training may be provided by an employer for some of the most basic computer operations, such as data entry; some companies send their employees to classes held by the computer equipment manufacturers.

ADVANCEMENT

Advancement possibilities in this field are almost unlimited. A beginner can progress from junior programmer to programmer to systems programmer or systems analyst, with additional experience and sometimes advanced training. Some of the top programmers and analysts form their own consulting firms or otherwise operate as free-lance trouble-shooters. A certificate of data processing (CDP), which is conferred by the Institute for Certification of Computer Professionals upon candidates with five years' experience who have passed a five-part exam, is useful for those seeking advancement to the highest levels. It is also a good credential for those contemplating self-employment.

SUCCESSFUL PART-TIMER

At the ripe old age of eighteen, Arthur Magnus of New York City is earning between $8 and $10 an hour as a free-lance computer programmer and consultant. It all began, Arthur recalls, when he was in sixth grade and his teacher devoted one week to computer study. "I thought it was all very elementary, but it got me interested in reading up on the subject myself. That's how I learned," he maintains. Practical experience at his high school's student-run computer center landed Arthur his first job: working weekends to help a teacher set up a program. That was in 1977. Today Arthur's clients include the New York School of Computer Technology, where, the precocious teenager confides, "I teach the teachers how to maintain their systems." Arthur plans to enter the University of Pennsylvania to study — what else? — computer science.

FOR FURTHER INFORMATION

The American Federation
  of Information Processing
  Societies
210 Summit Avenue
Montvale, NJ 07645

Data Processing
  Management Association
505 Busse Highway
Park Ridge, IL 60068

Word Processor

EARNINGS

Full-time salaries begin at about $170 a week and can run as high as $250 or more. On an hourly basis, some word processors make as much as $15.

TRAINING

On-the-job training is widespread, particularly as businesses build or expand word-processing centers. Some high schools and vocational and business schools offer word-processing courses, and more and more junior colleges are establishing programs.

ADVANCEMENT

A person with word-processing training can become a console operator. This type of work requires the ability to spot the causes of equipment breakdowns. With additional experience, and usually training, a word processor can advance to programmer. The rate of promotion is difficult to gauge, since the field is extremely new and there is tremendous variation from one industry to the next as well as from company to company.

SUCCESSFUL PART-TIMER

Forty-eight-year-old Denise DeGoumois operates the so-called thinking typewriter on temporary assignments secured through the Robert Half agency in New York. She learned the skill — which earns her between $7.50 and $9.00 an hour — simply by reading a manufacturer's "how-to" manual. Previously Denise worked full-time in the editorial department of a retirement journal, and later as a temporary secretary. But she soon realized that she could increase her earnings by switching to word processing. "I'm an independent person, so I've decided to work with a temporary agency," Denise explains. "This way, I have more control over my schedule. I'm making more money now than I ever could as a secretary. Word-processing equipment," she adds with a laugh, "has liberated me."

FOR FURTHER INFORMATION
Write to the sources listed on page 132. For a list of accredited vocational schools that teach data and word processing, write:

National Association of Trade and Technical Schools
2021 L St., N.W.
Washington, DC 20036

Education

Though the national over-supply of teachers remains critical, surprisingly good part-time possibilities do exist within the world of education. Ironically, many of these opportunities exist because of the declining enrollments and slashed school budgets that have plagued hundreds of school districts and rendered thousands of full-time teachers unemployed. Lower budgets often mean using part-timers where full-timers once held jobs.

ELEMENTARY AND SECONDARY SCHOOLS
Such familiar part-time jobs as teaching nursery-school or kindergarten students or filling in as a substitute teacher who is

willing to drop everything and run in at a moment's notice have always been, and remain, possibilities for the would-be part-time teacher. True, pay for substitutes is often abominable —as low as $25 a day. But by putting in their time as substitutes for one or two semesters, some teachers who seek regular teaching posts find themselves in a favorable position when jobs once again open up. According to the Bureau of Labor Statistics, shortages in the currently overcrowded elementary education field should soon begin to appear. (This is already happening in parts of the country experiencing population influxes and in growing young communities everywhere.)

Teaching kindergarten and "subbing" aren't the only opportunities for part-time work at public and private schools. Good jobs are available for those teachers who have special training. Today's top fields are reading, music or art, speech, special education, science, vocational education, mathematics, and guidance. Foreign languages are another. In the United States today, an estimated 3.5 million schoolchildren speak English as a second language. Bilingual programs have been established in many parts of the country, and there is a shortage of teachers qualified to run them.

School districts that want to offer diverse subjects and curriculum enrichment but that have no budgets to hire full-time staff members are the obvious potential users of well-qualified educators. Private and parochial schools also need these specialists, and to a lesser extent so do nursery schools and day-care centers. Many certified teachers with specialized training will also find part-time work in junior or senior high schools.

"Schools in San Diego . . . are advertising in Los Angeles and San Francisco newspapers for bilingual teachers. Detroit's school system, . . . like many others, is desperate for mathematics teachers . . . Vocational education teachers are in such short supply in New York City that high-school students are being steered away from classes in such subjects as electrical

> *insulation and business machine repair . . . Schools
> in Boston are hiring seniors from Harvard, Boston
> University and other institutions of higher education
> to work as substitute teachers, at $36.56 a day."*
>
> — GENE I. MAEROFF, "Shortages of Teachers Develop
> in Time of Layoffs," *New York Times*, September 29,
> 1980.

Another part-time possibility that exists at the elementary-school level is a form of job sharing that is frequently called "partnership teaching." Elementary-school teachers often have an easier time convincing school administrators to give their innovative work schedule a try than do most other pairs who seek to share a full-time position. For a detailed guide on how to select an appropriate teaching partner and how to approach school districts with such a plan, see the Catalyst booklet "Education" (C 8), which is part of the Career Opportunities Series. The booklet is available from Catalyst, 14 East 60th Street, New York, NY 10028; cost, $2.

COLLEGES AND UNIVERSITIES

At the college level, the part-time schedule as we know it is the norm. Full-time professors are often required to teach only nine to twelve hours per week. Some assistant professors or instructors may conduct classes only two or three times per week — an ideal arrangement for the person doing academic research or outside consulting work. Part-time teachers (often hired without the possibility of receiving tenure) are increasingly used by institutions that are faced with declining enrollments or budget problems.

Another way to secure a part-time position in academia is job sharing, which is being considered by more and more colleges. Husbands and wives who wish to pursue research and/or child raising in addition to their teaching careers often seek shared positions. Small liberal arts schools in particular seem to be receptive to the idea. Among those institutions of higher learning that have already hired two people to share one full professorship are Bucknell University, Gustavus

Adolphus College, Hamline University, Hampshire College, and Wells College. Gretl S. Meier, a nationally recognized expert on job sharing, estimates that some fifty to sixty colleges have already implemented job-sharing programs, but that most of the schools have only one or two such posts at a given time.

The Project on the Status and Education of Women of the Association of American Colleges in Washington, D.C., has identified a number of U.S. colleges that have initiated variations of part-time policies "that significantly improve the status" of part-time faculty in general. Among them: Central College, Iowa; Colgate University, New York; Cornell University, New York; Harvard University, Massachusetts; Rutgers University, New Jersey; University of Wisconsin, Wisconsin; Wells College, New York; Wesleyan University, Connecticut; and Yale University, Connecticut.

Continuing Education — Perhaps the greatest number of teachers seeking part-time positions will find them in academic surroundings outside traditional elementary schools, junior and high schools, or regular college programs. Most will find numerous opportunities in continuing education: the teaching of adults throughout the United States. Today one out of every three college students is over twenty-five years old; adult education is booming. For example, current projections are that by 1990, 50 percent of college students on Long Island will be over twenty-five.[3]

In response to the skyrocketing increase in adult education programs, colleges are already meeting and anticipating the needs of adult learners for flexible courses, varied classroom locations, and choices of schedules — which certainly benefits those who might be teaching those students. In the New York area, for example, Adelphi University has held classes at the Port Authority bus terminal, at La Guardia and Kennedy airports, and at public libraries throughout Long Island. Weekend programs for husbands and wives are popping up everywhere, with arts and crafts for the children while Mom and

---

3. See Diane Greenburg, "More and More, College Begins at 40," *New York Times,* June 29, 1980.

Dad are busy studying. New York University now has a mid-town Manhattan campus where workers can take any of dozens of courses during their lunch hours. Even the Long Island Railroad has experimented with classes for bleary-eyed commuters. And almost every two- or four-year school now offers an incredible array of evening and weekend courses on everything from advertising to zoology.

Specialization and willingness to adapt to a changing educational environment are the keys to finding part-time jobs in the ever-popular teaching field. That doesn't mean that finding a good job will be easy; it won't, even if you begin your job hunt six or seven months in advance (which you should). But if you think about the special skills you offer and of some special learning facilities that would be able to use those skills, you might just connect with a good part-time teaching position.

Teacher, Elementary or Secondary School

EARNINGS

The average salary for elementary-school teachers is just over $14,000 a year; for secondary-school teachers, just under $16,000.

TRAINING

A bachelor's degree is required, often with the stipulation that a master's degree be obtained within a certain time period (for example, four or five years). State certification is required in all states.

ADVANCEMENT

Advancement depends on experience, additional degrees, or even the completion of extra courses. Promotion to the administrative level is possible.

Teacher, Nursery School or Day-Care Center

EARNINGS

Salaries run from $9000 to $14,000, depending on education

and experience; directors or top management staff receive more.

TRAINING
Teachers need a one-year certification in early childhood education, offered by community and junior colleges, or a two-year associate's degree, which can lead to a higher starting salary (about $2000 more).

ADVANCEMENT
Experience leads to higher salaries; however, some teachers hope to run their own day-care or nursery facilities or to set up child-care programs where none exist, such as in inner-city areas or headquarters of major corporations. Several years' experience is usually required to convince corporate executives, potential lenders, or funding agencies that you can run the operation successfully (check with the Small Business Administration).

Teacher's Aide

EARNINGS
Aides receive from minimum wage to about $5 an hour; the figure is higher in schools with educational requirements for teacher's aides.

TRAINING
There is tremendous variation in requirements. Some schools demand only a high-school diploma and may set income or residential restrictions for job-seekers. Other school districts may offer a formal training program or require postsecondary training, such as completion of the teacher's aide program at one of roughly four hundred community colleges throughout the country.

ADVANCEMENT
Usually slight increases in salary come with additional experience. Becoming a regular teacher requires obtaining a bachelor's degree and state certification.

SUCCESSFUL PART-TIMER

Juanita Coen, fifty-six, of East Islip, New York, has worked as an aide at the John F. Kennedy Elementary School for the past twelve years. She helps out with such clerical duties as typing, photocopying, and mimeographing. She also relieves kindergarten teachers during their lunch breaks. Money is not what drew Juanita to her job; under current provisions of a New York State law, teacher's aides are only allowed to earn $3000 a year. (That regulation may soon be changed.) Instead, she points out, the schedule was perfect for her while her own two children were in school. Juanita has never had to work in July or August and has always had the same holidays as teachers do, including long winter and spring breaks. Because of the extremely low salary, Juanita admits, "It's pretty unusual to find a contented aide." But she enjoys her work immensely. Besides the convenient schedule and some benefits, one feature has made being a teacher's aide a good job for Juanita: the school is a three-minute walk from her house.

FOR FURTHER INFORMATION

Information on teaching careers and aide programs can be obtained from:

American Federation of
   Teachers
11 Dupont Circle, N.W.
Fifth floor
Washington, DC 20036

National Education
   Association
1201 16th Street, N.W.
Washington, DC 20036

For information about opportunities for work as a teacher's aide, contact your local board of education as well as private nursery, parochial, and other schools in your area.

College Teacher

EARNINGS

Salaries range from about $15,000 for instructors to over $40,000 for full professors.

TRAINING

A master's degree is almost always required; more often than not so is a doctorate, particularly if you plan to teach at a large four-year institution.

ADVANCEMENT

Promotion is dependent on the earning of a doctorate and/or on experience. Often, three years of teaching experience are necessary to move from instructor to assistant professor, three more to become an associate professor, and a combination of teaching experience and published works to receive a full professorship. When granted at all, tenure usually goes to those who have taught at a school for five years or more. Part-time or adjunct professors are rarely granted tenure at most schools.

FOR FURTHER INFORMATION

American Federation of
  Teachers
11 Dupont Circle, N.W.
Fifth floor
Washington, DC 20036

American Association of
  University Professors
One Dupont Circle, N.W.
Washington, DC 20036

Continuing Education Teacher

EARNINGS

Earnings range from $10 to $35 an hour; they are occasionally higher in specialized schools such as business institutes.

TRAINING

The training you need depends on the subject you teach. Most continuing education teachers are college graduates; some have advanced degrees. But for courses that require only expertise and the ability to communicate, there may be no degree requirements — in fact, experience in the field is sometimes more highly prized than academic credentials.

ADVANCEMENT
There is hardly any opportunity for advancement. Contracts are generally issued one semester at a time; there is little career growth potential. Some teachers maximize their income by teaching several courses or working at several different institutions.

SUCCESSFUL PART-TIMERS
Alan Ross, twenty-nine, is a New York City free-lance writer who gave up a full-time job teaching journalism at Hofstra University on Long Island to write full-time. To earn extra income, Alan teaches a journalism course for The Skills Exchange, a Manhattan-based adult education program that offers such divergent courses as "Commas and Semicolons" (a grammar course) and "How to Meet a Man" (aimed at New York's almost one million single females). Skills Exchange instructors conduct classes in their own apartments and receive $7.50 per student. The courses last one month.

There are usually between ten and fifteen students in each of Alan's sections; therefore, his income varies. "I plan to add a works-in-progress course for fellow writers," he maintains. That way, Alan can augment the average of $225 he earns for about ten hours of work each month.

FOR FURTHER INFORMATION
The best way to find out about openings for continuing education teachers is to contact the officials who head continuing education programs at various local colleges and universities. Also, write or call your local school-district headquarters to find out about positions in adult education programs offered at high schools. "Y's" and other community organizations can be another source of jobs, as can professional and trade associations, which may publish openings for positions throughout the year.

Engineering/Technology

GENERAL INFORMATION/PART-TIME PROSPECTS

Anyone who hasn't heard about the critical and growing shortage of engineers today has probably been off on a desert island somewhere. Engineers, and particularly electrical and electronics engineers, are among the most sought-after of all professionals; they are grabbed up by government and private industry as fast as engineering schools can turn them out.

For the person seeking part-time work in engineering, that means one thing: good news. Although permanent part-time positions are unusual in engineering, the U.S. government has begun hiring engineers who put in fewer than thirty-five hours per week. What's more, the Department of the Interior, the National Aeronautics and Space Administration (NASA), and the General Services Administration (GSA) are all participating in the new federal Part-time Direct Hire Program (for details, see "Opportunities in the Federal Government," page 270). And don't overlook municipalities in the hunt for a good permanent part-time job. New York City, the largest nonfederal employer of engineers in the country, recently opened almost all city jobs to alternative work scheduling.

Research and teaching present two other part-time opportunities for engineers, and consulting and free-lance design work should be readily available to anyone living in an area where there is a high concentration of electronics, computer, consumer product, or other industrial firms.

Even though permanent part-time work remains rare, temporary work for engineers and for trained engineering and science technicians is available almost anytime, anywhere. Microelectronics and computer firms, to name just two, are among the biggest users of engineers and other technically trained people to work on projects that last from a few weeks to a few months, sometimes longer. The prime areas for temporary work are northern California (particularly the Silicon Valley area near San Francisco), Boston, Dallas, Pittsburgh, Houston, New York, San Diego, Los Angeles, Detroit, Minneapolis–St. Paul, Chicago, and Denver.

Engineer

EARNINGS

Starting salaries run from $15,000 to $22,000; some consulting firms pay as much as $32,000 a year for those with minimal experience. The average engineer earns just over $31,000; those with ten years' experience can make upward of $50,000 a year. Engineers working for temporary agencies can expect hourly wages ranging from $10 to $25.

TRAINING

A four- or five-year bachelor's program is usually required. In the past, on-the-job training played a role in preparing engineers for increased responsibilities (see the example below), but today the bachelor's degree is usually the minimum requirement. A master's degree is sometimes needed for top-level entry positions, and a Ph.D. is a must for those who wish to teach.

ADVANCEMENT

Advancement comes with experience.

SUCCESSFUL PART-TIMER

Carol Watson, thirty-nine, is one of those rare individuals in the field of engineering — a successful electromechanical engineer who has had no formal engineering education. "I am self-educated and self-motivated," explains this mother of two, who learned her trade in Canada and in England where, she says, the field was dominated by women. "Of course, it's different today, but in the beginning I just bluffed my way through," she says, referring to her lack of formal training. "I got by with instinctive mechanical sense. Anyone with that kind of aptitude can pick it up."

Since 1965, Carol has done electromechanical packaging and design and also print circuit design for computers, medical equipment, "practically anything with motors." Today she does contract work, or job shopping, for the Manpower temporary agency. She works closely with other engineers and prefers projects that involve "high pressure." Carol, who lives in Buffalo, New York, earns between $12 and $16 an hour.

FOR FURTHER INFORMATION

Engineers' Council for
  Professional Development
345 East 47th Street
New York, NY 10017

National Society of
  Professional Engineers
2929 K Street, N.W.
Washington, DC 20006

Society for Women
  Engineers
United Engineering Center
345 East 47th Street
New York, NY 10017

Technician

There are probably as many types of engineering and science technicians as there are of health technicians. This section reflects earnings and training requirements for all of them. Among the fields that may interest a prospective technician are aeronautics; chemical engineering; radio and TV; air conditioning, heating, and refrigeration; pharmaceuticals; drafting; electronics; industrial engineering; and oceanography.

EARNINGS

Most technicians earn starting salaries of $10,000 to $14,000; for those with experience, earnings can run as high as $25,000.

TRAINING

Usually, an associate-level program at a two-year college or technical institute is essential. Vocational schools offer one- or two-year courses, and apprenticeships may also be available.

ADVANCEMENT

Experience leads to advancement.

SUCCESSFUL PART-TIMER

Francis Larkin is referred to as a technical genius by his fellow workers at the Cablevision TV studio in Woodbury, New York. The twenty-five-year-old modestly insists that his mechanical abilities only reflect an insatiable curiosity. "I love to play around with all the machinery I can get my hands on," he explains. Armed with an associate's degree and minimal experience at his high-school TV studio and at a museum that had some basic video equipment, Francis got a full-time job as head end operator at the new cable TV operation in 1975. During the next four years he learned to operate everything from a camera to a time-base corrector, and actually built much of the TV studio himself. "Whenever something needed to be done, I'd always volunteer. That way, I gained experience with the camera and master control equipment. I figured out the capabilities of all the new equipment the company bought, and I also did repairs."

In 1979 Francis decided to go back to school and enrolled in the video and film production program at New York University. He requested a switch to a part-time schedule. "I don't want this to sound funny or anything," he says shyly, "but they really had no choice but to agree. I was the only one who could do anything in the studio."

Management did agree. For a year Francis attended school full-time during the day and watched over the system by night. He worked Friday, Saturday, and Monday evenings from 5 P.M. to 2 A.M. His salary: $6 an hour. Recently, though, Francis's curiosity and hard work finally paid off. In September 1980 he was named director of programming at Cablevision.

FOR FURTHER INFORMATION

Careers
Washington, DC 20202
  Ask for "25 Technical
    Careers You Can Learn in
    Two Years or Less."

Engineers' Council for
  Professional Development
345 East 47th Street
New York, NY 10017

American Association of
  Community and Junior
  Colleges
One Dupont Circle, N.W.
Washington, DC 20036
  Ask for the directory of
    accredited schools.

National Association of
  Trade and Technical
  Schools
2021 L Street, N.W.
Washington, DC 20036
  *Ask for directory of accredited
    schools.*

Fashion/Beauty

GENERAL INFORMATION/PART-TIME PROSPECTS

When you think of part-time opportunities in the world of fashion, a whole range of occupations probably comes to mind. Illustration, advertising, photo styling, photography, modeling, sales, and administration (for instance, running a manufacturer's showroom) are all examples. Teaching fashion-related courses (such as sewing or pattern making) to students at fashion institutes, high schools, or adult education programs are other possibilities.

Permanent part-time jobs as fashion designers are rare. However, the enterprising individual may be able to land such a job (see example below). For those with talent and get-up-and-go, free-lance work may also be available. Fashion editors of women's magazines and other publications are always looking for new talent, people who can design the outfits or the knitted and crocheted garments featured in fashion spreads. Letters to fashion editors, accompanied by photographs of some of your creations, might just launch you on a successful free-lance career.

Keep in mind that work for magazines — and for that matter, almost all design work in the fashion industry — is based in New York, and to a lesser extent in California. However, anywhere that fabric, pattern, or clothing manufacturers set up shops or showrooms, or department stores advertise the clothing they sell, is the place to look for a good part-time job in fashion.

In the world of beauty, opportunities for permanent part-timers are far more widely available and more visible. Some 35 percent of all hairdressers, for example, work on a part-time basis. "For all the obvious reasons, women more than men seem to be the people that choose to work part-time," says Larry Butler, a successful hairdresser and for seven years the owner of a beauty parlor in Great Neck, New York. "Many of the women who work part-time have kids at home. Hairdressing offers tremendous scheduling flexibility and gives the women the chance to earn money on the busiest day, Saturday, when their husbands are home and able to watch the children."

In the past, Larry points out, most part-time opportunities were available only at the end of the week. That was when women had standing appointments for a wash and set, and beauty parlors were jammed from 8 A.M. to 8 P.M. Today the beauty business has changed. "Instead of coming in once a week to have their hair set," Larry says, "most women are interested in coming in for a haircut every three to six weeks. Or else they'll come in every four to eight weeks to have their hair dyed or, occasionally, for a permanent." Now women make appointments for almost any day of the week, particularly if the haircut has to be scheduled for a lunch hour or after work. So almost any day is appropriate for the prospective part-timer.

For those who prefer to work with male customers, here's a point worth noting: With the recent trend toward shorter hair for men, barbers and stylists who work on men's hair have had more work than they have had in years. As Elaine Louie wrote in the *New York Times* on September 7, 1980, "Many men are now going back to the old-fashioned barbershop. No massage, no shampoo, no appointment necessary." More opportunities exist there, too.

There are part-time possibilities other than working as a hair stylist in beauty salons, among them jobs as manicurists, shampooers, makeup specialists, masseuses (in the really fancy places), and even sales workers. Many beauty parlors now have boutiques on the premises. Whether the boutiques are run by the shop or exist in space rented from the owner, they need people to sell the jewelry, clothing, or accessories that they carry.

Finally, if you expand the definition of *beauty* to include fitness, as most of us do, you can immediately recognize other opportunities for part-time work — in health spas, exercise salons, private clubs, and even corporations.

Mary Ellen Fisenne, an industrious twenty-one-year-old student at Hofstra University in Hempstead, New York, has parlayed her own fitness, some background in gymnastics, and experience in exercise into a lucrative part-time job as an exercise instructor. Mary Ellen teaches coed classes as well as classes for women only, and includes slimnastics, yoga, and aquanastics (exercises in water) among her offerings. She has not one but three employers: Lucille Roberts Spas, where she has worked since 1977; the town of Hempstead; and now the corporate headquarters of Lufthansa Airlines in East Meadow, New York, where she conducts fitness classes for employees.

Mary Ellen earns about $100 a week for approximately twenty hours of work during the school year. In the summer she plans to start her own business, conducting exercise classes in Long Island beach clubs for a flat rate of $25 an hour or for fees collected from the students, of which a percentage will go to management. Eventually, Mary Ellen hopes for a career in communications. For now, she has found a lucrative sideline while she studies.

Fashion Designer

EARNINGS

Fashion designers can earn from $10,000 to the-sky's-the-limit. Free-lance designers selling to magazines may get from $100 to $500 per design, sometimes more.

TRAINING

Most employers favor students who have completed fashion design courses in schools specializing in the field; sometimes, on-the-job training or apprenticeship may be all that is required.

ADVANCEMENT

With talent, experience, and luck, a designer can advance. It may be necessary to move to different companies in order to do so; the business is highly competitive.

SUCCESSFUL PART-TIMER

John Gregory, twenty-nine, is a part-time designer at White Swan Uniforms in New York City. The company is one of the world's three largest nurses' uniform manufacturers; John, its only part-time designer. At first he worked full-time at White Swan for three and a half years and taught pattern making during the evenings at the Parsons School of Design in Manhattan. Then he was offered a position teaching pattern making at the Traphagen School of Fashion — but this job was during the day. John went to his boss and asked if he could switch to a three-day-a-week schedule, "just to get my feet wet with this teaching job." John's boss, whom John describes as "a gentlemen, a very nice person," agreed, but John admits that he did stretch the truth a bit by implying that his part-time schedule would only be for a while.

Over the next five months, however, John proved to his boss that he could put in five days' worth of work in three days. "I come in Friday after school and do some extra work so there'll be things in the works for Monday," he says. "The boss is happy, because I manage to keep my sample maker busy." John is happy because he has retained his $400-a-week salary and his benefits. ("I did voluntarily give up my vacation time," he confesses, "so I wouldn't feel too slimy.")

Like other designers, John recognizes that he could probably earn more money if he changed companies or resumed full-time work. But he says he prefers it this way. "If I was earning a really great salary and I had a couple of weeks when nothing was happening creatively, my boss might be tempted to say, 'Let's get rid of this guy.' I'd rather always be working for a small salary than occasionally for a fantastic amount." Besides, he adds, "I love my schedule just the way it is."

FOR FURTHER INFORMATION

Fashion Institute of
  Technology
State University of New York
227 West 27th Street
New York, NY 10001

The Fashion Group, Inc.
9 Rockefeller Plaza
New York, NY 10020

Cosmetologist

EARNINGS

Weekly earnings, including salary and tips, average $350 to
$450. After ten years' experience, cosmetologists can earn up-
ward of $500 or $600 a week. Beginners, however, may start
out as low as $120 to $150 a week. Usually part-timers who
work in beauty salons get to keep 40 percent of what they bill
for the day, plus tips. Some inexperienced workers earn a flat
fee of $25 or $30 a day, plus tips. In the high-powered New
York fashion and beauty industries, top hair and makeup artists can earn as much as $1000 to $1500 a day for a fashion
shooting.

TRAINING

All states require cosmetologists to be licensed, but other requirements vary. Usually a six-month to one-year course in
cosmetology at a state-approved school is necessary.

ADVANCEMENT

Advancement comes with experience and the building of a
steady clientele. Advancement generally means higher earnings. However, many top stylists move on to other beauty parlors, where they can make more money; some eventually open
their own salons.

FOR FURTHER INFORMATION

National Beauty Career Center
3839 White Plains Road
Bronx, NY 10467

Cosmetology Accrediting Commission
1735 K St., N.W.
Suite 1108
Washington, DC 20006
  Ask for a list of approved schools.

Food and Nutrition Services

GENERAL INFORMATION/PART-TIME PROSPECTS

Although permanent part-time positions are available, consulting and freelance opportunities abound throughout this small but high-paying field. Food manufacturers and processors, for example, require technologists to develop and test new products, and skilled home economists to come up with new and better ways to use them. They also need food stylists to make them attractive for advertising and public relations photos and booklets, and people to write directions and copy for packages and brochures. Similarly, food trade associations and food departments of magazines and other publications often maintain test kitchens, where recipes are tried and food features developed. All of these are sources of continuing and well-paying consulting work.

Various kinds of public and private institutions also need the services of people trained in food and nutrition. Hospitals, schools, nursing homes, clinics, and voluntary health agencies are just some of the facilities that require dietitians to help plan and supervise menus or to counsel patients or residents on proper nutrition and diet. Small institutions in particular may have the need but not the budget for full-time food specialists. They use consultants instead.

Next, of course, are part-time opportunities in the food preparation business. Schedules in restaurants, cafeterias, and other eating establishments vary widely, but a top-flight cook or chef can probably negotiate a suitable schedule, particularly if he or she works in a restaurant with predictable peak periods. Weekend work is often available.

Related fields, such as home economics, also offer good opportunities for part-time work. Nutritionists and home economists often work for federal, state, and local agencies, such as the cooperative extension service run by the U.S. Department of Agriculture. The home economists, 99 percent of whom are women, offer guidance to families and schoolchildren on everything from budgeting food and preparing meals to how to give up junk food and enjoy healthy snacks. Teaching in public and private schools and adult education programs is another natural for those with appropriate training and experience.

Food Technologist

EARNINGS

Food technologists are paid between $14,000 and $20,000 to start, depending on the degree they hold. Experienced technologists can earn as much as $30,000 a year. Free-lancers can earn $200 to $400 a day, sometimes more.

TRAINING

A bachelor's degree in food technology or chemistry is usually the minimum requirement for beginning jobs in the field. A master's degree or even a doctorate may be required by some of the top companies; it is usually a prerequisite for research and teaching posts.

ADVANCEMENT

Advancement is related to experience and/or education.

SUCCESSFUL PART-TIMER

Margery Einstein of Mercer Island, Washington, holds a master's degree in food science and biochemistry from Cornell University. After taking full-time jobs with General Foods, the federal government, and a clinic, Margery went to work at the Rainier Brewing Company in Seattle on a three-quarter schedule. "They wanted me to work full-time, but I knew it would be a demanding job that would turn into a fifty-hour-a-week commitment. So I asked for three-quarter time and got it. I think you have to be assertive," Margery maintains. "You have to convince them that you can do the job in the hours you say you can. In my case, I didn't have to do much convincing, though; they really needed me."

After five years at the brewery, working on flavor, color, and preservatives and devising analytical sensory tests, Margery decided to leave Rainier and go out on her own. "There wasn't a whole lot of challenge there. Besides, people called me up all the time — people from other companies — for advice. That's how I got the idea to do consulting on my own."

Today Margery's schedule ranges from six to eight hours all the way up to forty hours a week. She sometimes charges less than the going rate of $300 a day, because "I'd rather work from eight to noon at a lower salary than work a full day. I prefer the flexibility." When she knows she is going to get stuck working late, Margery asks her husband, a physician, to come home early. His support, she stresses, has been very important to her success as a consultant. The Einsteins have four children.

FOR FURTHER INFORMATION

Institute of Food Technologists
Suite 2120
221 North LaSalle Street
Chicago, IL 60601

Dietitian

EARNINGS

Beginners earn from about $12,000 to $15,000; experienced dieticians can earn as much as $30,000 a year. For self-employed dietitians with a bachelor's degree, the median salary was over $20,000 a year in 1978.

TRAINING

A bachelor's degree in food and nutrition or institution management is the usual minimum requirement. To become a registered dietitian (R.D.), a bachelor's-degree holder must complete an approved dietetic internship (six to twelve months) or a traineeship program (one to two years).

ADVANCEMENT
Usually advancement depends on advanced education, although higher-level administrative positions may be open to those with only additional experience.

SUCCESSFUL PART-TIMER
Helen Simons, sixty, of Country Club Hills, Illinois, has been working as a dietitian since 1948. After completing an internship with the Veterans Administration, she worked in hospitals in Idaho and Kansas, where she gained extensive experience in administrative work. She now teaches food management, nutrition, and other related subjects at Citywide College in Chicago. Helen also does consulting on the side, for fees ranging from $20 to $50 an hour. "Basically, this is a word-of-mouth business," Helen asserts. "I had no difficulty finding consulting assignments because I've been around a long time. Also," she continues, "professional organizations like the American Dietetic Association make referrals." Helen says that the reason she decided to get into consulting was simply that "I got bored." But she also decided to take the more challenging — and lucrative — consulting assignments in order to help put her daughter through law school.

FOR FURTHER INFORMATION

The American Dietetic Association
430 North Michigan Avenue
Chicago, IL 60611

Chef

EARNINGS
Salaries range from $4 to $8 an hour for cooks and chefs in small establishments to over $40,000 or $50,000 a year for top-name chefs in well-known restaurants and hotels.

TRAINING

Although many cooks and chefs learn their trade through an informal on-the-job training program, increasing numbers attend vocational schools with programs that can last at least two years. Formal three-year apprenticeship programs are also administered by the American Culinary Federation.

ADVANCEMENT

Experience is the path to advancement. Earnings may rise dramatically when a successful chef changes jobs.

SUCCESSFUL PART-TIMER

Bill Neilson, twenty-two, was working as a car salesman in Poughkeepsie, New York, when his wife, who holds a job at the Culinary Institute of America, took him to a food show at the school. From that moment on, Bill recalls, he was hooked on cooking. He quit his job selling cars and went to work in the kitchen of a local Howard Johnson's. Six months later, to gain more experience, he took a job at a Ground Round restaurant, where he worked for six months more. Then Bill moved on to Noah's Ark, a Poughkeepsie restaurant, where he became head chef. He worked full-time for eight months.

Since July 1980, Bill has been studying at the Culinary Institute. He attends classes from 7:00 A.M. to 1:30 P.M. Then, at 4:00 P.M., he heads over to Noah's Ark, where he works till 9:00. Although Bill now earns only $150 a week (compared to the $275 he made as a full-timer), he has retained the title of head chef, largely because he makes many of the specialties of the house, including various types of quiches and a widely acclaimed cheesecake. Despite the eleven and a half hours a day that he spends in a kitchen professionally, Bill is proud to point out he does half of all the cooking at home, too.

FOR FURTHER INFORMATION

Culinary Institute of
   America
P.O. Box 53
Hyde Park, NY 12538

The American Hotel and
   Motel Association
888 Seventh Avenue
New York, NY 10019

National Institute for the
    Foodservice Industry
20 N. Wacker Drive, Suite
    2620
Chicago, IL 60606

American Culinary
    Federation
Educational Institute
920 Long Blvd., Suite One
Lansing, MI 48910

Health Services

GENERAL INFORMATION/PART-TIME PROSPECTS

With the possible exception of education, there is probably no
field that lends itself to an under-thirty-five-hours-per-week
schedule more readily than health care does. Undoubtedly
one of the key reasons is that, except for the top-paying positions, the health-care field is dominated by women. (The actual figures: in 1980, only 11 percent of all physicians, 2 percent of all dentists, 3 percent of all optometrists, and 17
percent of all pharmacists were female. However, 98 percent
of all registered and licensed practical nurses were women, as
were 75 percent of physical therapists, 90 percent of occupational therapists, and 80 percent of all medical technologists.)
As we already know, fields in which demand is particularly
high and in which women are widely employed tend to have
the greatest number of part-time opportunities. Health care
is a prime example of both.

> *"To combat the [nursing] shortage, many hospitals*
> *are actively recruiting personnel through job fairs,*
> *advertisements in newspapers and professional jour-*
> *nals and visits to nursing schools. Some hospitals*
> *have offered flexible work hours, increased insurance*
> *benefits and larger blocks of time off as incentives,*
> *while others have achieved some . . . success by tout-*
> *ing their locations."*
>
> — MARYANN BIRD, "Nurses' Duties Are Expanding —
> and So Are Their Demands," *New York Times*, March 25,
> 1980.

Another reason for the widespread availability of part-time positions is that health care is one of those services that people need all the time, not just during the normal nine-to-five business day. So workers are needed to fill in on evenings and weekends, to provide twenty-four-hour-a-day coverage throughout the year.

Part-timers work virtually everywhere that health services are dispensed. Besides such familiar settings as government and private hospitals, nursing homes, community health departments, clinics, voluntary health agencies, public schools, research centers, colleges, and universities, there are women's health centers, corporate and union medical and dental centers, and even medical and dental facilities popping up in shopping malls. Then of course there is private practice. Not only doctors and dentists choose to go into business for themselves. Other specialists, such as occupational and physical therapists, speech and hearing pathologists, and nurse-practitioners, are increasingly deciding to hang out shingles of their own.

Temporary work in the health-care field is available almost everywhere. Registered nurses, LPNs, technicians, and medical support personnel find temporary agencies actively competing with hospitals for their services in some parts of the country. This is particularly true in Florida, Texas, Arizona, New Mexico, California, and other Sun Belt states.

Part-time opportunities are also available for such medical practitioners as optometrists and podiatrists, particularly for those willing to work on weekends. Opportunities for administrative support workers, such as health-care administrators and medical records technicians, are somewhat less abundant than for direct-care workers. However, part-time work can be found. Among the best bets are large hospitals and community clinics.

Medical students and interns should find no shortage of part-time and summer jobs, often listed with their school placement offices. Some hospitals now permit shared residencies, and residents can make extra money almost any time they want to by signing on for weekend duty at emergency rooms of local hospitals.

A note about supply and demand: Anyone who is contemplating a career in health services and who has yet to begin training should be aware of a report issued by the Graduate Medical Education National Advisory Committee in September 1980. Based on four years of study, the report concluded that by 1990, there will be a surplus of about 59,000 doctors in the United States. By the year 2000, there should be 130,000 doctors too many. However, while the study cited surgery, obstetrics/gynecology, radiology, and internal medicine as the four specialties soon to become the most crowded, it projected shortages in such areas as emergency medicine, general and child psychiatry, and nuclear medicine. Furthermore, critical shortages of doctors should occur in certain locations (such as rural areas) while much of the rest of the country will be oversupplied.

The reported recommendations to the Department of Health and Human Services included a 10 percent decrease in medical school admissions by 1984; termination of loans and scholarships to American students studying medicine abroad; and a decrease in the training of paraprofessionals (such as physician's assistants and nurse-practitioners), who relieve physicians of some of their duties.

If you're planning to enter one of the medical specialties, choose carefully. You would be well advised to check out possible sources of educational funding before you apply, and to check with professional associations regarding job prospects in your chosen field and in the geographical area in which you plan to work. Also, recognize that while the demand for nurses and other medical support people should continue to skyrocket, becoming a physician or even a physician's assistant is likely to get a lot harder during the next few years.

For information on the health services field in general, send for the free booklet "200 Ways to Put Your Talent to Work in the Health Field." Write to the National Health Council, P.O. Box 40, Radio City Station, New York, NY 10019.

Physician

EARNINGS

Doctors are clearly America's most highly paid professionals. Orthopedic surgeons top the list with annual earnings in 1977 of more than $91,000; general practitioners in private practice made just over $51,000 the same year. In 1979, hospital staff doctors on the average earned base salaries of $43,000. Radiologists made over $100,000.

TRAINING

Four years of medical school followed by one or two years of residency are required. Those seeking to specialize spend an additional two to four years of advanced residency training plus two years of practice before they can take the examinations to become board-certified. Physicians who decide to teach medicine often go on for Ph.D. degrees, as do doctors who conduct medical research.

ADVANCEMENT

Medical research, teaching, and publishing all enhance physicians' incomes. For those who open their own offices, incomes rise as the practice expands and their reputation becomes better established.

SUCCESSFUL PART-TIMERS

Esther Janowsky, M.D., is a professor of anesthesiology at the University of California at San Diego (UCSD) Medical School. As part of her responsibilities, she works in the hospital as an anesthesiologist. She also teaches residents and lectures at the university. The thirty-nine-year-old physician says she has known many other people who work in the medical profession on a part-time basis. She herself has worked part-time for eleven years, seven of them at UCSD. "At the very beginning, when I discussed this job, I said I was only interested in working part-time hours," she recalls. "I had no trouble establishing the schedule that I wanted." Dr. Janowsky works two and a half days each week: two full clinical days and one half-day for research and administration. Her annual salary is $30,000. It's easy to see why Dr. Janowsky prefers a half-time schedule to one that would be more demanding — she is the mother of four children, ranging in age from thirteen to two.

A staff physician at Pennsylvania's Norristown State Hospital, Judith P. Wilson, M.D., switched to a part-time schedule after she gave birth to her first child. Dr. Wilson, thirty-four, is one of several part-time physicians at the hospital; all the others are men. "I originally wanted to work part-time and the hospital said absolutely not. Then, after my child was born, I told them if they wanted me back, they'd have to take me part-time. The medical director was agreeable only because I suggested that I might eventually resume working on a full-time schedule." Dr. Wilson says she feels there has been some discrimination, in that she has lost her seniority and some benefits since switching to a part-time schedule. "Sometimes I feel I'm not taken seriously," she declares. "Other physicians resent my part-time schedule. They make remarks and seem quite perturbed when I say I enjoy being a mother." Right now, Dr. Wilson's plans are uncertain. "I can foresee a time when I would want to work full-time," she admits, "but then again, I may want another child. My husband doesn't want me ever to work full-time."

FOR FURTHER INFORMATION

American Medical
   Association
Council on Medical
   Education
535 North Dearborn Street
Chicago, IL 60610

American Medical Women's
   Association
1740 Broadway
New York, NY 10019

Dentist

EARNINGS

In 1977, oral surgeons earned a median income of almost $60,000 a year; general practitioners, just over $39,000.

TRAINING

Dentists need at least two or three and more likely four years of college prior to studying dentistry for four years at an accredited dental school.

ADVANCEMENT

As a private practice builds, so does income. Many dentists begin as associates in well-established practices; later, when they can afford to set up offices of their own, most do.

FOR FURTHER INFORMATION

American Dental
Association
Council on Dental Health
Education
211 East Chicago Avenue
Chicago, IL 60611

Association of American
Women Dentists
435 North Michigan
Avenue, 17th Floor
Chicago, IL 60611

Physician's Assistant or Nurse-Practitioner

EARNINGS

Most physician's assistants make from $12,000 to over $20,000 a year.

TRAINING

Requirements vary widely. Physician's-assistant programs generally last from two to four years, including clinical experience ranging up to an additional fifteen months or more.

ADVANCEMENT

Only with completion of medical school can one become a physician. Nevertheless, where physicians are in short supply — notably in rural areas — there may be good self-employment opportunities for nurse-practitioners and physician's assistants.

FOR FURTHER INFORMATION

American Medical
    Association
Department of Health
    Manpower
535 North Dearborn Street
Chicago, IL 60610

American Academy of
    Physician's Assistants
2341 Jefferson Davis
    Highway, Suite 700
Arlington, VA 22202

For a detailed description of good paraprofessional jobs in the
field of medicine, including a comprehensive section on physician's assistants, and on the varieties of available training
programs, see Sarah Splaver's book *Paraprofessions* (New York:
Julian Messner/Simon and Schuster, 1972). Some details are
dated, but the resource guide is excellent.

Registered Nurse (RN)

EARNINGS

Average beginning salaries throughout the United States
ranged from $13,000 to $14,000 a year in 1980, although
many new graduates are earning $16,000 or more in large
cities.

TRAINING

Two-year associate-level courses, three-year hospital training
programs, or four-year bachelor's degree programs are the
most common for nurses today. In every state, nurses require
a license to practice; completion of an appropriate program
in an approved school of nursing is a prerequisite for taking
the licensing exam.

ADVANCEMENT

With further training, a nurse may become a nurse-midwife
or a nurse-practitioner and assume some of the duties normally carried out by physicians, or even set up a private practice. Further education, particularly a master's degree, is usually required in order to enter research, teaching, or other
nursing specializations.

SUCCESSFUL PART-TIMER

Rosemary Grasso, twenty-five, holds the title of assistant head of cardiac care at Metropolitan General Hospital in Pinellas Park, located in Largo County, Florida. She puts in four eight-hour days, mostly in the hospital's coronary care unit (CCU), and earns $8.59 an hour plus a thirty-cents-per-hour differential for work actually done in the CCU. "Working forty hours a week was just too much of a hassle," says Rosemary, who is currently expecting her first child. "Earning less money was worth it; I needed the peace of mind." After the baby arrives, Rosemary plans to continue working, on what is known as a *pro re nata* (as needed) basis. Since Metropolitan General Hospital has established a pool of nurses who can be called in temporarily, making the transition from permanent part-time to temporary work should be easy for Rosemary. "The majority of nurses who work here are on full-time schedules," she says. "But qualified nurses are so scarce that my guess is no one seeking part-time work would be turned away."

FOR FURTHER INFORMATION

American Nurses
   Association
2420 Pershing Road
Kansas City, MO 64108

American College of Nurse-
   Midwives
1012 14th Street, N.W.,
   Suite 801
Washington, DC 20005

Career Information Services
National League for
   Nursing
10 Columbus Circle
New York, NY 10019

Dental Hygienist

EARNINGS

Earnings range from $12,000 to $19,000 a year.

TRAINING

An associate's degree from a two-year college is usually required of hygienists working in dentists' offices; school and public health hygienists often need a bachelor's degree. All hygienists must be licensed to practice.

ADVANCEMENT
Salaries increase with experience.

FOR FURTHER INFORMATION

American Dental Association
Council on Dental Health Education
211 East Chicago Avenue
Chicago, IL 60611

Physical Therapist

EARNINGS
Starting salaries range between $10,000 and $13,500; with experience, workers can earn from $17,000 to as much as $30,000.

TRAINING
A bachelor's degree in physical therapy is required. All states require therapists to pass a state board examination and to be licensed. In some cases, those with bachelor's degrees in other subjects may take a twelve- to sixteen-month certificate program that qualifies them to take the state board exam.

ADVANCEMENT
Public and private hospitals employ the largest number of physical therapists; salaries rise with experience. However, self-employed therapists who contract to work with nursing homes, schools for the disabled, or voluntary health agencies may earn significantly more than staff personnel do.

SUCCESSFUL PART-TIMER
Joanne Crowell is director of physical therapy for Baltimore County, a job that is part-time, she says, "because there isn't a budget for a full-time person." She earns just over $10 an

hour and her schedule, which is completely flexible, usually amounts to thirty-four hours per week on the job. When she has spare time, Joanne works as a temp for Upjohn HealthCare Services at a per-patient rate of $20. The average visit, she maintains, lasts about forty minutes. Joanne works mainly with geriatric patients, particularly those interested in receiving necessary treatments at home. The need for physical therapists who can work with older patients is particularly great, Joanne believes.

FOR FURTHER INFORMATION

American Physical Therapy Association
1156 15th Street, N.W.
Washington, DC 20005

Occupational Therapist

EARNINGS

Salaries range from $14,000 for beginners to $25,000 for experienced therapists; occasionally, earnings can reach $30,000 or more.

TRAINING

Completion of an approved four-year bachelor's program plus certification by the American Occupational Therapy Association entitles an individual to become a registered occupational therapist (OTR). For occupational therapy assistants with four years of work experience, registration is also possible.

ADVANCEMENT

Newly graduated therapists usually begin working at hospitals, nursing homes, community mental health centers, schools or camps for handicapped children, and so on. Some may advance to supervisory or administrative positions; others become self-employed and work for a variety of health- and mental-health-care facilities.

FOR FURTHER INFORMATION
American Occupational Therapy Association
6000 Executive Boulevard
Rockville, MD 20852

Medical Technician, Technologist, Related Specialists

This group takes in a wide variety of health-care workers, many of whom have somewhat similar educational training and earn comparable salaries. Among them are electrocardiograph (EKG) technicians, electroencephalograph (EEG) technicians, operating-room technicians, medical laboratory workers, medical record technicians, radiologic (x-ray) technologists, and respiratory therapists.

EARNINGS
Starting salaries range from $6500 to $10,000 for those with one or two years of training and no experience. For those who complete three- or four-year programs, salaries are considerably higher, as are earnings for more experienced workers.

ADVANCEMENT
Education, experience, and certification lead to advancement.

SUCCESSFUL PART-TIMERS
Patricia Harris, thirty-seven, is chief microbiologist at General Hospital of Everett in Everett, Washington. She has worked under several job-sharing arrangements since 1972 and currently works thirty-two hours per week. Patricia, who holds a master's degree in clinical microbiology, earns $11.50 an hour. She also recently began doing consulting work on her days off, helping out at hospitals that don't have the budget for a full-time microbiologist. Her consulting work nets her $25 an hour. Originally Patricia worked full-time at General Hospital, but after she and a colleague both had babies, they decided to approach the administration with the idea of a job-

sharing arrangement. "They were really reluctant at first," she says. "But our example proved the value of job sharing, and it generated lots of pressure for more opportunities here. We really have 'part-timed' this lab up since then."

Nancy Kelley of Dunby, Vermont, works weekends as a veterinary technician at the nearby Rutland Veterinary Clinic. Nancy, who is thirty, has no formal training in veterinary medicine or technology. She holds a degree in art and has done some free-lance commercial artwork on occasion. Nevertheless, her interest in veterinary medicine came about quite naturally. She and her husband, Rick, own a ten-acre farm inhabited by calves, sheep, pigs, chickens, ducks, turkeys, and a dog and cat. "When the veterinarian arrived to care for the animals, I was interested in what he was doing," Nancy says, "so I just kept asking questions. That way, I learned to do some things myself." For a while, Nancy put in time as a volunteer for the Vermont Fish and Game Department (inspecting the jawbones of deer to determine their ages), and she has worked for three different veterinary clinics during the past three years. She now works Saturdays and Sundays, 7 A.M. to 3 P.M., and she is paid $3.50 an hour. "I know I'm settling for a low salary," she says, "but I just couldn't work full-time and still take care of everything I have to do on the farm. I'm willing to sacrifice the money for that."

FOR FURTHER INFORMATION
There are as many sources of information on careers in the medical technical fields as there are job descriptions. Consult the various career guides for details about the specific technical careers that interest you. Some of the best sources of information for many of these diverse occupations are:

American Optometric Association
Paraoptometric Guidance Department
243 North Lindbergh Boulevard
St. Louis, MO 63141

National Association of Emergency Medical Technicians
P.O. Box 334
Newton Highlands, MA 02161

American Medical
  Association
Department of Allied
  Health Evaluation
535 North Dearborn Street
Chicago, IL 60610
  *Ask for a free copy of
  "Education for Allied
  Health Careers."*

The American Society of
  Radiologic Technologists
55 East Jackson Boulevard
Chicago, IL 60604

Association of Surgical
  Technologists
Caller No. E
Littleton, CO 80120

American Medical Record
  Association
John Hancock Center, Suite
  1850
875 N. Michigan Avenue
Chicago, IL 60611

American Society for
  Medical Technology
5555 W. Loop South
Bellaire, TX 77401

American Society of EEG
  Technologists
32500 Grand River Ave.,
  #103
Farmington, MI 48024

American Hospital
  Association
840 North Lake Shore Drive
Chicago, IL 60611
  *Ask for information on EKG
  technicians.*

American Association for
  Respiratory Therapy
1720 Regal Row
Dallas, TX 75235

American Veterinary
  Medical Association
930 North Meacham Road
Schaumburg, IL 60196

Licensed Practical Nurse (LPN)

EARNINGS

Most LPNs earn from $7000 to $10,000 per year; private
nurses, considerably more.

TRAINING

Generally, a one-year course at a junior or community college
is necessary; training programs are also offered at local hos-

pitals, health agencies, and vocational schools. State licensing regulations vary, but almost all states require completion of a state-approved training program.

ADVANCEMENT
Advanced education leads to promotion. However, salaries can rise with experience, as do those of LPNs working for temporary agencies.

SUCCESSFUL PART-TIMER
Elizabeth Liggett, thirty-seven, of Virginia Beach, Virginia, is an employee of the Upjohn HealthCare Services Company. She works in patients' homes, in hospitals, and in nursing homes, usually putting in an eight-hour day but sometimes only one hour per day. She averages about $5 an hour but gets more for weekend and holiday work. Elizabeth now prefers to work three or four days a week as a temporary worker, but has worked full-time and permanent part-time schedules in hospitals and nursing homes. "There's such a variety of jobs and you meet so many interesting people that I really think this is one of the best fields to be in. Also, you can choose your own shift. There's so much work out there," Elizabeth declares, "that I don't think an LPN could collect unemployment. No one would believe she couldn't find a job."

FOR FURTHER INFORMATION

National Federation of
  Licensed Practical Nurses,
  Inc.
250 West 57th Street
New York, NY 10019

National Association for
  Practical Nurse Education
  and Service, Inc.
122 East 42nd St., Suite 800
New York, NY 10017

National League for
  Nursing
10 Columbus Circle
New York, NY 10019

Medical/Dental Assistant

EARNINGS
Beginners earn $8000 to $10,000 a year; those with more experience or who work in large medical or dental offices earn higher salaries.

TRAINING
Usually a one-year program at a community or junior college or at a vocational school is a requirement. Two-year associate's degree programs are also offered. In a relatively few cases, on-the-job training may be available, but employers increasingly prefer formal education.

ADVANCEMENT
Salaries rise with experience.

SUCCESSFUL PART-TIMERS
Roxanne Welch, nineteen, holds so many different part-time jobs that it's amazing she can keep track of her schedule. She works ten hours a week as a medical assistant in an internist's office, handling secretarial and clerical duties as well as some lab work. In addition, she works three hours each weekday as a teacher's assistant at the New York School for Medical and Dental Assistants, from which she graduated in March 1980. As if that weren't enough, she puts in sixteen hours a week selling cosmetics at a drugstore. The job at the doctor's office pays $4.50 an hour; at the school, she earns $5 an hour; and selling cosmetics, she gets $3.50 an hour plus commissions. "I don't think I'd be able to work a nine-to-five day," she claims. "I find this schedule easy because I never get bored." Roxanne plans to attend Molloy College on Long Island to study nursing. She hopes that with a nursing degree she will be able to continue her flexible schedule.

Brenda Conroy, another Long Island woman, works from 5 P.M. to 9 or 10 P.M. three nights a week at Family Dental Services in Levittown. After attending government-subsidized dental training classes at night for about a year, Brenda, a former supermarket employee, became eligible to work as a chairside assistant. "I work next to the dentist, almost as a second pair of hands," she says, describing her responsibilities. "I hand him instruments, do some mixing and preparation, and, most important, try to make the patients feel comfortable." The thirty-five-year-old mother of two earns $4 an hour.

FOR FURTHER INFORMATION

The American Association
  of Medical Assistants
One East Wacker Drive
Chicago, IL 60601

American Dental Assistants
  Association
666 North Lake Shore
  Drive, Suite 1130
Chicago, IL 60611

Commission on
  Accreditation of Dental
  and Auxiliary Educational
  Programs
211 East Chicago Avenue
Chicago, IL 60611

Interior Design

GENERAL INFORMATION/PART-TIME PROSPECTS

There is no question that the top opportunities for part-timers in the interior design field are in starting and building a successful interior design service. Designers spend a great deal of time and can earn a great deal of money accompanying clients to showrooms, browsing through furniture galleries, or assembling swatches of wallpaper and fabric. Those who work when and for whom they want can make as much as $300 to $500 a day, plus commissions. For individuals who have yet to establish their own businesses, shopping and consulting services may attract clients who lack confidence, need "inside" contacts, and are willing to pay $25 to $50 an hour to someone who can provide both.

If working on your own has no appeal, you may find it possible to work for one of the decorating companies that have contracts to design interiors for banks or offices, shopping malls, schools, or even model rooms in new houses, condominiums, or luxury co-op complexes. Head for the major growth areas in the United States for the best chance to line up new accounts or jobs. Department or furniture stores are probably the best bets for those just starting out or for people who want to combine sales experience with design work.

Interior Designer

EARNINGS

Salaries run from $125 per week plus commissions for beginners to between $12,000 and over $50,000 for those with experience, a good reputation, and affluent clients.

TRAINING

A number of two-year associate programs in interior design are offered by community and junior colleges. In addition, professional schools of interior design offer three-year programs, and some four-year schools award bachelor's degrees. After having completed formal education and several years' experience, most designers choose to join the American Society of Interior Designers (ASID) or the American Institute of Interior Designers (AID), which have membership requirements that may include passing an examination.

ADVANCEMENT

Salary or commission increases with experience; the highest earnings and prestige are for those in top companies or owners of private firms.

SUCCESSFUL PART-TIMER

Barbara L. Cohen, fifty-two, is one interior designer who has made it big as a free-lancer. For consultations with clients and for her personal design services, she charges $50 an hour or $250 for a four- or five-hour day. Barbara, who lives in Westbury, New York, also works as an adjunct instructor at New York Institute of Technology's department of interior design. She says she is particularly wary of the part-time label when it is applied to people in her field, because so many untrained women become self-appointed designers. "The term *part-time designer* has a bad connotation," she says. A designer must have some professional training, and clients must understand that this training justifies the fees that professionals get. Most of the work in her field is seasonal, Barbara contends, although the amount of business available is closely related to the state of the economy. The best times of the year for picking up free-lance assignments? Barbara says, "People seem to develop an interest in redoing their homes around holiday times."

FOR FURTHER INFORMATION

American Society of Interior
  Designers
730 Fifth Avenue
New York, NY 10019

Institute of Business
  Designers
National Headquarters
115 Merchandise Mart
Chicago, IL 60654

Law

GENERAL INFORMATION/PART-TIME PROSPECTS

This is an increasingly good field for women, who now represent about 10 percent of all attorneys. Lawyers are among the nation's best-paid professionals; average 1980 earnings for those in private industry topped $50,000 a year.

The best opportunities for part-time work are in teaching and in private practice, and the best opportunities for private practice are in small towns and suburbs. Large cities have recently experienced a glut of law-school graduates, and the trend is expected to continue. Other law-related possibilities include free-lance work for legal aid societies or other nonprofit organizations that provide assistance for those who can't afford private counsel. In the legal publishing field, opportunities exist for lawyers to write and edit trade magazines, newsletters, and legal digests. Local government provides still another opportunity: positions such as city mayor or town councilor are often highly sought after. Such jobs are particularly accessible to trained lawyers, who are required to put in little time and who may greatly enhance their incomes and prestige.

For law or prelaw students, part-time positions may be

available in law firms, legal departments of private and non-profit corporations, and government agencies; some students will also find work as clerks for prominent judges. Summer internships are also obtainable; see your adviser, the department chairperson, or the school's placement office early in the fall semester to find out about application deadlines.

Lawyer

EARNINGS

In 1980, beginners averaged $16,000 a year, with the highest starting salaries (roughly $37,000) going to those signing on with top Wall Street firms. Heads of the foremost law firms or prominent corporate attorneys can earn as much as $250,000 a year, or more. On an hourly basis, the majority of attorneys charge between $25 and $100; some of the more famous lawyers in the United States command far more than that. For example, the legendary "palimony" whiz Marvin Mitchelson hires himself out for $125 an hour, on top of a five-figure retainer. Louis Nizer and Melvin Belli reportedly charge over $300 an hour, and Alan Eagleson, Toronto lawyer and "superagent" for many of professional hockey's top players, gets $500 an hour just for negotiating a player's contract. On a somewhat more modest scale, respected law professors who teach bar-exam review courses get from $250 to $500 for a three-hour lecture; some earn as much as $700.

TRAINING

Lawyers need three years of postgraduate study, resulting in the J.D. (juris doctor) or LL.B. (bachelor of law). Those who have done well at prestigious schools are grabbed up first, as are those with specialized training. Lawyers with a strong background in some other field, such as banking or insurance, are in an enviable position when they graduate from law school.

ADVANCEMENT

Lawyers advance through experience and specialization. Partnership in a legal firm offers significant increases in annual earnings.

SUCCESSFUL PART-TIMER

Beth Don, an attorney for the U.S. government, holds a senior-level Government Service ranking of GS-15 and earns over $24,000 a year. She works from 9:00 A.M. to 2:30 P.M. four days a week, while her young son is at school. Beth, who works in the Office of Special Counsel, has held other part-time jobs as an attorney for the U.S. government, including associate general counsel of the Merit Systems Protection Board and special assistant to the vice-chairman of the Equal Employment Opportunity Commission in Washington, D.C. Her next step up, to the Senior Executive Service, is a move that Beth foresees difficulty in attaining. "I already applied for one job for which I was well qualified and was told, 'How would it look to Congress to put a part-timer at the head of a government agency?' I think that's ridiculous, and has been since the invention of the telephone."

Though Beth would like to break into the highest level of legal service on Capitol Hill, she maintains that at present her part-time status is more important to her. "My husband and I just bought some property that we expect to make into a farm, so I have time to take care of what is now our garden. What's more," she adds, "by working only part-time, I've never had any trouble with my son. Nor have I had any guilt, which a lot of my friends who work full-time suffer with. I look at part-time work as the best of all possible worlds."

FOR FURTHER INFORMATION

American Bar Association
Information Services
1155 East 60th Street
Chicago, IL 60637

Paralegal

EARNINGS

Salaries range from $9000 to $15,000 for up to one year's experience, and up to $20,000 or more for those with several years' experience or supervisory responsibility.

TRAINING

Since the field is so new, there are few established criteria for paralegal programs. Some courses last only thirteen weeks; they are the ones offered by private business schools and public continuing education programs. However, the American Bar Association recommends a two-year course at a junior or community college. For those planning eventually to obtain a bachelor's degree and go on to law school, the two-year paralegal program would probably be more advisable. Vocational training may or may not be transferable for bachelor's degree credits. Check with four-year schools in your area.

SUCCESSFUL PART-TIMER

Carol Buckalew, twenty-nine, works for a private law firm in Philadelphia. She does everything from routine secretarial work and taking minutes of meetings to research on complex legal matters in the firm's law library. Carol, who holds a degree in political science from Temple University, took a thirteen-week course at Philadelphia's Institute for Paralegal Training and got a job right away. She has worked at the same law firm for over seven years, six of them as a full-timer. After the birth of her son, though, she switched to two eight-hour days per week. "I also take some work home," Carol admits. As a part-timer, Carol has received raises; she now makes just under $10 an hour.

FOR FURTHER INFORMATION

American Bar Association
Special Committee on Legal
  Assistants
1155 East 60th Street
Chicago, IL 60637

National Association of
  Legal Assistants
3005 East Skelly Drive
Suite 122
Tulsa, OK 74105

National Federation of
  Paralegal Associations
Benjamin Franklin Station
P.O. Box 14103
Washington, DC 20044

The Institute for Paralegal
  Training
235 South 17th Street
Philadelphia, PA 19103

Library Science

GENERAL INFORMATION/PART-TIME PROSPECTS

Part-timers now account for nearly one-quarter of all librarians, and the American Library Association officially passed a resolution approving permanent part-time employment in July 1975. As libraries continue to diversify their services above and beyond simple book lending, the opportunities for part-timers with special skills — or just bright ideas — will increase accordingly. Innovators in the field are discovering that there is a lot more a librarian can offer than a knowledge of the Dewey decimal system. Special programs for children require librarians to conduct story hours, demonstrate crafts, and even help teach reading. More and more libraries are also offering seminars on everything from career counseling for teenagers to art appreciation — projects that part-timers can both conceive and conduct. If driving a book-filled bus isn't your idea of a career in library science, maybe you should think again. Bookmobiles, or traveling libraries, have become a popular community service. Once again, the required commitment is less than full-time, and opportunities are plentiful in suburbs and rural areas.

Opportunities are also available for traditional librarians — but the more specialized your training, the more easily you will find them. Expertise in an academic area, such as political science or languages, combined with a general library science degree is sure to put you in a good bargaining position for a job at an academic library attached to a college or university. Academic employers in particular are eager to save money at every opportunity and therefore might be amenable to a partnership or job-sharing arrangement. Scan the help-wanted ads (sometimes the library listings are in a special section with education).

A much larger segment of the profession — 40 percent — works in public school libraries. Although these jobs are considered full-time, they actually require only twenty-five to thirty hours a week. Moreover, public school librarians, like teachers, work only nine months a year and enjoy the added free-time bonus of regularly scheduled school holidays. To find out about these jobs, check with your state or local board of education.

Another possibility worth investigation is part-time work in a specialized or business library that serves a particular company's private research needs. Banking, food, and oil are just a few of the industries that regularly maintain staffed libraries. And for those seeking work with the U.S. government, we should note that the Library of Congress has actively encouraged the use of part-timers since the spring of 1977.

Overall employment prospects are even better for library support people, mainly technicians and assistants who may type file cards, operate media equipment and computers, maintain special information files, and help library visitors find the materials they seek. Currently, more than half of all library technicians and assistants work part-time.

Librarian

EARNINGS
Starting salaries range from $9000 to $12,000, while those librarians with experience can earn upward of $24,000.

TRAINING
A master's degree in library science is a requirement for employment in all but the smallest school and public libraries. A Ph.D. is a plus for those who plan to teach or try for a top administrative post. In addition, most states require public school librarians to be certified both as teachers and librarians.

ADVANCEMENT
Promotion comes with experience, or sometimes with a transfer to another job.

SUCCESSFUL PART-TIMER
Jane Holland of McLean, Virginia, is an example of a librarian with such top-flight skills that eighteen years after she had

retired from her job, she was called and asked to return on a part-time basis. Jane had worked as a cataloguer in the massive State Department Library in Washington, D.C., for four years as a full-timer, but resigned when she got married. When Jane got the call offering her the same position, she decided she was ready to get back to the responsibilities that the job entailed, but that a five-hour, four-day-a-week schedule would be ideal. "I'm really glad I chose to come back," she affirms. "Library work has always been my choice, and at this time in my life, part-time work is my preference. I enjoy it, and it's challenging, too."

FOR FURTHER INFORMATION

Office for Library Personnel
   Resources
The American Library
   Association
50 E. Huron Street
Chicago, IL 60611

Special Libraries Association
235 Park Avenue South
New York, NY 10003

Library Technician or Assistant

EARNINGS
Experienced, trained technicians earn $12,000 on average; those without formal training may start at $3.50 to $4.00 an hour.

TRAINING
Requirements vary widely. Some employers prefer applicants who hold an associate's degree in the field, while others consider on-the-job training to be just as valuable.

ADVANCEMENT
Those with expertise in a particular field (medicine, law, education) are most likely to command the best salaries and be assigned the most interesting tasks. With education, advancement to librarian is possible.

FOR FURTHER INFORMATION

Council of Library
  Technical Assistants
8600 South Wentworth
  Avenue
Chicago, IL 60621

Council on Library-Media
  Technical Assistants
Cuyahoga Community
  College
2900 Community College
  Avenue
Cleveland, OH 44115

Office Work

GENERAL INFORMATION/PART-TIME PROSPECTS

Working in a huge typing pool or shoving papers into file cabinets all day is hardly anyone's idea of a fun way to earn good money. But add specialized training or the ability to take dictation to your list of qualifications, or learn to operate stenotype or word-processing equipment (see "Data Processing," page 130), and you can have your pick of good jobs in almost every major city in the United States. So critical is the shortage of well-qualified secretaries and other office workers that companies everywhere are resorting to job fairs and even bounties to lure prospective employees. Many companies that are otherwise reluctant to hire part-timers offer a warm welcome to highly qualified clerical workers who request reduced work schedules.

Those individuals who wish to find temporary secretarial work will also find the going easy. Skilled temps can walk into any agency any day of the week and have a job the very next day.

> *"It's worse than ever," says Mark Rosen, owner of Jo-Lane, an employment agency. "Any secretary who walks in here and has some steno and typing, I'll send her on as many interviews as she wants."*
> — CRAIG UNGER and SHARON CHURCHER, "Intelligencer," *New York*, October 6, 1980.

Bookkeepers will also find a wide choice of part-time jobs. Small businesses and retail stores of all types are the most logical places to look for work; about one-third of all bookkeepers work for retailers or wholesalers.

A final note: Office work may or may not be your ultimate career goal. If it is, and you simply wish to work a reduced schedule, you will find the opportunities limitless. If it isn't, office experience can nevertheless be quite valuable. For example, if you simply want to see what goes on in a particular industry before you invest time, money, or both to get the necessary training to enter the field, a secretarial position offers a good way to get a feel for the business, related work experience to put on your résumé, and possibly some useful contacts.

Although it is no longer necessary for a woman to use a secretarial job to get her proverbial foot into any business door, clerical jobs do remain entry-level steppingstones in many of the so-called glamour fields. Television, radio, motion pictures, and advertising are a few. Publishing is another; talented editorial assistants (both female and male) can, and often do, work their way up and become top editors. So don't rule out doing a stint as a secretary, particularly if you are a student and you are undecided about future career goals. An office job, like a sales job, can offer much to the person with the good sense to take advantage of the benefits it may provide.

Shorthand Reporter

EARNINGS

Most shorthand reporters who work in large cities are paid on a per-page basis — usually from $1.25 to $1.50 per page, plus a flat attendance rate of as much as $10. Depending on his or her skill, a reporter can record between thirty and fifty pages per hour. If the reporter works for a reporting service, the transcription is done by someone else at the office, freeing the reporter to continue doing what he or she does best.

TRAINING

Most courses last from six months to two years and are offered at private business schools and shorthand reporting schools. Some states require court stenographers to obtain certified shorthand reporter (CSR) accreditation.

ADVANCEMENT

Speed and accuracy are the secret; usually, it takes a year or two of practice before the shorthand reporter can work up to top speed and pay levels. The best jobs usually require dictation speeds of at least 225 words per minute.

SUCCESSFUL PART-TIMER

Rolf Bergman, fifty-seven, has been a shorthand reporter for the past twenty-seven years. He now owns the Acme Reporting Service in Manhattan and usually has between eight and ten other shorthand reporters on call. Rolf and the other men and women at Acme often work for prosecutors and defense attorneys, recording testimony of witnesses outside courtrooms or actually taking down every word spoken during a trial. In addition, they record minutes of stockholders' meetings and hearings of all types.

In discussing opportunities in the field, Rolf emphasizes the need for a shorthand reporter to be available much of the time. "If I get a call from some woman who says, 'Only call me on Mondays and Wednesdays after 1 P.M.,' well, she's not going to find much work. Unless, of course, there's an emergency and she just happens to be available." You don't need to work a thirty-five-hour week in the business, he emphasizes, but flexibility is certainly one key to success.

FOR FURTHER INFORMATION

National Shorthand Reporters Association
18 Park Street S.E.
Vienna, VA 22180

Legal, Medical, Executive Secretary

EARNINGS

Salaries range from $10,000 to as much as $35,000 a year.

TRAINING

One-year courses are offered at private business or vocational schools as well as at junior and community colleges. In some cases, however, high-school graduation is the only requirement, or a high-school diploma plus several months' additional schooling.

ADVANCEMENT

Legal and medical secretaries require additional training to enter the fields of law or medicine as paraprofessionals. Depending on the type of business in which they work, however, executive secretaries may have the chance to advance to other positions or even to management jobs. Obviously, if specific technical education is required for advancement, the executive secretary, like the legal or medical secretary, would have to obtain it.

SUCCESSFUL PART-TIMER

Christa Settle, thirty-six, has worked as an executive secretary for the Manpower temporary agency since 1968, when she moved to Dallas from Bayreuth, Germany. She works only about three months each year and spends the rest of her time traveling, either to Germany or accompanying her husband on business trips. Christa received her secretarial training at a two-year business school in her native country. (She learned to speak English when she was eight years old.) After completing her formal training, she was certified both as an executive secretary and an interpreter for foreign correspondence. Christa worked full-time for an electronics corporation in Germany for four and a half years; when she met her husband, an American businessman, Christa quit her job.

It was after she and her husband moved to Dallas that Christa decided to work as a temporary. "I thought it would be a good way to find out all about our city — to see different parts of it, different businesses, and meet new people. It's amazing what I've learned about American business over the years." Although Christa says she has been offered permanent positions "everywhere I work," she prefers the diversity of working as a temporary. "I do it because I enjoy it; but of course, it's nice to have some extra money." She earns about $6 an hour working for various private and government agencies, among them the U.S. State Department. "I've always been satisfied with the work I've done," she says.

FOR FURTHER INFORMATION

National Secretaries
  Association (International)
2440 Pershing Road
Kansas City, MO 64108

National Association of
  Legal Secretaries
  (International)
3005 East Skelly Drive
Tulsa, OK 74105

National Association of
  Executive Secretaries
9401 Lee Highway, Suite
  210
Fairfax, VA 22031

Association of Independent
  Colleges and Schools
1730 M Street, N.W.
Washington, DC 20036
  *Ask for directory of business
  schools.*

A number of organizations are also working to upgrade the professional status of secretaries and to improve working conditions. Among the more prominent are:

9 to 5 Organization for
   Women Office Workers
140 Clarendon Street
Boston, MA 02116

Women Employed (WE)
37 South Wabash Avenue
Chicago, IL 60603

Cleveland Women Working
   (CWW)
1258 Euclid Avenue
Cleveland, OH 44115

Women Office Workers
   (WOW)
680 Lexington Avenue
New York, NY 10022

Women Organized for
   Employment
127 Montgomery Street
San Francisco, CA 94104

Also check your telephone directory to see if there is a local chapter of Working Women, the National Association of Office Workers, a national group that is rapidly expanding throughout the country.

Bookkeeper

EARNINGS
Bookkeepers make from $9000 to $15,000 a year, and sometimes more with additional administrative responsibility.

TRAINING
A high-school diploma is usually the minimum requirement for beginning jobs. Some employers prefer business school or junior college graduates, or those with some experience in accounts payable, accounts receivable, or payroll records.

ADVANCEMENT
Bookkeepers advance through experience and with the assumption of more responsibility for handling tax and other financial records. Additional education is usually required for advancement to the level of accountant.

FOR FURTHER INFORMATION

Association of Independent Colleges and Schools
1730 M Street, N.W.
Washington, DC 20036
  Ask for directory of business schools.

Personnel

GENERAL INFORMATION/PART-TIME PROSPECTS

Personnel administrators frequently know better than other employers about the benefits of hiring part-timers. Finding topnotch workers who will produce at a high level is their job, after all. Moreover, many have seen the government studies and reports that confirm what their own experience has probably shown them — that the myths about part-timers being uncommitted are just that, myths. Therefore, if you're looking for a part-time job in the personnel field, you are likely to find potential employers sympathetic. If you already work in personnel, you have the added advantage of knowing where good part-time jobs may be located. That's just how Winifred Gilmore, a position classification specialist with the U.S. Department of Transportation, found her $22,765-a-year job. "I knew where to shop around," explains the forty-year-old mother of two, who puts in thirty hours a week doing management research in Washington, D.C. Winifred, who also worked part-time at the Office of Personnel Management, notes that personnel jobs in the government are often open to part-timers and job sharers.

Personnel Worker

EARNINGS

Beginners start at about $12,900, while experienced job analysts earn up to $25,000 a year. Top executives, of course, earn considerably more.

TRAINING

A bachelor's degree is becoming increasingly important to land a good entry-level position. Those with degrees in either personnel or public administration are considered the best qualified. However, any liberal arts major is usually acceptable. Secretaries and clerks, too, are sometimes given the chance to advance to administrative posts. Regardless of education, all new employees receive on-the-job training in interviewing techniques and methods of salary evaluation.

ADVANCEMENT

Trainee job analysts can eventually advance to upper-level jobs as employment managers, wage and salary administrators, training directors, and labor relations directors. Promotions in this field tend to come rapidly — and so do raises. Even six months' on-the-job experience can make a big difference.

SUCCESSFUL PART-TIMERS

Mary Mullen and Dorothy Schmitz started their job-sharing arrangement by taking advantage of an experimental program in Wisconsin known as Project JOIN, which opened certain government positions to part-time workers. They share the $7.23-an-hour job of research analyst at Wisconsin's Department of Employment Relations in Madison. The job was formerly held by one full-time employee, Mary recalls, but when Project JOIN applied to the U.S. Labor Department for funds to conduct a study of alternative work patterns, the department suggested that the project carry out a part-time experiment in its own administrative offices. So in 1977 the position was converted to a shared job, with each worker assuming different responsibilities.

Since Mary formerly worked as a research analyst for her state's Department of Natural Resources, she has continued to handle research in her new job. In addition, she processes all of the detailed questionnaires that pertain to alternative work patterns throughout the Wisconsin state government. Dorothy takes care of other personnel responsibilities in the office. The two women work out their own schedules, each putting in about twenty hours a week.

FOR FURTHER INFORMATION

American Society for
   Personnel Administration
30 Park Drive
Berea, OH 44017

American Society for
   Training and
   Development
P.O. Box 5307
Madison, WI 53705

Sales

GENERAL INFORMATION/PART-TIME PROSPECTS

Sales as a part-time career has much going for it. Educational requirements are usually not stringent; often minimal training or related experience may be all that is necessary to enter the field. It is also possible to start in an entry-level position and work your way up to a high-income job.

In fact, sales is one of the few careers that offer women a good way to make really big money, particularly since affirmative action programs have opened sales positions in many new fields. The Bureau of Labor Statistics reports that female sales engineers, or industrial salespersons, attained income parity with men in the same field as far back as 1970. There aren't many women in other fields who have done as well! Here are some other encouraging statistics in those sales areas that lend themselves most readily to part-time scheduling:

◆ Insurance — Roughly 10 percent of all agents and brokers in the United States are women; almost one-third of all managers in the insurance business are female.

◆ Manufacturer's representatives — About 10 percent are women, but the number of females working as sales reps is growing rapidly. According to the Research Institute of America, only 15 percent of the nation's five hundred largest manufacturing companies had women in their sales forces in 1972; by 1975, it was 38 percent.

◆ Real estate — About 41 percent of all agents and brokers are women; the majority of agents, both male and female, now work part-time.

◆ Travel — Half of the nation's travel agents are female; 22 percent of all travel agencies are owned by women.

Although schedules are flexible in each of these fields, it's almost axiomatic that the more time you put in, the more money you stand to earn. Also, expect peak periods and slow seasons during which your schedule — and income — may vary markedly.

Another word about time: At the beginning, you may have to train on a full-time basis; later you can adjust your schedule to meet your needs. Expect much of your work to be done during the evenings and weekends, particularly if you choose to work in real estate or insurance. Travel agents may also have a great deal of weekend work. Manufacturers' representatives must often concentrate their efforts during the regular business day. However, they are free to set up whatever schedules they want and work whenever they choose, provided they meet their productivity requirements.

The best opportunities in all of the sales fields are in large urban and suburban areas. Rapidly growing small communities also offer great potential.

Insurance Sales Worker

EARNINGS

Earnings range from $11,000 a year starting salary to over $35,000 a year. Independent brokers can earn substantially more.

TRAINING

A college degree is usually preferred, though not always required. Most companies offer some on-the-job training.

ADVANCEMENT

Earnings increase in direct proportion to the amount of insurance sold. Management positions may be open to successful salespeople, but many individuals prefer to continue selling rather than move into an office position.

FOR FURTHER INFORMATION

Institute of Life Insurance
277 Park Avenue
New York, NY 10017

Institute of Health
  Insurance
277 Park Avenue
New York, NY 10017

Insurance Information
  Institute
110 William Street
New York, NY 10038

National Association of
  Insurance Women
Furlong Insurance Agency
280 N.W. 42nd Avenue
Miami, FL 33126

National Association of Life
  Underwriters
1922 F Street, N.W.
Washington, DC 20006

Manufacturer's Representative

EARNINGS

In salary and/or commissions, manufacturers' reps earn from $6000 to $50,000 or more.

TRAINING

It depends on the firm. A college degree is sometimes required of those entering in the field. If the product you are selling is one that requires technical knowledge (such as pharmaceutical products or microelectronics components), you may also need a master's degree or at least some specialized or additional training. Some firms require reps to travel extensively, either during their training periods or once their territories are assigned.

ADVANCEMENT

With additional sales, earnings increase. Sometimes promotion within the company may result from a solid background in sales.

FOR FURTHER INFORMATION

Sales and Marketing Executives International
Career Education Division
380 Lexington Avenue
New York, NY 10017

If you're a woman planning to enter this lucrative field, you may want to obtain a copy of Barbara A. Fletcher's *Saleswoman: A Guide to Career Success* (Homewood, Ill.: Dow Jones/Irwin, 1978).

Real-Estate Sales Worker

EARNINGS

Real-estate salaries range from nothing to $50,000 a year or more. Earnings are tied closely to the state of the economy and to a rise or decline in mortgage rates, construction, and house sales. Extreme fluctuations in income are common in the field. According to a 1978 study by the National Association of Realtors, full-time real-estate agents averaged about $15,000 a year; those working fewer than thirty hours a week, $5000. Full-time brokers averaged almost $30,000 a year. The Women's Council of the National Association of Real Estate Boards reported that only 44 percent of female brokers and 16 percent of real-estate saleswomen are entirely dependent on income derived from sales.

TRAINING

Every state requires real-estate agents and brokers to be licensed. A high-school degree is essential for sales agents, as is the passing of a written test, usually based on thirty hours of classroom instruction. Those seeking a broker's license must generally complete ninety hours of formal training, pass a more rigid exam, and have from one to three years of selling experience.

ADVANCEMENT

The more listings obtained and houses, commercial buildings, or plots sold, the higher the income. Those with extensive experience may branch off into real-estate appraisal, property management, mortgage financing, or other specialties. Licensed brokers are eligible to open their own offices; many do.

FOR FURTHER INFORMATION

National Association of
    Realtors
430 North Michigan Avenue
Chicago, IL 60611

Women's Council of
    Realtors
430 North Michigan Avenue
Chicago, IL 60611

National Institute of
    Realtors
Department of Education
155 East Superior Street
Chicago, IL 60611

Travel Agent

EARNINGS

Travel agents usually make between $9000 and $15,000. Beginners may earn as little as $150 to $200 per week, with no commissions. Later they may earn a base salary of, say, $175, plus 20 percent of the commissions that their agency takes in, depending on the amount of sales they generate. Commissions to the agency range between 5 percent and 20 percent depending on what the agents sell — airline tickets, hotel bookings, package tours, and so forth. In addition to actual earnings, however, very attractive travel discounts are available to agents. Airlines may allow travel agents to fly at 75 percent off regular airfare; some hotels even offer free accommodations. Travel benefits can easily add several thousand dollars a year to an agent's total take.

TRAINING

Many travel agents begin by getting jobs as reservations clerks or by learning basic skills at a branch office of a major travel chain. Some attend travel and tourism classes offered by adult or continuing education programs or travel agency schools. Usually there are no formal educational requirements, nor are there licensing procedures.

ADVANCEMENT

As an agent generates more sales, the proportion of the agency's commissions that he or she receives will rise. Those travel agents with experience and a good following may open their own agencies.

FOR FURTHER INFORMATION

American Society of Travel Agents
1300 19th Street, N.W.
Washington, DC 20036
   Ask for the names of approved travel agency schools in your area.

❧ 6 ❧

Part-Time Jobs for Special People

In the preceding chapter, "Today's Best Part-Time Jobs," I presented each field with every prospective job-hunter in mind, whether female or male, twenty or seventy years old. I mentioned special opportunities that might be relevant to one job-seeker but not another (for example, on-campus opportunities) where appropriate. But for the most part, I discussed the fields in terms of their availability to anyone with the proper training.

In this chapter, we will take into account the needs of special groups of part-time job-hunters. Senior citizens are considered separately, as are handicapped workers, since both groups have special resources available to them. Similarly, jobs for those with no formal training or experience are highlighted — with the obvious caveat that these are positions with extremely limited potential. Then there is a section on part-time work for students: money-making jobs both on and off campus. Finally, I have included pointers for those individuals seeking employment for the summer only. Opportunities for women and men who wish to work at or from their homes will be discussed in the chapter "The Work-at-Home Option."

Part-Time Work for Senior Citizens

Today, there are 24 million people in the United States who are over sixty-five years of age. Senior citizens now account for a full 11 percent of the U.S. population, and their proportion is expected to grow to over 12 percent by the year 2000.

Over one-eighth of today's senior citizens hold paying jobs. Most of those jobs are part-time, and according to a recent Harris survey, three times as many older people would continue to work if suitable employment were available. Some 46 percent of all retirees say they would like to be working, claims the Work in America Institute.

Clearly, there is a difference between the motivations of those seeking work today and of those who sought to continue working beyond the age of sixty-five in days past. Today's senior citizens have been denied the economic security that their decades of hard work and careful saving should have provided them. Double-digit inflation took care of that. Inflation continues to render people sixty-five and older afraid that those monthly Social Security or pension checks, plus whatever money they have managed to save, won't be enough to see them through their years of retirement without serious financial hardship. Economic worries are a prime motivation for many seeking to stay on their jobs or to find gainful employment once they have retired.

But it would be a gross disservice to characterize all of the people over sixty-five in today's work force as individuals who are there solely to keep up with the staggering cost of living. Americans are living longer. Senior citizens today are healthier and more vigorous than their predecessors of several decades ago were. Today's older people are simply not content to settle back and allow the rocking-chair stereotype to prevent them from continuing to be productive and valued members of their communities.

"I said calling me 'chairman' was fine. They can call me 'Hey, you' if they want to. It's the job I do that matters."

— HELEN BUTTENWIESER, first elected female board chairperson of the New York Legal Aid Society, at the age of seventy-four. Quoted in Judy Klemesrud's "At 74, Lifelong Achiever Has a New Job," *New York Times*, November 26, 1979.

Of course, not all senior citizens choose to make their continued contributions at paid jobs; but many do. They want to establish or maintain friendships and ongoing relationships with coworkers. They want the feeling of belonging that makes the work environment a home away from home for millions of other Americans. They want to experience the feeling of satisfaction brought on by doing a good job.

In 1967, the Age Discrimination in Employment Act went a long way toward ensuring that older workers who wish to secure and keep their jobs can continue to do so. An amendment to that act, which went into effect January 1, 1979, raised the mandatory retirement age from sixty-five to seventy.

In the past ten to fifteen years, numerous organizations have begun to address the needs and problems of senior citizens with regard to income, health, and now employment. Programs providing jobs and job counseling for senior citizens exist almost everywhere. For the American over sixty-five who would like to work, there are now opportunities that didn't exist even four or five years ago. To keep abreast of all developments that have particular relevance to people over the age of fifty-five, you should consider joining the American Association of Retired Persons (AARP) (national headquarters: 1909 K Street, N.W., Washington, DC 20049). The extremely reasonable annual membership fee of $4 includes a subscription to *Modern Maturity,* an excellent, comprehensive publication that deals with employment opportunities for older workers, among its many other features.

Other resources worth noting are:

◆ Administration on Aging (AoA), U.S. Department of Health and Human Services, 330 Independence Avenue, S.W., Room 4551, Washington, DC 20201. Ask for the leaflet "Publications of the Administration on Aging" as well as the "Directory of State Agencies on Aging." The AoA is the U.S. government's chief clearing-house for all information pertaining to programs for the aging in America. It offers an incredible amount of material.

◆ National Council on Aging, Inc. (NCOA), 1828 L Street, N.W., Washington, DC 20036. Another information clearing-house, this is a nonprofit rather than a government organization. Ask for information about the National Organization of Older Workers Employment Services, an organization that represents many local nonprofit employment services funded by combined federal and state resources. Also ask about the Senior Community Services Aides program, which offers part-time jobs to seniors in various settings throughout the country.

◆ Gray Panthers (national headquarters: 3635 Chestnut Street, Philadelphia, PA 19104; telephone (215) 382-3300). Since 1970, this organization, with groups located in thirty-five states plus the District of Columbia, has been fighting age, sex, and racial discrimination, among many activities. The Gray Panthers stress the importance of taking action when the needs of senior citizens (and other groups as well) aren't being properly met. This is a vital, committed organization.

◆ Urban Elderly Coalition (national headquarters: 1828 L Street, N.W., Suite 505, Washington, DC 20036; telephone (202) 857-0166). Twenty-four of the nation's largest cities formed the UEC to help cities deal with inner-city housing, crimes against the elderly, health care, transportation, and employment opportunities. The UEC also offers professional services to help local offices on aging aid senior citizens who live within their jurisdictions.

◆ National Caucus Center on the Black Aged, 1424 K Street, N.W., Suite 500, Washington, DC 20005; telephone (202) 637-8400.

♦ National Association of Spanish Speaking Elderly, 3875 Wilshire Boulevard, Suite 401, Los Angeles, CA 90010; telephone (213) 487-1922.

♦ National Indian Council on Aging, P.O. Box 2088, Albuquerque, NM 87103; telephone (505) 766-2276.

Another must for senior job-seekers is the Senior Community Service Employment Program (SCSEP), which was established to foster and help create part-time jobs for individuals over fifty-five with low incomes and limited employment prospects. SCSEP projects are located in all fifty states, the District of Columbia, Puerto Rico, and all U.S. territories. As of June 1980, funding for the program was supporting 52,250 jobs! According to the Employment and Training Administration (ETA), which oversees the project, 52 percent of the jobs provide such services to older Americans as nutrition, recreation, health and home care, transportation, and so forth. The remaining 48 percent are aimed at helping the community at large. Senior citizens work in day-care centers, schools, hospitals, programs for the handicapped, beautification, conservation and restoration projects, and fire prevention programs. Participants may work up to 1300 hours per year (the average is twenty to twenty-five hours per week) and earn at least the federal minimum wage. For information, contact the Office of National Programs (Attention: Older Worker Work Group), ETA, Department of Labor, 601 D Street, N.W., Room 6122, Washington, DC 20213; or ETA's Office of Information at the same address, Room 19418; telephone (202) 376-3172.

Still another possibility is temporary employment. Keep in mind that, in addition to the numerous general temporary agencies, there is one that specializes in mature workers and is called, appropriately, Mature Temps, Inc. (national headquarters: 1114 Avenue of the Americas, New York, NY 10036; telephone (212) 869-0740).

Mature Temps has thirteen offices around the country, in Washington, D.C.; Chicago; Baltimore; Boston; New York City; Philadelphia, Bala Cynwyd, Plymouth Meeting, and Malvern, Pennsylvania; Dallas and North Dallas, Texas; Los Angeles and Pasadena, California. At any given time, there are roughly four thousand temps working for the firm; their ages range from eighteen to eighty. ("We actually have some people over eighty working at various offices," claims a New York spokesperson.) Most of the jobs are clerical in nature, but there are blue-collar positions, and consulting assignments may be available for those seniors with solid business experience. Salaries are competitive.

Finally, a note for those seniors fortunate enough to live in the Seattle area: FOCUS, Inc., one of the nation's leading part-time advocacy groups, recently began a special project to promote part-time employment for older workers. Details can be obtained from FOCUS, 509 Tenth Avenue East, Seattle, WA 98102; telephone (206) 329-7918.

For an extensive bibliography related to the subject of work and older Americans, send for *The Older Worker: A Selected Bibliography,* edited by Stephen R. McConnell and Leslie A. Morgan. Copies can be obtained by writing to the Ethel Percy Andrus Gerontology Center, Publications Department, University of Southern California, University Park, Los Angeles, CA 90007; cost $2.95 plus 40¢ handling.

Help for Handicapped Workers

One of the best resources for handicapped persons seeking employment is the *Directory of Organizations Interested in the Handicapped,* which can be obtained by writing to the People to People Committee for the Handicapped, 1522 K Street, N.W., Room 1130, Washington, DC 20005. The directory lists over one hundred voluntary and public agencies and contains descriptions of their functions, programs, and publications.

Other useful publications include:

◆ *Access: The Guide to a Better Life for Disabled Americans,* by Lilly Bruck (David Obst Books/Random House, 201 East 50th Street, New York, NY 10022; 1978, $5.95). Employment is only one of the subjects covered in this excellent guide.
◆ *Training Programs and Placement Services: Vocational Training and Placement of the Severely Handicapped* (Olympus, 1670 East

Thirteenth South, Salt Lake City, UT 84105; 1978, $16.95).
A complete rundown of over 150 programs listed by region
and state, with detailed descriptions.

♦ *Vocational Opportunities: Vocational Training and Placement of
the Severely Handicapped,* by Paul F. Cook, Peter R. Dahl, and
Margaret Ann Gale (Olympus, 1670 East Thirteenth South,
Salt Lake City, UT 84105; 1978, $7.95). Discusses both phys-
ical and emotional disabilities and the jobs suitable for people
with various handicaps.

♦ *The Help Book,* by J. L. Barkas (Scribner's, 597 Fifth Avenue,
New York , NY 10017; 1979, $9.95). Contains an extensive
list of resources for handicapped individuals, including a
state-by-state listing of agencies for the handicapped plus
names and addresses of private organizations dealing with visual, hearing, speech, and other specific handicaps.

For the disabled worker seeking vocational counseling
and/or employment, various agencies can provide assistance.
The organization with which people are probably most familiar is J.O.B. (Just One Break), 373 Park Avenue South, New
York, NY 10016. J.O.B. has helped over ten thousand disabled men and women find jobs since 1959, and serves as a
free employment agency and research center; it also maintains a listing of qualified handicapped men and women who
are looking for work.

Help may also be obtained from any of the following federal agencies:

President's Committee on
  Employment of the
  Handicapped
Vanguard Building, Room
  600
1111 20th Street, N.W.
Washington, DC 20036

Rehabilitation Services
  Administration
U.S. Department of
  Education
330 C Street, S.W., Room
  1427
Washington, DC 20201

President's Committee on
  Mental Retardation
Washington, DC 20201

The Always-Available, "No Experience Necessary" Jobs

A job as a gas-station attendant, cashier, food counter clerk, or another of the positions in this category definitely *won't* be your ticket to power and prestige. What it *will* bring you is a low salary and limited opportunity for advancement, which in turn means that it will probably give you the chance to meet new coworkers each week. Why? Because workers in low-paying occupations tend to leave them quickly; a high turnover rate is often the surest indicator of a "no-future" job.

Besides anticipating low pay, little advancement possibility, and a steady stream of coworkers, you should expect the work to be tough. While ringing up sales at a fast-food restaurant or hefting warehouse crates may not require you to tax your brain, it probably will demand physical stamina. And even if lifting heavy objects isn't involved in the job, being on your feet all day could be. Furthermore, unlike working in a quiet office, driving a cab or even baby-sitting for a couple of active preschoolers can be nerve-frazzling under the best conditions. Finally, there are the hours. Work may be available only during weekends or late at night, when you least feel like heading off for four or five hours on the job.

The best thing to be said about most of the following part-time jobs is that they are there for the taking when necessity arises. They can offer permanent employment to the person with minimal skills or ambition, or provide a short-term solution to a personal cash-flow problem.

Busboy/Busgirl and Dishwasher

GENERAL INFORMATION

This is often considered the lowest of the low-level jobs; the work can be dirty as well as difficult. Roughly half of all such workers are students, who come and go with great frequency. Jobs may be somewhat more desirable in better restaurants, where working conditions tend to be better, and in fast-food places, where cleanliness is a marketable commodity.

EARNINGS

Pay is among the worst around: usually minimum wage to about $4.50 an hour. Occasionally busboys and busgirls, or "dining room attendants" as they are sometimes called, do receive a share of the tips earned by waiters and waitresses. In a good week, that could add up to as much as $65 to $80, on a full-time basis.

TRAINING

Training occurs on the job.

ADVANCEMENT

Busboys and busgirls are sometimes promoted to waiter or waitress. Dishwashers may occasionally become cook's helpers or even short-order cooks.

FOR MORE INFORMATION

Contact restaurants directly. To line up future jobs at resorts or vacation places, apply several months before the peak season begins.

Cashier

GENERAL INFORMATION

Growing numbers of retail outlets and restaurants, coupled with longer shopping hours in stores and supermarkets, are providing new jobs all the time. What's more, turnover is high, which means that replacement jobs crop up constantly. Many cashiers work during evenings and weekends, with highest demand during holiday seasons. Wear comfortable shoes.

EARNINGS
Beginners often earn minimum wage, with salaries predictably higher in urban areas. Many cashiers belong to unions, such as the United Food and Commercial Workers International. Where there is unionization, salaries are higher — from about $4 to over $8 an hour in some cases.

TRAINING
Most cashiers receive on-the-job training, particularly in stores that have installed optical or magnetic scanning devices and other equipment hooked into computers.

ADVANCEMENT
Advancement usually occurs only in terms of salary. Occasionally cashiers may switch to selling positions in department stores, which may enable them to earn salary plus commission.

FOR MORE INFORMATION
Contact your local office of the state employment service, or speak directly to store owners or personnel officers about job openings.

File Clerk

GENERAL INFORMATION
File clerk is the lowest entry-level job in most offices. Clerks spend the day sorting, labeling, filing, and retrieving. What they file is usually paper, but it can also be phonograph records, videotape cassettes, mail, or what-have-you. To say the least, the work is often deadly dull.

TRAINING
A high-school diploma is usually required; typing is preferred. Most firms provide on-the-job training for a few days.

ADVANCEMENT

In large offices, advancement to a supervisory level is sometimes possible. Other promotions may be to receptionist or typist. About the only way to climb up from the lowest rung on the office ladder is to show enthusiasm and aptitude for learning and doing more. In particular, take advantage of opportunities to learn to operate more sophisticated office equipment. That way, if you can't get a promotion, you can at least prepare for a better job somewhere else.

FOR MORE INFORMATION

See your state employment service. Also check want ads for part-time situations. Clerk and typist jobs are among the most plentiful listed under the heading "part-time."

Food Counter Clerk

GENERAL INFORMATION

To estimate the demand for people to work in food establishments, you need only look down any city street or take a leisurely drive through the suburbs. You will see them all: fast-food restaurants turning out hamburgers, fried chicken, pizza, roast-beef sandwiches, fish and chips, tacos, clams and seafood, hero sandwiches, and that good old American favorite, hot dogs. And for dessert? Why there's ice cream, of course — soft, hard, and in any of several dozen flavors and forms.

Part-time opportunities abound right now, and there should be more in the future as busy mothers continue to enter the work force and as eating out becomes even more widespread than it already is. For high-school and college students in particular, the fast-food boom has meant a boom in income-earning possibilities.

EARNINGS

Most counter workers earn minimum wage, but other benefits include free meals and occasionally tips.

TRAINING

Some fast-food restaurants offer minimal training for all employees, using booklets and audiovisual aids. The bulk of the training is simply on-the-job experience.

ADVANCEMENT

Some of the larger chains operate formal management training programs, which can pave the way to higher-level supervisory positions.

FOR MORE INFORMATION

Contact food establishments. For information about food service careers, write to:

Educational Director
National Institute for the
   Food Service Industry
20 North Wacker Drive
Chicago, IL 60606

Culinary Institute of
   America
P.O. Box 53
Hyde Park, NY 12538

Gas-Station Attendant

GENERAL INFORMATION

The trend toward self-service gas stations, along with our national effort to conserve gasoline, will limit the growth of job opportunities. However, turnover is quite high and jobs are frequently available.

EARNINGS

Earnings vary considerably, from minimum wage to as much as $6 an hour. Some attendants earn commissions on products they sell in addition to gasoline. The best salaries are found in metropolitan areas.

TRAINING

A driver's license is a must. Also, a general understanding of how cars work, plus some sales ability, is helpful. Applicants should be familiar with the local area in order to give directions to motorists, and with simple arithmetic in order to keep accurate records of money taken in. Training is often received on the job, although many high schools do offer formal programs.

ADVANCEMENT
Most major oil companies offer two- to eight-week training programs for service-station managers. Further training could also lead to a job as a mechanic, sales representative for an automotive products company, or even district manager for an oil company.

FOR MORE INFORMATION
Contact your local office of the state employment agency, or approach service-station owners directly.

Guard

GENERAL INFORMATION
Unfortunately, the rising rate of crime and vandalism will increase the need for people to guard schools, stores and shopping centers, plants, and parks. As increased apartment building security becomes more widespread, so will the need for people to monitor the surveillance equipment that is often installed in hallways and elevators. Many retirees are hired, and preference is given to those with military or police backgrounds.

EARNINGS
The average pay in 1980 was just under $4 an hour. The highest salaries were in the North Central states; the lowest, in the South. Hourly wages for security guards in the manufacturing field were $5.42; in transportation and public utilities, $5.68; in banks, $4.41; and in private security firms, sometimes as low as minimum wage.

TRAINING
A high-school diploma is preferred but not necessary. Sometimes guards receive training in first aid or in the use of fire-

arms. Occasionally, technical training related to sophisticated alarm systems may be offered by employers.

ADVANCEMENT
Promotion opportunities are limited. Promotions to supervisory positions are possible; sometimes, experience is transferable to related police work.

FOR MORE INFORMATION
Contact local employers (such as department-store security offices, private security companies, manufacturing plants) or your state employment office.

Interviewer

GENERAL INFORMATION
We as a nation are consumed with curiosity about ourselves and our neighbors. Which candidate do people plan to vote for? Which TV shows do we watch? What do Catholics, Jews, Protestants think about sex education in public schools? What brands of beer do we drink? How much confidence do we have in current government economic policies? Which would we rather have with chicken, stuffing or mashed potatoes? There seems to be no limit to the questions government and private corporations ask, and no end to our desire to know the answers.

If you possess a natural curiosity — a willingness to track down the answers to questions ranging from "How many people live here?" to "Which deodorant (toothpaste, hair dye, cake mix) do you normally buy?" — you may actually find a ready and enjoyable source of part-time income.

EARNINGS
Pay for interviewers, or enumerators, as they are sometimes called, ranges from $3.10 to $4.50 an hour, plus a gas and mileage allowance if you must use your car. Those who ask questions for Uncle Sam can make up to $400 a month; interviewers for private market-research firms may make more,

particularly if they are paid on a per-questionnaire basis and they put in a lot of time. Count on some productivity requirement, however, if you expect to remain on the payroll. Companies know how many "not-at-home's" there should be on an average Wednesday evening. Also, count on little or no income at Christmastime — 'tisn't the season for market research and government surveys.

TRAINING
Little training is available. You will probably be provided with a packet of instructions or training materials. If you are working for a local market-research firm, you may also be asked to attend a seminar for several hours to familiarize yourself with proper interviewing techniques and with how to fill out the required forms. You may also be given a test survey to complete before you are accepted as a regular.

ADVANCEMENT
There is not much likelihood for advancement; perhaps you may be promoted to a supervisor of other interviewers if you live in a large metropolitan area.

FOR MORE INFORMATION
If you are interested in asking questions for the U.S. government, write to:

U.S. Department of Commerce
Social and Economic Statistics Administration
Bureau of the Census
Washington, DC 20233

If market research for private firms interests you, head to the library and consult *The Bradford Directory of Market Research Agencies*. Also check your local Yellow Pages under "market research and analysis" or "educational research." If conducting Gallup polls is your desire, write to:

Princeton Survey Research Center
53 Bank Street
Princeton, NJ 08450

Parking-Lot Attendant

GENERAL INFORMATION

High turnover provides most of the job opportunities that exist, since increasing numbers of parking lots are of the park-it-yourself variety. More work is available at night, particularly at hotels and restaurants that utilize valet parking.

EARNINGS

The starting salary is often minimum wage; it is higher where workers are unionized. Most attendants also receive tips, which can exceed salary.

TRAINING

High-school graduates are preferred, particularly those who have studied driver education. Workers must be able to operate cars with standard as well as automatic transmissions.

ADVANCEMENT

Sometimes, promotion to manager is possible.

FOR MORE INFORMATION

National Parking Association
1101 17th Street, N.W.
Washington, DC 20036

Sales Worker — Retail Trade

GENERAL INFORMATION

Rising sales volume, longer store hours, and high turnover will provide many opportunities for people who would like to work part-time throughout the year or only during peak seasons, such as during the pre-Christmas rush.

Even if selling is to be a stopgap income provider, one advantage you should consider is that it offers terrific experience which can be used in almost any other job you ever take. For example, learning to deal with the public, and particularly how to handle difficult customers, can hold you in good stead regardless of the career you ultimately choose. Moreover, minimal selling experience is often all you need to land a high-paying or salary-plus-commission position in, say, a boutique or specialty store. It can also be the key to landing one of the most lucrative of all sales jobs — manufacturer's representative, where you can parlay that low salary into $25,000 or more per year.

EARNINGS

Nonunion starting salary is usually the federal minimum wage. Stores in major cities are often covered by union contracts. In 1979, beginning full-timers earned from $3.13 to $6.62 an hour; for those with two years' experience, $7.12 an hour was the average.

Some sales workers also earn commissions, usually 2 percent to 5 percent, on such items as cosmetics, jewelry, and cameras. Among the highest salary-plus-commission incomes go to those selling automobiles, major appliances, and furniture. In addition, many stores (most department stores) offer employees a 10- to 20-percent discount on all store merchandise — a nice extra.

TRAINING

High-school graduates are preferred. Some stores may require aptitude tests; others offer several hours or days of formal and on-the-job training.

ADVANCEMENT

Retail sales remains one of the few fields in which top-flight employees can advance to executive-level jobs. Though many retail chains select their management trainees from among new or recent college graduates, the training programs are often open to employees, too. Furthermore, sales workers can be promoted to department manager, buyer, floor manager, and even store manager.

FOR MORE INFORMATION

Contact the personnel office of local stores you may be interested in working for. Keep in mind that many stores begin their pre-Christmas hiring in September; apply early. Also, for further information write to:

The National Retail Merchants Association
100 West 31st Street
New York, NY 10001

or your state or local merchants' association.

Sell _Their_ Products and _Your_ Service

Many people dismiss retail sales as one of the go-nowhere jobs of all time. For those who don't have the imagination to use sales work to their own advantage, that is probably true. But for the creative and ambitious part-timer, a sales job can offer more than just basic training for some planned or as-yet-unknown career. It can provide a quick way to build up concrete accomplishments to list on any résumé of the future — for example, such desirable inclusions as "Sold a wide variety of clothing accessories to an average of seventy customers per day," or "Increased sales in the department by 30 percent," or "Sold over $1500 worth of cosmetics each week." These are the kinds of specifics that convince _any_ potential employer that you are a person who is goal-oriented and who achieves.

Moreover, working behind a sales counter or out on the selling floor can help the would-be entrepreneur line up potential customers for a free-lance business that he or she may be planning to operate. Here's how it might work. Let's say you take a job in a garden and nursery center or a plant store, and you decide you want to set up the Green Thumb plant-care or the While You're Away vacation plant-watering service to make some extra cash. If you have proven yourself to be a conscientious salesperson and you can show your employer that your proposed service has a potential for boosting merchandise sales (or at least that it doesn't compete with services the store already offers), the boss might be willing to help you out by advertising your service on a sign tacked behind the cash register, or by letting you mention the proposed service to customers or hand out your business cards with sales receipts. What's more, in exchange for your purchase of whatever supplies you need at his or her store, the owner might be willing to offer you a generous discount.

Here are just a few examples of how you might use a local selling job to help you launch a successful free-lance enterprise.

Store You Work At	Related Services You Might Offer
Party goods and rental	Party planning — running children's birthday parties; coordinating business luncheons, at-home weddings, organization affairs; party entertainment
Hardware, lumber, or home products	Handywork — small household repairs; interior or exterior painting
Women's clothing	Wardrobe coordination; alterations
Stationery	Typing; bookkeeping
Beauty parlor or beauty supply	Private makeup sessions for bridal parties
Food specialty, delicatessen	Helping at parties, bartending
Toy or children's clothing	Play groups; baby sitting
Pet	Feeding and care of pets for owners who are away on vacation

Neither the selling jobs nor the free-lance services mentioned here are likely to make you rich. But together, they offer you the chance to earn a steady income plus extra cash when you have the need, inclination, and time.

Stock Clerk

GENERAL INFORMATION

Though jobs will be available because of high turnover, increased automation and slowed growth in the manufacturing industry will combine to lower the number of new jobs that open in the future. Computers are increasingly used for inventory control, and storage systems are now sometimes automated, which points to more — and higher-level — job possibilities for those familiar with the new technology.

EARNINGS

Weekly earnings in 1978 were $226, on the average. Today that works out to about $250 a week for full-timers. With experience, salary increases.

TRAINING

Minimal on-the-job training is provided. Where there is computer tie-in, training in the automated systems is likely.

ADVANCEMENT

Supervisory positions may be accessible to those who begin as stock clerks; eventually, perhaps, promotion to warehouse manager might be possible.

FOR MORE INFORMATION

Contact your local office of the state employment agency or potential employers.

Taxi Driver

GENERAL INFORMATION

Driving a cab, which has been recently celebrated in song by Harry Chapin and in the movies and on TV by actors Robert De Niro and Judd Hirsch, remains an easy way to make a buck — or a grueling one, depending on whom you ask. For the philosophical, talkative cab driver of old, it's a way to meet interesting people. For the student in need of cash or the out-of-work actor or Ph.D., driving through the traffic-clogged streets of a major city during rush hour in lousy weather can be a headache that won't quit. Many cab drivers work only a couple of days a week or on a temporary basis (for several weeks at a time) and then stop. When they need money again, they go back to the taxi.

EARNINGS

Customarily, drivers working for fleet owners keep 40 percent to 50 percent of the meter income plus all tips. That means an average day's take-home pay of $40 to $70. Union contracts in 1978 guaranteed drivers from $14.00 to $18.50 per day. Some drivers rent their cabs on a daily or weekly basis; after they have paid the rental and gasoline costs, they keep everything they earn.

TRAINING

A state-issued chauffeur's license is almost universally required. In addition, drivers may need to have a special operator's license issued by the police department, safety department, or public utilities commission. Besides having a license free of serious traffic-violation convictions and a relatively clean personal record, drivers may have to prove their knowledge of traffic regulations or of the best ways to get to major landmarks and tourist attractions. Sometimes the cab companies issue written tests. There is no formal educational requirement, although applicants for jobs must write legibly and be able to read at an eighth- or ninth-grade level.

ADVANCEMENT

Occasionally, taxi drivers may advance to supervisory positions within the firms for which they work.

FOR MORE INFORMATION

Contact your state motor vehicle department, police department, and potential employers.

Usher

GENERAL INFORMATION

Showing people to their seats before a performance or sporting event is simple work that is rough on the feet and legs (particularly when you must repeatedly trek up to the top rows). However, for some music aficionados or avid sports fans — particularly students — walking up and down the aisles for less than an hour before curtain time or kickoff is a small price to pay for the opportunity to see concerts, movies, plays, tournaments, or other performances they might otherwise not be able to see. Sometimes ushers are even allowed to sit during the event!

EARNINGS
Pay ranges from minimum wage for ushers in small-town movie theaters to as much as $20 for professional sports events; tips, if any, can be a substantial extra.

TRAINING
Training occurs on the job.

ADVANCEMENT
Sometimes ushers are promoted to supervisor. In some cases they get jobs in the box office or ticket booth, where the work may be somewhat less fatiguing; tips, obviously, are no longer a possibility.

FOR MORE INFORMATION
Contact theater, stadium, or concert hall personnel offices to inquire about openings.

Waiter/Waitress

GENERAL INFORMATION
Part-time work is almost always available in almost all restaurants. Turnover is extremely high, primarily because about 25 percent of all waiters and waitresses are students, who may not wish to work for more than a couple of months at a time. The work is quite strenuous, which also helps account for the rapid change in personnel.

EARNINGS
Hourly rates, excluding tips, range from about $1.50 to $4.00

or $4.50. For many waiters and waitresses, however, tips exceed hourly wages by quite a bit. In some particularly fine restaurants, earnings can reach upward of $400 a week. Another plus is free meals.

TRAINING
Training takes place on the job. However, at least three months' experience is usually required by larger restaurants and hotels. Restaurant associations, some chains, and even public and private vocational schools may provide classroom training.

ADVANCEMENT
After gaining initial experience in coffee shops or small cafés, some workers move on to jobs in larger, more expensive restaurants. Places that serve wine or liquor are prime choices, since tips tend to be higher. Advancement opportunities may include promotions to supervisor, host or hostess, or even maître d'hotel.

FOR MORE INFORMATION
For information about opportunities in the food services field, write:

National Institute for the
    Foodservice Industry
20 North Wacker Drive,
    Suite 2620
Chicago, IL 60606

The American Hotel and
    Motel Association
888 7th Avenue
New York, NY 10019

Culinary Institute of
    America
P.O. Box 53
Hyde Park, NY 12538

American Culinary
    Federation
Educational Institute
920 Long Blvd., Suite One
Lansing, MI 48910

. . . and On and On

These aren't the only go-nowhere jobs that provide employment for millions of part-time (and full-time) workers; there are many others. The following list contains sixteen more little- or no-future jobs, along with the current hourly wages that employees earn. Suffice it to say that for most of these jobs, as for the jobs just described in greater detail, getting ahead means getting more training —and getting out.

Baby sitter $1–$5
Custodian/janitor $4–$7
Dispatcher (truck) $8–$8.50
Laborer $8
Meter reader (parking) $4
Meter reader (utilities) $6–$7
Private household worker $3.50–$5
Receptionist $4–$5
School-bus driver $4–$6
School crossing guard $4–$6
Shipping and receiving clerk $6
Telephone solicitor $3.10–$4
Telephone/switchboard operator $3.50–$4.50
Ticket seller $3–$4
Toll collector $6–$7
Typist $4.50–$6

Money-Making Jobs for Students

With tuition and other college expenses soaring ever-upward, it is getting harder and harder to pay all the bills and still have money left over for an occasional movie or a post-midterm splurge. Today, over 40 percent of all students hold part-time jobs they obtain through their college placement offices. Many more get jobs on their own, applying directly to local businesses or otherwise finding ways to turn their skills into cash during the school year.

How can you earn part of your college tuition or living expenses? Here is a rundown of some of the popular and the more innovative ways in which young men and women are making money on and around campuses across the country. Also, a complete, step-by-step job-hunting guide for today's students is provided.

On-Campus Jobs

According to spokespersons from numerous student employment offices throughout the nation, on-campus jobs for students are actually more abundant than is generally assumed. Not all of the available jobs are equally attractive, of course; nor are they all necessarily there exactly when you might want them.

The overwhelming number of on-campus jobs are clerical in nature. They involve office work of one type or another: sorting mail, filing school forms, answering phones, typing, and general fetching, among others. Every academic department in a university usually has its own office. So do admissions and student health services, counseling services, libraries, registrars' and security offices, campus bookstores. All of them need help; all hire students. Similarly, professors who have received research grants may be looking for students to assist them with research, writing, typing, or proofreading.

Among the more frequently mentioned nonclerical workers are cafeteria or snack-shop employees, library assistants, student security guards, and dormitory assistants (usually upperclassmen who act as administrators for their dormitories in return for free room plus a modest salary). At some schools, stagehands who work on drama department productions and people who put out student newspapers are salaried. In Laramie, Wyoming, for instance, the editor-in-chief of *The Branding Iron,* the University of Wyoming's student publication, earns $65 a week.

The Top Dozen On-Campus Jobs

In May 1977, *Changing Times* magazine published the results of a survey of available jobs at eighty-two colleges and universities across the country. Some 40 percent of all college students, the researchers found, put in an average of thirteen hours per week at part-time jobs obtained through their college financial or placement offices. The jobs most frequently found on college campuses? In order: clerk-typist, science lab assistant, library assistant, food service worker, mail clerk, lifeguard, data-processing assistant, dormitory assistant, cashier, tutor, research assistant, and campus tour leader. The highest-paying jobs? Tutor, teaching assistant, and research assistant.

Some of the best on-campus jobs, such as research, laboratory, or teaching assistant positions, may be offered through the federal college work-study program. Under this program, authorized by the Higher Education Act of 1965, colleges or other approved employers are reimbursed 80 percent of the earnings of eligible students plus a small administrative fee. During the 1978–79 school year, over one million jobs at over three thousand approved institutions were funded by the program. Not every student can participate, however. Under the provisions of the work-study program, students applying for jobs must demonstrate financial need. In fact, many work-study jobs are part of a total financial-aid package that may also include grants or loans. Eligibility to participate is for one year only, and there is a restriction on the number of hours per week that students can work. To be considered for a work-study job, apply to your school's employment or financial-aid office.

Even if you can't land a plum job through the work-study program or find a position working for some professor destined to win a Nobel Prize, remember that plenty of other jobs are available. Their average pay ranges from $2.65 to $5.00 an hour. Most can be had practically for the asking, and many offer more than just the potential to earn a few bucks.

Virginia Brown, a 1980 graduate of Boston University (BU), is a good example of a student whose on-campus jobs paid off in a big way. Virginia, an urban studies major, held three different part-time jobs during her last two years at BU. She worked as a telephone solicitor for the college's Office of Alumni Development, earning $5.00 an hour, and also as the coordinator for continuing education for BU's School of Nursing, where she earned $3.10 an hour. In addition, she held an off-campus position at a Boston law office, typing legal briefs for eight hours each week and earning $3.75 an hour. During her senior year, Virginia was hired as a sales representative for the Xerox Corporation in Lexington, Massachusetts. "The part-time work played a significant part in helping me to obtain the job," she says in retrospect. "I was able to show them my résumé, and they could see that I'd worked hard and that I'd already had the experience of holding a wide variety of positions."

Almost any job that lets you demonstrate initiative, a talent for organizing or managing, or the ability to work well with people can come in handy at a later date.

Off-Campus Jobs

While most colleges focus their efforts on providing on-campus jobs for students, others specialize in placing young men and women in jobs with local businesses, where students often stand to earn considerably more money than they would working on campus. One such college is Roosevelt University in Chicago, where an estimated 90 percent of the student body works at paying jobs outside the school.

Since Roosevelt is located in the heart of the busy Chicago Loop business center, there are plenty of local companies willing and eager to hire students during the school year, explains Arthur Eckberg, the school's director of placement. What's more, the incredible success that Roosevelt has had in placing young women and men is due to the fact that the university employs someone who works on a one-to-one basis with the students, lining them up with appropriate positions.

Here's how the Roosevelt placement system works. Job listings from the community are posted on a school bulletin board. If a student is interested in one or more of the jobs, he or she applies to the Job Development Office. There the student meets with Lana Grey, who could best be described as a part-time part-time-job developer (she works three days a week). Grey screens the students and sends them out on as many interviews as possible.

"Most of the jobs are clerical or sales-related," says Grey, a thirty-three-year-old mother who graduated from Roosevelt with a degree in vocational counseling. "Better-paying positions are available to business majors [Roosevelt has a large business school] and particularly to those who can work as accounting or bookkeeping assistants. We also have an internship program," she points out. "Companies seeking what they call 'potential graduate employees' will hire a student to work part-time during the school year and usually full-time during the summer. If the employer is satisfied, the student will be offered a job after graduation."

General Mills is one company that now takes advantage of the excellent job placement program at Roosevelt University. Tom Lyndel, office manager of General Mills's Chicago office, is an enthusiastic supporter of the program. "Internship gives the student the opportunity to experience the business world from the inside. If the student proves successful, we're happy to invite him or her to join the firm."

Cheng Huang, a twenty-one-year-old accounting major and a member of Roosevelt's class of '81, was accepted as an intern at General Mills in 1980. During previous summers, Cheng had worked in a factory in his hometown, Addison, Illinois, doing wiring and inspecting work for $4 an hour. The General Mills position pays him $1100 a month. "I decided to go to the job placement office and to see Lana Grey," he recalls, "but I had no idea I'd end up with anything like this."

The advantage of looking for an off-campus position, of course, is that you can hunt for exactly the job you want rather than settle for whatever on-campus job happens to be available when you get to the placement office. That doesn't mean that those off-campus positions likely to be found by relatively inexperienced students are necessarily going to be much better than the standard clerical and sales positions found at many schools. But at least you have a better shot at working in the field of your choice, where you can combine earnings with pertinent experience and the chance to make contacts that could be useful later.

Answering want ads or working through a local temporary employment agency are two of the easiest ways to secure appropriate jobs. Contacting potential employers directly can be an even better approach for the young man or woman with a ready supply of persistence.

Keep in mind that by taking an off-campus job, you do not need to lock yourself into a fixed schedule every week. You can, of course, take a job that requires you to show up every morning or on Tuesdays and Thursdays. But you can also find a job that requires you to work occasionally. Or you can hold several part-time jobs at once, depending on your schedule and other commitments.

Annette Guarisco of Merrick, New York, found three lucrative part-time jobs that allow her to work when she wants to. A twenty-two-year-old accounting major at Hofstra University, Annette decided to attend a clinic sponsored by the Nassau (County) Board of Women Officials so she could become certified to officiate at junior varsity volleyball games at Long Island high schools. She signed up for the sessions (cost: $20), attended classes once a week for three weeks, and then passed a written and practical test. That was it — Annette was certified as an apprentice official. During her senior year, she officiated at various games "which last an hour, tops." She earned a neat $20 per game.

Now Annette is attending law school and still officiating to earn extra money. After another year as an apprentice, she can take the test to be certified for varsity games. She will also be eligible for a state rating, which will enable her to work anywhere in the country. Best of all, she will earn $27 a game.

Besides officiating, Annette works for $10 an hour as a calisthenics instructor for the town of Hempstead. During the summer she works as a bookkeeper at a Long Island tennis club, where she puts in four hours a day and earns $6 an hour. But supervising athletic games for $20 apiece is certainly the job that holds the greatest appeal for this future attorney.

If you are interested in officiating at high-school, junior-high, or even Little League games, a phone call to a local board of officials or someone in the physical education department at a nearby public or private school should be all that's necessary to find out about requirements in your area. As Annette mentions, ratings are available in other sports, too, such as field hockey, swimming, track, and soccer (which pays the most, $31 per game).

Off-Campus Boss, On-Campus Job

It is hard to imagine that there is much money to be made by tacking up magazine subscription forms around campus from time to time during the school year. Yet according to Brenda Blackwood of the Campus Rep Program of Time, Inc., working as a campus representative can be a simple way for any college student to earn as much as $500 per semester. If a student wants to apply for a position, he or she simply writes a letter to the company (Campus Rep Program, Time, Inc., College Bureau, Time and Life Building, Rockefeller Center, New York, NY 10020). The application is forwarded to the appropriate area manager, who may be in charge of students in one or more states. If a rep is needed in the area, the student has the job.

Each student rep is supplied with campus rate cards —small envelopes with subscription blanks inside — which he or she puts up around campus. When another student takes a form and sends it in along with subscription money, a code printed on the form identifies the rep who posted it. The rep gets $2.50 for each subscription sold.

The Time program has been in operation for some twenty-five years and there are currently about nine hundred student reps. A single campus, says Blackwood, can accommodate as many as five. One of the reasons the program is so successful, she says, is that student subscription prices to Time, Inc., publications are considerably lower than normal rates. For example, a year of *Time* is $18.20, compared with the usual $65.

Bill Bornemann, a former college rep, worked for Time and also for a Michigan-based magazine distributing company while he was a full-time student at St. Peter's College in Jersey City, New Jersey. In 1972, Bill worked not one, but *twenty-five* college campuses. He earned over $9000 that year. (He also held jobs as a substitute teacher in Jersey City at $35 a day, and he loaded trucks at night!) Today, the ambitious thirty-one-year-old is an area manager for Time's Campus Rep Program. He is in charge of between fifty and ninety students in New Jersey, Delaware, and Pennsylvania. He also owns Campus Marketing Services of Red Bank, New Jersey, a business that deals with advertising on college campuses. Why did he get started in magazine sales on campus? For the same reason he still works in the field: "I just like money."

Ken Bloom, a member of Temple University's class of '83, is another successful magazine magnate who comes from a long line of magazine sales wunderkinder. Ken inherited his job from his brother, who had inherited it from their older sister. Ken became a campus rep while he was a sophomore in high school. He now works for Bill Bornemann.

During 1979, Ken, then only eighteen, earned over $2000 posting subscription cards for *Time, Newsweek, Playboy,* a film-developing service, and a private magazine-distributing company that handles between 70 and 140 magazine titles. Ken says he works only about four or five hours a week, and that he could easily take another part-time job. "But there's no way I could earn as much from any part-time job that pays by the hour."

Similar to and potentially even more lucrative than campus magazine sales is sales of newspapers through vending machines and student subscriptions. Chris Baders of the New York Times School and College Service in New York City explains: "Student salespeople buy their own papers at a discount: sixteen cents each for vending machine copies; eleven cents for student subscription copies. They in turn sell the papers at retail cost: twenty-five cents in vending machines, and fifteen cents by subscription. Their profit is the difference." (High-school reps, she adds, can do the same thing and earn even more money, because they pay only thirteen cents a copy.)

Needless to say, somewhat more work is involved in handling newspaper sales than in simply posting up subscription rate cards around campus. The *New York Times* (which offers its service "in the northeast quadrant," as far south as Washington, D.C.) delivers papers daily to the campus. The student must then distribute the copies, fill the vending machines, and empty coin boxes. He or she is billed for the papers at the end of the month.

On an average college campus, Chris says, "reps can make $100 and more per week for about an hour's work each day." Similar opportunities undoubtedly exist for distributing newspapers in other parts of the country. One phone call to a major newspaper in your area would enable you to find out about the possibilities.

Enterprising Students

On any campus there are students who offer goods and services to other students and make extra money for themselves. Typing and tutoring are two well-known standbys. Providing transportation (for instance, shuttling students to airports) and entertaining at campus parties are two others. To get jobs, students usually use the familiar methods of posting index cards on campus bulletin boards, placing ads in the student newspaper, or mimeographing flyers and sticking them in mailboxes or under windshield wipers. But consider how students at Columbia University have capitalized on their own talents and organized a money-making venture that could work on virtually any college campus.

Columbia Student Enterprises is a clever, thriving campus business that has been in operation since 1977. It is under the immediate direction of the Office of Student Employment of the university. Eugene Kisluk, who is employed by Columbia, oversees the operation. However, as he is quick to acknowledge, each of the member agencies has at least one student manager who is directly responsible for that agency's day-to-day activities. Some agencies are one-person operations; others employ a number of students. Each agency pays 15 percent of its profits to Columbia Student Enterprises to cover operating costs, printing, investment capital, and other expenses. The whole venture is a kind of cooperative for young entrepreneurs.

To give you an idea of the types of services that might be offered during any semester, here is a rundown of the different member agencies listed in the Columbia Student Enterprises 1979–80 spring brochure. Included are details taken from the brochure, or descriptions provided by Kisluk or student managers, of what the agencies offer and how much their members can earn.

◆ *Bartending Agency* — Bartending is available throughout the New York metropolitan area. All participating students are trained in a mixology course. (See "Special Skills Agency," page 227.) Bartenders average about $10 an hour.

◆ *Birthday Cake Agency* — At the beginning of each school year, manager Gary Adams, from Creve Coeur, Missouri, sends around brochures to the parents of all Columbia College students. The parents place their orders for their children's cakes and enclose checks. The cakes, bought from a local bakery, range from $8.25 to $12.00 each, which includes a 30 percent markup for Gary. He will deliver a cake anywhere within a fifteen-block radius.

◆ *Bookcover Agency* — The agency compiles, prints, and distributes ten thousand bookcovers free of charge to Columbia students. The bookcovers are distributed at the beginning of every semester to dormitories and other spots on and off campus. Profits come from advertising.

◆ *Calligraphy Agency* — As you would expect, this agency offers "a fine penmanship service to the University community."

◆ *College Services Agency* — Students place and stock postage-stamp vending machines throughout the campus.

◆ *Columbiana Agency* — This agency sells caps, pennants, and other items at athletic events.

◆ *Computer Agency* — The computer agency designs programs to meet the needs of businesses and individuals.

◆ *Desk Blotter Agency* — Like the bookcover agency, this is an advertising gimmick. About eight thousand desk blotters are distributed to students throughout the university. The blotters offer ready references to campus activities throughout the academic year. Two students have worked on the project for three years and have averaged $4000 a year profits.

♦ *Floor Refinishing Agency* — For fifty cents a square foot, the students will sand, stain, and seal any hardwood floor over one hundred square feet in size. As an extra, they will come back one month later to wax it. The service is offered within a ten-block radius of the school.

♦ *Grade Retrieval Agency* — This is a new one, conceived, begun, and operated by prelaw student Paul Locker, who is now at Harvard Law School. Students from out of town or local students "who don't want to make a special trip or trudge around to the various departments" to gather information on their course work supply their Social Security numbers (in order to ensure confidentiality) and ask for the grades they would like to know. Using a program that a computer-science major designed for $15, Paul feeds the information into a computer, which "throws out" the class grades. Subscribers are charged fifty cents per grade, with a two-grade minimum.

♦ *Messenger Service Agency* — Messages are delivered on campus or within Manhattan. Rates, the brochure advises, are competitive.

♦ *New York Times News Service* — "With a daily circulation of better than 1000 newspapers our agency represents the largest college account in the metropolitan area." The agency employs a number of students, and seeks those "who can brave the early morning hours."

♦ *Notary* — The notary provides services to the college community and to the general public.

♦ *Photographic Agency* — For parties, family portraits, portfolios, or coverage of events, this agency offers "top-quality photos at reasonable prices."

♦ *Shirt Agency* — Columbia shirts sold at a great savings, plus the promise of more items to come during the school year.

♦ *Special Skills Agency* — This agency offers courses outside the standard academic curriculum such as "Bartending" and "How to Tutor Effectively." A new addition for 1980 was "Ice

Skating," and "Cooking" is anticipated for the future. Most courses last six weeks and cost $40.

♦ *Student Advertising Agency* — "We will distribute literature or advertise your product throughout the Columbia campus."

♦ *Student Publishing Agency* — In September 1980 the agency put out the first edition of the "Columbia Student Guide to New York City," a 250-page guidebook distributed free to Columbia students and subsidized by an anticipated $30,000 worth of advertising.

♦ *Student Record Agency* — This agency offers unusual phonograph records that are generally not available. "The slant will be to various forms of 'folk music.' "

♦ *Student Travel Services Agency* — The travel agency sells Greyhound bus tickets to all parts of the United States and Canada, at whatever special rates may be available at the time of sale. It saves students long hours of traveling downtown and waiting in lines at the Port Authority bus terminal.

♦ *Student Typing Agency* — This agency's work is obvious.

♦ *Tutoring and Translating Agency* — Services are available to anyone in the New York metropolitan area. Hourly rates are high: from $8 to $20, depending on the project.

As you can see, a little organization and a lot of ingenuity can go far toward providing students with terrific part-time jobs. As Gene Kisluk says, during the first year you have to put in a lot of time getting the operation established. But after that, it practically runs itself. Most students, he claims, work about five hours a week.

Job-Hunting Guide for Students

This guide will help ensure that you will land one of the better on- or off-campus jobs. Bring solid skills or at least some paid or volunteer work experience to your job hunt. As a rule, you can expect to earn from $4 to $6 an hour if you can type, and the same or more if you can organize and keep the books of a small business. Waiting on tables can bring in $50 to $100 a week (at $1 to $3 an hour, plus tips). Bartending will earn you a higher hourly wage ($4 to $8, sometimes more), but the tips will be lower. If you can program computers, you can expect to make as much as $10 to $12 an hour. Best of all, if you are capable of interpreting or translating one or more languages, you may be able to earn as much as $15 to $20 an hour.

Some hints:

FOR ON-CAMPUS JOBS

Most on-campus jobs are filled on a first-come, first-served basis. Arrive early.

Check with professors or department heads to line up possibilities for research associate or paper-grading jobs which may not be listed in the placement office.

Keep looking at ads posted on bulletin boards around campus, such as at the placement office or perhaps in a student center or lounge. Sometimes a good job will pop up almost out of nowhere. And if things are really slow, you will find no shortage of stopgap money-makers such as baby sitting, yard work, helping at parties, and so forth.

FOR OFF-CAMPUS JOBS

If it's a clerical or sales job you are after, check the help-wanted ads in your local paper, where most part-time typist or Gal or Guy Friday positions will be advertised. Check with local banks and insurance companies, which tend to be particularly receptive to hiring college students. Don't forget the temporary agencies.

Write a brief résumé. Mention any paid work experience you might have had. If you haven't had any, highlight good grades, honors, extracurricular activities, and volunteer experience. The point is to stress achievements and accomplishments wherever possible. Put down anything that is relatively true (no one is going to check on the number of customers you waited on each night while you worked in a restaurant). Include anything that makes you look good. You want to show potential employers that you are eager and dependable — a can't-be-beat combination, particularly if you are inexperienced.

Page 230 gives an example of a résumé that lists only the

most routine part-time jobs. Nevertheless, the specifics in each job description help create the impression of a hard worker who gets along well with people and who is achievement-oriented. These are good impressions to try to make. (As you can see, "education" is the first heading listed in the sample résumé. Normally, experience is listed first. However, since this student has strong grades and weak work experience, it is a good idea for her to put education right at the top. If your previous jobs are more impressive than your academic credentials, you may want to reverse the two headings on your own résumé.)

Carole Jane Ward
603 Richmond Road
Viola, New Jersey 82646
(201) 483-1964

RÉSUMÉ

EDUCATION

Sept. 1980 to present

Student at Fairleigh Dickinson University, Teaneck, New Jersey. Major: Accounting. Grade point average: B+. Served as freshman orientation counselor.

EXPERIENCE

Jan. 1981 to May 1981

Pedowitz Department Store
60 Atlanta Avenue
Teaneck, New Jersey

Salesperson. Worked three nights a week in the furniture department. Sold over $15,000 worth

of merchandise during
four-month period.

Sept. 1980 to Dec. 1980

Dave Shor's Restaurant
330 Durward Turnpike
Teaneck, New Jersey

Counter attendant.
Waited on an average of
60 to 80 customers per
night in busy downtown
location.

July 1980 to Aug. 1980

Camp Stan-Lee
Sylvan Lake, New York

Counselor at YMCA
camp for disadvantaged
children. Supervised 11
campers ranging from
eight to ten years old.

PERSONAL DATA

Date of Birth: December 22, 1962
Marital Status: Single
Health: Excellent
Special Skills: Speak Spanish; type 60
                         words per minute

REFERENCES

Available upon request.

If you're answering want ads or sending your résumé to
likely employers, enclose a covering letter that is brief and to
the point. One possibility for such a letter is the following:

Mr. Jeffrey S. Jawer
Jawer and Stearn Company
1412 Hemlock Avenue
Madison, New Jersey 84880

Dear Mr. Jawer,

I am an accounting major at Fairleigh Dickinson University in Teaneck and am seeking a part-time position as a bookkeeper or junior accountant during the current school year. I'm hoping that you may be in need of someone to help you two or three days a week.

As the enclosed résumé indicates, I held part-time jobs throughout my freshman year and worked during this past summer. I would welcome the opportunity to discuss employment possibilities with you.

Thanks for your consideration, and I look forward to hearing from you.

Sincerely yours,

Carole Jane Ward

If you do manage to get several interviews, or you decide to take the "walk-in-off-the-street" approach to job-hunting, look the part. This point has been belabored to death, but the fact is, people *are* judged by appearance, whether we like it or not. In his book *Jobs 80–81* (New York: Paragon, 1979), William N. Yeomans puts it this way: "Before you go for the interview, get into your best clothes. Check everything to be sure you look as good as you possibly can at that time. Remember: The interviewer is going to make a judgment quickly about you, and much of his decision is going to be based on how you look. Don't louse it all up from the beginning by being a slob."

If you do take the direct approach and walk into stores and offices around town, don't simply ask, "Do you have any part-time jobs available?" Why not? First, doing so sets you up for an easy and immediate "no." Second, the employer may look at you and see only a warm body, someone to do all the dirty work that no one else has been willing to do.

Instead, ask to see the person in charge when you enter and hand the prospective employer your résumé when you walk in. Say something like, "I'm majoring in accounting at Fairleigh Dickinson and thought you might be in need of someone to help you with your record keeping on a part-time basis." Or "I'm studying graphic arts at Pratt and I'm looking for a part-time job doing illustration or paste-ups and mechanicals, and I was hoping you might be in need of someone who can work up to twenty hours a week." Or, "I'm studying retailing at UCLA and I'm interested in finding a part-time job that combines selling with some administrative responsibility. Can you use a good student who has already had some work experience?"

Use the approach that's easiest for you. Be sure to suggest a specific job — the job *you* want. Help the employer to see you in a specific position from the moment that he or she lays eyes on you. That way, even if an opening is not available, the employer might say, "Well, I don't need a bookkeeper, but you know, I really could use someone who could check up on back orders and handle correspondence and fill in for me when I have to go into town to buy new merchandise." And there you have it — a job offer.

By presenting yourself as already qualified in some way, you immediately give the impression of being competent. And an exchange based on the supposition that you are competent is far more likely to lead to a job offer than an open plea for employment is. Whether you get a direct offer or just the suggestion that you see a friend of the employer's who may have an opening, it's a positive response. Either way, you are now in the position to accept or reject whatever comes of it.

If the employer's initial response is at all positive, say something like, "Why, that really sounds interesting. I'd like to hear more about it." Then let the employer sell *you* on the job he or she has in mind. On the other hand, if the job isn't for you but you want to keep the door open, say, "Thanks for the offer, but since accounting is my major, I would like to get a job that will give me some experience in the field. However, if I don't find anything within a couple of days, I'd be delighted to talk with you some more. Why don't I stop by again on Thursday morning to let you know what's happening.

Leave the door open whenever possible. If you get a flat no when you approach an employer, ask if he or she expects any openings to become available in the near future and if you may check back in a week or two. Thank the person you have spoken with, and be sure to leave behind a copy of your résumé in case he or she should think of something within the next few days. If you have said you're going to call back, do so.

If you decide you simply want to offer typing, translating, home repair, baby-sitting, or any other services that are usually in demand on and around college campuses, tack up index cards all over the place — in churches and synagogues, community centers, supermarkets, community bulletin boards, anywhere you think people who might be interested in your service will see them. If you have access to a mimeograph machine or inexpensive printing, you might want to print up flyers and hand them out or distribute them around town. Make your pitch clever, if possible. Come up with a catchy name for your service. Use some bright design or decorative detail to catch people's attention. To protect yourself, *never* include your full name and address; use only the details you wish to make known, plus a phone number where you can be reached.

Finally, don't overlook the strength-in-numbers principle when you are trying to launch a money-making venture. Talk to your friends at school about setting up something like the venture that Columbia University students now run. Decide on the various services you might offer. Think how you could recruit other students who may have talents and skills that complement those of the organizers. Next ask a professor in the business school or department for some pointers on setting up such an organization. Then speak to your class adviser or someone in administration and ask about getting some financial assistance, or even the use of school equipment, to help launch your student services business. Before long, and with any luck at all, you will be on your way to running a successful enterprise that will benefit not only the school community, but yourselves as well.

Tips for Summer Job-Hunters

"This seems to be the kind of job you really can't get unless there's someone you know. Everyone I know who's a desk assistant at ABC News has gotten their job through their connections. After all, it doesn't take a great deal of brilliance to rip paper off the wires."

— DAVID KISSINGER, eighteen, son of former secretary of state Henry Kissinger, referring to his $180-a-week summer job. Quoted in the *New York Post*, June 12, 1980.

Every year, as every student knows, it gets harder and harder to find a good summer job. According to the Bureau of Labor Statistics, the number of employed young people grows by some three million each year. No wonder the search for a summer job can be tough. Yet the news needn't be all that discouraging. For the high-school or college student with the sense to begin the job hunt early (around Thanksgiving is a good time) and with the persistence to stick with it through "no openings" and "try us later," there will probably be a good job waiting when the warm weather comes. Here are the best ways to begin and follow through on the search for a rewarding job.

Decide what you can do, what you want to do, and where you want to do it. Finding a paid job in your chosen career may take considerable effort; so may locating *any* job, if your geographical requirements are stringent. Consider how much money you need to earn (say, for tuition), or whether you are willing to take a summer internship that pays little or nothing in return for the experience. If you can pinpoint your desires and requirements, your job hunt will be more focused and probably more successful than if you decide to wait and take just any job that comes along.

Start early. Late fall isn't too soon to begin exploring next summer's possibilities. According to John Losa, an interviewer with the New York State Job Service, the earlier an inquiry appears, the more opportunities there are. The smart job-seekers, says Losa, come in during the fall or early winter "and have a nice, large listing to choose from."

Check opportunities with Uncle Sam. The student seeking a summer job with Uncle Sam will find that most government application deadlines come in mid-January, long before most students even begin to think about summer jobs. Send for "Summer Jobs — Opportunities in the Federal Government, Announcement No. 414," which is revised each year and is available from any local office of the Federal Job Information Center (see "U.S. government" in the telephone book's white pages), usually around December first. The booklet names the agencies that offer positions, the requirements, filing deadlines, and general salary information.

If you are seeking a student internship, see your college placement officer as soon as possible. Under the Federal Summer Internship Program, students apply to their college placement officers, who interview applicants and nominate those they feel are qualified. Then comes an interview with the agency itself, plus the requirement that students submit two recommendations and a brief essay. Kay Sternenberg, a graduate of Trinity College in Burlington, Vermont, and a graduate student at the University of Vermont, worked during the summer of 1980 as a program officer for the International Communications Agency (ICA). Kay says she probably got her job because of her writing skills, knowledge of government, and the fact that she worked in Washington during the previous summer in the civilian personnel division of the Air Force. Her salary at ICA: $216.30 per week.

Two other internship programs are worth noting: (1) The Federal Junior Fellowship Program for college-bound high-school seniors. The program is open only to students in the top 10 percent of their classes, and there are usually income requirements (information should be available at local high schools). (2) The Congressional Intern Program, under which applicants may work for their legislator, or for any of a number of congressional committees. Contact your representative for details, or write to the Congressional Intern Program, Washington, DC 20515.

Consider summer jobs offered by large corporations. Each summer, Public Service of Bloomington, Indiana, hires students who work at the electric company as customer service representatives. They start at $4.36 an hour. According to supervisor Peggy Spitzer, the only qualification necessary for customer service jobs is a high-school diploma. She stresses that the company looks for those "with customer contact skills" because 95 percent of the work entails dealing with the public. Marva Donald, a twenty-year-old health administration major at Indiana University, doesn't view her part-time job with Public Service as a stepping stone to a career with the utility; however, she does recognize that it offers her more money than her previous summer positions working as a bookkeeper and at a fast-food restaurant, "plus experience working with people in an office-type atmosphere."

Contact resorts and amusement parks. The pay is low, usually around minimum wage, but the larger amusement parks and resorts do hire thousands of students each summer as attendants or to work in snack shops and gift shops, among other places. For example, Disney World in Orlando, Florida, hired some two thousand high-school and college students during the summer of 1980, and Six Flags Over Texas, in the Dallas vicinity, employed about four thousand young men and women.

Don't overlook clerical jobs. Typing and filing are probably not anyone's idea of a great way to fill three months of vacation time. Yet jobs with temporary agencies are plentiful, diverse, and, best of all, pay from $4 to $6 an hour or more, depending on the skills you have to offer. If operating a computer happens to be one of the skills you possess, you can easily earn $10 or more per hour.

Are you a potential camp counselor? One way to cash in while you enjoy sun, fun, and exercise is to work at a summer camp. Expect salaries ranging from $500 to $1200 for the summer, depending on whether you are a general counselor or someone offering specialized skills in lifesaving and water safety, arts and crafts, drama, tennis, dance, and so on. For information about camping jobs, write to the American Camping Association, Bradford Woods, Martinsville, IN

45151. For $5.95, the ACA will send you a packet of information, including a list of some 2500 member camps. You may also wish to contact the Association of Independent Camps, 55 West 42nd Street, New York, NY 10036, as well as your local "Y," Boy Scouts or Girl Scouts, or other community organizations that sponsor summer camps.

Consider volunteering. Often the really good jobs, such as lab positions for premed students or future biologists and chemists, go to exceedingly bright students with top grades who are willing to work for no pay. If you can afford to forgo the income, working as a volunteer can pay off in other ways. As Kay Sternenberg points out, "If you work free one summer, you get paid the next." That is often true. If paid work within your chosen field is impossible to get, a good volunteer position can offer invaluable experience, good contacts, and references, plus the prospect of a salaried job during the coming school year or next summer. Contact your college placement office, department chairperson, community volunteer referral agency or the United Way, the board of education, or local government headquarters to inquire about positions. You may also be interested in obtaining a copy of *Invest Yourself,* a directory of volunteer and service programs in North America and on five other continents. The book sells for $3 (including postage and handling) and can be obtained by writing to the Reverend J. Wilbur Patterson, Commission on Voluntary Service and Action, Room 1126, 475 Riverside Drive, New York, NY 10015.

Work abroad. Salaries in foreign countries are often much lower than they are in the United States. What's more, jobs for American students are often hard to come by and are almost always at the very lowest levels. Nevertheless, if you think you want to try to find a job abroad, the best way to begin your job hunt is by writing to the Council for International Educational Exchange. CIEE publishes a wide variety of excellent publications revised each year. Write to CIEE at 205 East 42nd Street, New York, NY 10017.

Don't forget the old standbys. Fast-food restaurants, public parks, beaches, ice-cream companies that operate trucks, retail stores, restaurants, and supermarkets all hire students during the summers. For the self-motivated, there are always the create-it-yourself jobs. For instance, you might offer your services as a mother's helper, gardener, house watcher, dog walker, tutor, baby sitter, party helper, car washer, or home companion. Robert Cipriano, a member of the Drew University class of '82, explains how taking a job as a laborer for the summer can pay off: "All of my friends were either working for nothing or for minimum wage, in do-nothing jobs. So I decided if I was going to make some money, I'd better start scouting around. I asked everyone I knew about summer jobs, and as it turns out one of my father's clients was a stonemason who needed a helper for the summer. The work is really hard, but I'm earning over $200 a week. For a student working during the summer, that's quite a bit of money."

Look professional when you look for a job. Blue jeans may be acceptable *on* the job, but they are not when you are *looking* for the job (see page 232). Dress neatly, and bring along a résumé or any summary of work experience that indicates your willingness to work hard and your enthusiasm (see sample résumé, page 230). If at all possible, have available the names and phone numbers of three adults who have agreed to serve as character references.

Stick with it. If a potential employer tells you to come back in two or three weeks, do so. If you are not told to call or stop back, ask if you may, and do so. If you get a negative response, ask if there are likely to be openings in the future. If you get no encouragement whatsoever, ask the employer for the name of someone else who may be looking for help, and ask if you may use his or her name when you call to inquire about openings. Don't be a pest, but do be persistent. It is better to be thought overeager than to be forgotten.

For further information, *The Summer Employment Directory* lists some six thousand jobs with over nine hundred employers, most of whom are managers, owners, or personnel directors of resorts and summer camps. The paperback should be available in most bookstores for $6.95. You may order the directory from Writer's Digest Books, 9933 Alliance Road, Cincinnati, OH 45242.

❧ 7 ❧

Who Is Hiring
and Who Isn't

❧————◆◆————

*"One probable reason for lower turnover, absentee-
ism, and recruitment costs is that a good supply of
able, intelligent, willing, and motivated employees exists but is available only on a part-time basis. Employers who want to take advantage of it, however,
must first shed old ideas that all employees must work
nine to five, five days a week. Relaxing full-time requirements for certain positions could well pay off."*
— "Improving Productivity with Part-time and Temporary
Help" (New York: Research Institute of America, 1979).

The Private Sector

Those in Favor

By now you should have a fairly good idea of the types of
businesses, companies, agencies, and organizations that tend
to be receptive to the idea of hiring part-time workers. As you
saw in "The Way It Was and Will Be," most of those in the
so-called service industries, and particularly firms that offer
extended hours or experience predictable business peaks during the day or week, are likely to use part-timers. So are those
that keep their operations running during weekends and hol-

idays. Many of the fields discussed in "Today's Best Part-Time Jobs" are such service fields.

In addition to those companies that have periodic bursts of activity, say during lunchtime or on Friday evenings, are companies and institutions that have difficulty recruiting workers on a continuing basis. The health-care field is full of them; so is the data-processing industry. "Personnel people are sitting in parking lots of rival companies trying to grab computer programmers on their way to work," says Carol Parker of Job Sharers, Inc., in Arlington, Virginia. In New York, Leslie Ginsburg, vice-president of a data-processing consulting firm, claims that during the summer and fall of 1980 he was inundated with calls from programmers offering to hire themselves out for $150 to $250 a day. Ginsburg reports that there was no shortage of takers.

Other companies that have been coming around to the idea of hiring workers on reduced schedules include those whose employees are subjected to extremely high levels of boredom or mental and emotional stress during their workdays. "Some jobs are highly demanding, so much so that they cry out for part-time workers or short shifts," observed the Research Institute of America in its study "Improving Productivity with Part-time and Temporary Help" (New York: Research Institute of America, 1979). Thanks to studies such as this one, employers of factory workers, prison guards, social workers, and air traffic controllers, for example, have become increasingly mindful of the losses they sustain because of excessive stress and fatigue among workers on full-time schedules. Washington researcher Lorraine D. Eyde has also highlighted the kinds of jobs now usually done on a full-time basis that would benefit from part-time scheduling and are likely to become more open to such scheduling in the future.[1] Among them are positions in economics, the physical sciences, math, and statistics, as well as such public-sector jobs as police officer and firefighter.

---

1. Lorraine D. Eyde, "Flexibility Through Part-Time Employment of Career Women in the Public Service" (Washington, D.C.: U.S. Civil Service Commission, Personnel Research and Development Center, June 1975), pp. 6–8.

Clearly, even among those firms that have been reluctant to adopt reduced work schedules, things seem to be changing. "The private sector is beginning to open up," maintains Barney Olmsted of New Ways to Work, in San Francisco. "It's true that opportunities are greater where there's an organization actively promoting part-time work, but word is beginning to spread among private corporations that there are benefits to hiring part-timers."

"People are more willing to talk about job sharing," adds Nancy Inui of FOCUS, Inc., in Seattle. "They may want to know who else is doing it, and they may not want to be the first on their block to try it, but they're increasingly receptive to the idea."

An interesting sidelight to the who's-hiring question is mentioned by Carol Parker. "In my experience," she says, "it seems that companies that are based on the West Coast or that are national in scope tend to be more receptive to the concept of alternative work scheduling than other firms are. They are more familiar with the idea to begin with." Carol also feels that regional differences play a part in determining who welcomes part-timers. "Washington, D.C. tends to be extremely conservative," she points out, "whereas Seattle, Washington, is more open and innovative and therefore better represented by top-level part-timers."

"The best bets everywhere seem to be in companies with a certain management style," adds Nancy Inui. "Companies that believe in the philosophy 'happy workers are better workers' are all for alternative scheduling. On the other hand, rigid companies — in any field, anywhere — are likely to be among the least receptive to the notion. It's not anything you can always identify ahead of time," she says, "but things like strict dress codes are usually a giveaway."

Certainly, the experts agree, the number of private-sector employers receptive to hiring part-timers is still not as large as any of us would like. But the number is growing. As you can see from the following list, many types of companies in most parts of the country are now willing at least to consider the idea of part-time scheduling. Among them:

Banks
Hospitals
Real-estate agencies
Department stores
Voluntary health agencies
Accounting firms
Travel agencies
Law offices
Health clubs
Day-care centers and
    nursery schools
Beauty parlors
Libraries
Railroads
Rehabilitation centers
Engineering firms
Advertising agencies
Child guidance centers
Printing and graphic-design
    companies
Hotels
Personnel agencies
Sports complexes
Art galleries
Women's centers
Museums
Prisons and halfway houses
Continuing education and
    adult education programs
Credit card and other
    finance companies
Doctors' and dentists' offices
Insurance companies and
    agencies

Resorts
Security companies
Public and private
    elementary and secondary
    schools
Repair services
Airlines
Family service agencies
Nursing homes
Nonprofit organizations of
    all types
Data-processing companies
Amusement parks and
    recreation facilities
Bus companies
Theaters, concert halls, and
    other entertainment
    centers
Small retail stores of every
    description
Car rental firms
Veterinary hospitals and
    animal shelters
Clinics of all types
Magazine and book
    publishing companies
Market research firms
Vocational centers
Temporary employment
    agencies
Public utilities

These, then, are the employers you are likely to find on any list of those most likely to be hiring part-timers. Let's look at some specific firms that serve as examples of these employers.

Twenty-five Top U.S. Companies That Hire Part-Time Workers

Company and Headquarters	Where Jobs May Be Offered	Types of Jobs and Benefits Offered
Avis (Automobile and truck rental and leasing) 1114 Avenue of the Americas New York, N.Y. 10036	Primarily at reservation headquarters in Tulsa, Okla.; North American headquarters in Garden City, N.Y., and 1400 rental locations throughout the country.	Rental agent; collection; microfilming; driving (moving cars from one location to another); some clerical. Benefits: Holiday pay only after 1000 hours.
Connecticut General Life Insurance Hartford, Conn. 06152	At company headquarters, plus various branches throughout the U.S. Main offices in New York, N.Y.; San Francisco and Santa Barbara, Calif.; Houston, Tex.	Secretarial; bookkeeping; other clerical; maintenance and support (night staff). Benefits: Full after 6 months; must work 20 hours per week.
Continental Illinois National Bank and Trust Co. 231 S. LaSalle Chicago, Ill. 60693	At head office, two main branches in Illinois, plus major subsidiaries in Houston, Tex.; Cleveland, Ohio; New York, N.Y.; California; and Boca Raton, Fla.	Secretarial; accounting; bookkeeping; a few managerial positions, such as trust administration, personnel, mortgage processing and new accounts representative. Benefits: Prorated for staff part-timers.

Where to Apply	Comments
At main offices located at airports, or nearest Avis office. 200–400+ part-time employees	Best opportunities are outside the New York area. Many rental locations operate 20 to 24 hours per day; many opportunities exist in most locations for night work. Always looking for qualified people.
Write to: Sally Kiehnle, Supervisor of Employment, Connecticut General Life Insurance Co., Hartford, Conn. 06152 400	Hires some women on "family hours" schedules; limited experimenting with job sharing. Also maintains roster of "intermittents" for short-term assignments or vacations.
At personnel office of local branch; check telephone directory. 1500	Very progressive program for senior citizens; currently employs 250 people over age 70. Small but growing program for professional women, in real-estate division, customer service, personnel. Also maintains "Ready Work Force" of about 350 people on call to work 2 to 3 days per week during vacations, special projects. Work-study programs for high-school and college students.

Company and Headquarters	Where Jobs May Be Offered	Types of Jobs and Benefits Offered
Control Data Corp. (Computer and financial services) 8100 34th Ave. S. Minneapolis, Minn. 55440	15 locations in the Minneapolis–St. Paul area; principal branches in Palo Alto, Calif.; Atlanta, Ga.; New York, N.Y.; Greenwich, Conn.; Baltimore, Md. (Commercial Credit Co.)	Programming; professional and technical positions in computer sciences; maintenance; bookkeeping; secretarial. Benefits: Prorated.
Eastman Kodak (Film, cameras, photographic supplies) 343 State St. Rochester, N.Y. 14650	At main offices in Rochester, and some 20 branches around the country, including Dallas, Tex.; Chicago, Ill.; Cleveland and Dayton, Ohio; Wellesley, Mass.; Washington, D.C.; New York, N.Y.	Keypunch operator and bank teller (in company bank); receptionist; secretarial; cafeteria and maintenance staff; process work in photo labs all over the country. Benefits: Prorated.
Emery Air Freight (Air freight and express service) Wilson, Conn. 06897	At 102 offices in every major city and airport, including Chicago, Los Angeles, New York, and smaller cities as well.	Telephone sales; secretary; typist; dock work; clerical. Benefits: Prorated for staff part-timers. Must work over 20 hours per week.
Equitable Life Assurance Society (Life insurance) 1285 Ave. of the Americas New York, N.Y. 10019	Largest concentration in regional service centers in Chicago, Ill.; Fresno, Calif.; Columbus, Ohio; Charlotte, N.C.; Fullerton, Calif. About 800 local offices in the country.	Mostly clerical; some lawyers, research investment analysts. Benefits: Prorated.

Where to Apply	Comments
At personnel office at each branch; check telephone directory. 4000	Innovative program for part-timers includes training at all levels. Hires disabled workers who can work at home using computer terminals. Operates a bindery in Selby, Minn.; staffed entirely by part-timers.
At personnel office at each branch; check telephone directory. 1500	Peak hiring after Christmas and major holidays, as well as during summer.
Contact the local office of Emery in any city. 700	Strong promotional possibilities for those within the company, including part-timers. Also maintains temporary work force (no benefits). Peak hiring varies according to location.
At personnel office at each branch; check telephone directory. 750	Hires women returning to work, as well as high-school co-op students. Hires "limited" or half-time workers, plus "modified limited," who have flexible schedules and put in 10 to 15 hours per week.

Company and Headquarters	Where Jobs May Be Offered	Types of Jobs and Benefits Offered
Honeywell Inc. Microswitch Division (Photoelectric devices) Honeywell Plaza Minneapolis, Minn. 55408	At factory in Massachusetts. Honeywell's 375 other offices may or may not use part-time workers. Each employee relations manager establishes local hiring guidelines.	Mechanical assembly work. Small number of secretarial positions. Benefits: Prorated.
Howard Johnson (Food and lodging) One Howard Johnson Plaza Boston, Mass. 02125	At some 1000 locations around the country, including 650 Howard Johnsons', 135 Ground Round restaurants; 130 Howard Johnson Motor Lodges; 32 Red Coach Grill restaurants.	Service positions: waitress; utility and maintenance work; fountain positions; other customer service. Benefits: None
IBM (Business machines; information processing) Old Orchard Rd. Armonk, N.Y. 10504	At several company divisions in Westchester, N.Y., plus other large branches in San Jose, Calif.; Raleigh, N.C.; Poughkeepsie, N.Y.; those with cafeteria and medical facilities	Food service work; security; nursing. Benefits: Prorated.
K Mart Corp. (Discount department stores) 3100 W. Big Beaver Rd. Troy, Mich. 48084	In each of 1446 stores nationwide.	Bookkeeping; merchandise assistant; cashier; cafeteria and grill operation. Benefits: Prorated.

Where to Apply	Comments
Apply directly to Microswitch Division headquarters, 401 Elm Street, Marlborough, Mass. 01752. Applications accepted all the time. 100	Pilot program began in 1972; now a model for other assembly-work companies. Most workers are mothers, who work 4 to 6 hours per day. Extremely flexible for school schedules, children's illness.
At local Howard Johnson or affiliated restaurant. 25,000	Over 24 hours per week is considered full-time, in restaurants. Many employees are students. The majority of general managers started out as part-timers. Company encourages applications at all times.
At personnel office of local division, plant, lab; check telephone directory. 400	Also maintains "non-regular" list of employees who work less than 90 days at a time; used for vacations and special short-term projects. Workers in this group include engineers, computer programmers, technicians.
Each store has its own personnel office; check telephone directory. 43,000	On-the-job training offered in all stores. Peak hiring season is Christmas.

Company and Headquarters	Where Jobs May Be Offered	Types of Jobs and Benefits Offered
Kentucky Fried Chicken (Quick-service restaurants) P.O. Box 32070 Louisville, Ky. 40232	At 4500 stores in U.S.; 600 in Canada.	Food service and customer service. Benefits: Prorated in company-owned stores for those working over 30 hours per week. Franchise owners determine benefits in their own stores.
Levitz Furniture (Furniture retailing) 1317 N.W. 167th St. Miami, Fla. 33169	At home office, accounting office in Philadelphia, Pa., plus group offices (San Francisco, Calif.; Seattle, Wash.; Chicago, Ill.; Boston, Mass.; Los Angeles, Calif.; St. Louis, Mo.) and at 71 branches.	Cashier; data processing clerk; warehouse operator. Benefits: Prorated.
Lockheed Missiles and Space Co. (Aerospace research, development, manufacturing) 1111 Lockheed Way Sunnyvale, Calif. 94086	At headquarters, plus principal offices in San Francisco Bay area; Sacramento, Santa Cruz, Calif.; Charleston, S.C.; Silverdale, Wash.; Huntsville, Ala.; Vandenberg AFB.	Mostly security force; switchboard operator; computer programming. Benefits: Prorated for staff part-timers.

Where to Apply	Comments
Apply at local KFC store. 75,000	Many daytime workers are mothers; many full-time managers began as part-time workers. One-third of all managers are women.
At nearest Levitz office or store. 400	Maintains ongoing work-study programs with high schools and colleges within 25 miles of all large offices and stores.
Write to: Employment Office, Lockheed Missiles and Space Co., 1111 Lockheed Way, Sunnyvale, Calif. 94086. 200	Maintains list of "call-ins" who work up to 20 hours per week. Limited summer intern program for college students.

Company and Headquarters	Where Jobs May Be Offered	Types of Jobs and Benefits Offered
McDonald's (Fast-service restaurants) One McDonald Plaza Oak Brook, Ill. 60521	In 4605 U.S. and 304 Canadian restaurants.	Food preparation and sales. Benefits: Prorated for those over 25 who work over 1000 hours in a 12-month period in company-owned stores; varies in individually owned stores.
Montgomery Ward (Retail chain) 619 W. Chicago Ave. Chicago, Ill. 60607	In 420 retail stores throughout the country, including large stores in Chicago, Los Angeles, Baltimore, Minneapolis–St. Paul, Oakland, Dallas–Fort Worth, Kansas City.	Most positions are for sales force; also, cashier, some stock clerk, secretarial. All departments use part-timers. Benefits: limited. All employees, both part-time and temporary, receive 15% discounts on fashions and related accessories; 10% on other merchandise.
Quaker Oats (Diversified manufacturers of grocery products and toys) Merchandise Mart Plaza Chicago, Ill. 60654	At offices in Chicago, western New York (Fisher Price Toys); and at about 100 Magic Pan Creperie restaurants throughout the country.	Primarily positions in restaurants: waiters and waitresses; some clerical; assembly work. Benefits: Prorated.

Where to Apply	Comments
All hiring done locally; inquire at nearest McDonald's. 220,000	Continuous training at all levels; most jobs held by high-school and college students.
Stop in a local store to apply. Don't call. Come in as soon as possible for Christmas hiring. 50,000	Peak hiring periods are Christmas, summer and mid-July (back-to-school hiring). Extremely flexible in terms of schedules.
Apply at any local office of Quaker Oats, Fisher Price, or Magic Pan Creperie. 500	Opportunities for temporary and seasonal work exist primarily at Fisher Price Toys. Otherwise, opportunities are on a year-round rather than seasonal or peak basis.

Company and Headquarters	Where Jobs May Be Offered	Types of Jobs and Benefits Offered
Ralston Purina (Pet food; livestock and poultry feed) Checkerboard Square St. Louis, Mo. 63188	At Ralston Purina offices throughout the country, plus at 1015 Jack-in-the-Box restaurants; 63 Continental restaurants.	In Ralston Purina offices, majority of jobs are secretarial, bookkeeping, typist and other clerical positions. In restaurants, food preparation or service. Benefits: Prorated for those who work more than 20 hrs./wk.
Ramada Inns (Hotels and inns) 3838 East Van Buren St. Phoenix, Ariz. 85001	At 650 Ramada Inns at roadsides, city centers and airports throughout the U.S.	Mostly restaurant work; room help; groundskeeper; bellboy; some office work. Benefits: Prorated for those working more than 20 hours per week.
Sears, Roebuck & Co. (Retail chain) Sears Tower Chicago, Ill. 60684	In 865 retail stores and 2835 catalogue stores throughout the U.S.	Sales; customer service; bookkeeping; secretarial; programming; delivery; cafeteria; maintenance; product repairs. Benefits: Prorated, except for medical insurance (none).
Travelers Corporation (Diversified financial institution) One Tower Square Hartford, Conn. 06115	At about 100 field locations throughout the country.	Keypunch; data entry; typing; file clerk; statistical clerk; mailroom; some cafeteria positions. Benefits: Prorated.

Where to Apply	Comments
Write: Corporate Employment, Ralston Purina Co., Checkerboard Square, St. Louis, Mo. 63188 700+	About 99 percent of all part-time positions are for those who work full days, a few times per week. The employment figure of 700 is for Ralston Purina only. Restaurants account for substantially more part-time opportunities, depending on location.
At the Ramada Inn nearest you. 9000	Peak hiring seasons depend on location. Winter hiring is greatest in California, Florida, Arizona, and other southern locations. Company always looking for competent full- and part-time workers.
At any large local store with a personnel office; contact store manager in smaller stores. 200,000	Every worker receives at least some training; comprehensive sales training program. Peak hiring time from end of September through December.
Contact local offices with personnel departments; check telephone directory. 1000	Best opportunities are in the largest cities, which have major corporate offices (Boston, New York City, Chicago, and Los Angeles).

Company and Headquarters	Where Jobs May Be Offered	Types of Jobs and Benefits Offered
Trans World Airlines (Airline) 605 Third Ave. New York, N.Y. 10016	At most TWA offices, including principal branches in New York; Los Angeles, San Francisco, Calif.; Chicago, Ill.; St. Louis, Mo.	Reservation agent; customer service agent (including ground hostess); ticket agent; some clerical. Benefits: Prorated for regular part-timers.
Upjohn HealthCare Services (Health care to individuals in institutions and at home) 3651 Vanrick Dr. Kalamazoo, Mich. 49001	Through 240 offices in U.S. and Canada. Work may be in private homes, nursing homes, hospitals, or in conjunction with insurance company rehabilitation programs.	Registered and licensed practical nursing; physical and occupational therapy; nutrition; homemaker–home health aide; housekeeping; cleaning work. Benefits: Prorated.
Wells Fargo Bank (Retail and commercial bank) 420 Montgomery San Francisco, Calif. 94104	In 370 branches throughout the state of California. Largest branches in San Francisco, Los Angeles, Sacramento, San Diego, and Fresno.	Data processing; some real estate; tellers; administrative; computer operations; clerical; secretarial; accounting. Benefits: Prorated according to length of service and hours worked.

Where to Apply	Comments
At local TWA offices; check telephone directory. 900	Besides regular part-timers who usually work 4 hours per day in winter and 5 to 6 hours per day in summer, TWA hires "contingents" who work from April to September. Peak hiring time for regular part-timers, March and April.
Contact local office of Upjohn Health-Care Services, listed in both white pages and Yellow Pages. 55,000	For free booklet, "Opportunities in Health Care," write: Upjohn HealthCare Services, at headquarters. Extensive training and in-service education. Eager to hire women returning to work.
Write: Personnel Office, Wells Fargo Bank, 420 Montgomery, San Francisco, Calif. 94104. 2600	Employs many students for fall and summer seasons. Many part-timers are women with children. Company particularly responsive to needs of this group — also uses flexible scheduling where possible.

Company and Headquarters	Where Jobs May Be Offered	Types of Jobs and Benefits Offered
Western Air Lines (Airline) 6060 Avion Dr. Los Angeles, Calif. 90045	In 46 cities in 16 states and western Canada and Mexico. Largest offices in Los Angeles, Miami, San Francisco, Honolulu, Anchorage, Minneapolis–St. Paul, Denver.	Customer and passenger service at airports; some part-time positions in reservations; at ticket counter; baggage handling. Benefits: Prorated.

The preceding table appeared in an article I wrote for the November 20, 1979, issue of *Family Circle* magazine. As you can see, the table highlights not only the employers but the types of jobs they offer to people who wish to work reduced schedules. (The figures in the "Where to Apply" column represent the number of part-time workers employed by each corporation at the end of 1979.) Please note that the table was not and is not intended to be a current job directory. Spokespersons at all of the included companies did indicate that they planned to continue hiring part-time workers in the future. But that doesn't necessarily mean that job openings exist at this exact moment. Use the list as a general guide, and also as a starting point for identifying similar companies in your own area — firms that are likely to be hanging out a welcome sign to those who wish to work fewer than thirty-five hours a week or would like to put in a few days, weeks, or months now and then on a temporary basis.

You may also want to check your library for a copy of the first edition of *Alternative Work Schedule Directory,* published in 1978 by the National Council for Alternative Work Patterns, Inc. (NCAWP). The directory, which sells for $25, is available from NCAWP, 1925 K Street N.W., Washington, DC 20006. It lists 290 public and private employers that use various alternative work schedules, including flexitime, compressed work weeks, permanent part-time, and job sharing.

Where to Apply	Comments
Contact local office of Western Air Lines. 500	There is some seasonal hiring, depending on the location and time of year. Best bets for winter would be in Miami, Los Angeles.

Now that we have taken a harder look at those companies in favor of utilizing or at least experimenting with such alternative work patterns as permanent part-time jobs or job sharing, let's consider the nay-sayers in the private sector.

Those Opposed

"It stands to reason that part-timers are more productive than full-timers," says Gilbert L. Black of the Research Institute of America, referring to the ability of part-time workers in blue-collar jobs to get more done in less time. "They're working at peak capacity while they're on the job, as opposed to full-time workers, who can't produce at top levels all day long."

Despite the apparent logic of Black's statement, the fact remains that companies in the mining, construction, and manufacturing industries have been among the slowest to implement part-time scheduling. Of their employees, only 2.2 percent, 5.0 percent, and 3.4 percent, respectively, work part-time.

One notable exception to the general rule is the Selby bindery plant in St. Paul, Minnesota, which is owned by Control Data Corporation of Minneapolis. The Selby plant's early shift is staffed primarily by mothers of young children; the late shift, by high-school and college students. By capitalizing on the high energy level and productivity of its employees, the management of the Selby bindery now spends half of what it used to pay an outside contractor for collating, binding, and mailing.

Similarly, Honeywell, Inc. began a pilot program for part-timers at its Microswitch Division in Marlborough, Massachusetts. "Formerly, workers were bored to death," says Louise Hale, personnel manager of the plant, which makes photo-electric and proximity-sensing devices, small circuit boards, and other components. "So we thought we'd try hiring mature people who were eager to work a reduced schedule." Mothers in the community were offered the chance to work four to six hours a day at the plant. The women were automatically given leave during school vacations, and if a child became sick, the mother got time off with no difficulty. "The program has been so successful," says Hale with justifiable pride, "that it's now a model for other assembly-work companies in New England and in other parts of the country."

Of course, not just manufacturing firms are reluctant to offer reduced work scheduling or would benefit by using more part-timers. As Gilbert Black points out, each year numerous corporations move their offices to different parts of the country, or simply pick up and head to the suburbs. Most of these firms would be a lot better off if they were more flexible, Black argues. "Many don't realize that they should be hiring part-timers instead of relying on temporary workers," he contends. "They don't understand that there's a lot of talent out there: a huge, well-qualified labor pool that they could be availing themselves of."

Why are employers still reluctant to give part-time scheduling a try? Managers who don't use part-timers often say that a particular job doesn't lend itself to part-time scheduling (although Nollen, Eddy, and Martin concluded that almost any job can be scheduled on a part-time basis). Or they maintain that their costs would increase substantially, despite all of the evidence to the contrary. Employers reason that if it takes twenty weeks to train a full-timer and forty weeks to train someone working half-time, and if the average employee stays on the job eighty weeks, hiring the part-timer will cost them considerably more. As John D. Owen, the labor expert from

Wayne State University, notes, this assumption alone "helps to explain the reluctance of managers to hire part-timers for jobs that require much training."[2]

Yet the fact is that part-timers, particularly those who have *good* jobs, exhibit a lower turnover rate than full-timers do — though this is simply not accepted by many prospective employers. Neither is the fact that the quality of the part-time work force is usually higher than that of the work force at large; as John Owen indicates, the part-time work force consists mainly of mature, experienced, and well-educated workers who tend to be quick learners and who may also bring special skills or abilities to their jobs, which may actually *lower* training costs.

The myths die hard. As Nollen, Eddy, and Martin found (see "The Way It Was and Will Be," page 35), managers who have not yet employed part-time workers tend to emphasize the negatives: higher anticipated training and recruitment costs, higher absenteeism, the need for more managers to supervise the extra workers, higher costs for prorating and paying fringe benefits, higher record-keeping costs. But managers who have had the experience of hiring part-timers usually find that extra costs are insignificant and generally are more than made up for by the benefits of higher productivity, lower turnover and absenteeism, improved employee morale, and greater loyalty to the company.

Unions Still Skeptical

"Girls and women are just learning that the hourly wages for the trades are way above wages in traditional women's work; and besides enjoying their work, they are getting paid more than double the

---

2. John D. Owen, "An Empirical Analysis of the Voluntary Part-time Labor Market" (Washington, D.C.: U.S. Department of Labor, Manpower Administration, Office of Research and Development, August 31, 1977), p. 21.

amount paid clerical workers, receptionists, and women in health jobs with the same amount of education."

— JOYCE SLAYTON MITCHELL, *I Can Be Anything* (New York: College Entrance Examination Board, 1978).

In the chapter "The Way It Was and Will Be," we looked at several interesting statistics about the earnings of women who are members of labor unions. Women who work full-time and who belong to unions earn roughly 40 percent more than their nonunionized counterparts do. Among unionized part-timers, earnings are 50 percent higher. And yet only 10 percent of all female part-timers belong to unions. The principal reason, as noted in the same section, is that few unions really want part-timers.

Why not? First, to expand on the points made in the earlier chapter, they are afraid that increased use of part-timers will eliminate the payment of overtime to full-time workers already on the job. In many cases, they are right. One of the key advantages to employers of "using part-timers during regular working hours, or in place of regular workers after hours," as cited by the Research Institute of America, is that it "enables many companies to eliminate overtime in many chronically overloaded situations."[3]

A second union objection to the use of part-timers is that the seniority system, which protects workers who have been on the job for a long time, would be eroded if such measures as involuntary work sharing (shortened work weeks at lower pay) were widely adopted as an alternative to layoffs. Here again, the unions are right. However, many civil-rights and women's advocacy groups claim that the seniority system *should* be modified, since it tends to protect only white males. The groups argue that minority workers and females are always the last hired and consequently the first to go during

---

3. "Improving Productivity with Part-time and Temporary Help" (New York: Research Institute of America, 1979), p. 17.

periods of economic slowdown. Therefore, shortening work weeks for everyone is a much more equitable way to solve the problem of reducing the work force during bad times than laying off already disadvantaged groups is.

A third key objection that unions have to the hiring of part-timers is based on their fear that part-time work shifts could become mandatory for everyone. In other words, once employers recognized the benefits of, say, two minishifts as opposed to one eight-hour shift, they might try to force everyone to come in for only four to six hours a day. Fourth, unions argue that by supporting more opportunities for part-timers, they would be undermining their attempts to have the official forty-hour work week reduced to thirty-five hours — a move, they maintain, that would add five million full-time jobs to the economy.

Union opposition to the idea of part-time work, whether well founded or groundless, helps in large part to explain why so few opportunities for part-timers exist in the building trades, skilled crafts, and other high-paying nontraditional fields that have offered so much hope to a tiny but growing number of female workers during the past few years. For that reason, let's take a look at some of the other objections voiced by union officials in order to understand further why most unions still do not have signs welcoming part-timers at the entrances to their union halls.

"The nation's unions are not entirely pleased with the accelerating trend toward part-time workers, relatively few of whom become union members. But some unions, notably the Retail Clerks International Association, have stepped up their efforts to organize part-timers."

— Work in America Institute Inc., *World of Work Report,* Vol. 2, July 1977.

John Zalusky, an economist with the AFL-CIO in Washington, D.C., and one of the nation's most prominent union officials, explains some of the issues at stake. "We have no phobias against part-time workers," he is quick to answer when asked about union opposition to part-timers. "We represent a lot of them, particularly in the retail field and the longshore and seafaring trades. And we do a good job of representing them. My attitude toward part-timers is positive, where the job requires part-time workers. Then we're supportive. Where we differ is in taking an existing job presently occupied by one person and making it into two jobs. The reason we're opposed to that," he says, "is that there are a lot of people looking for full-time work who can't get it. There are three million part-time workers who would rather be full-time."

Another point Zalusky makes is that employers use part-timers not only because they can pay them less money and offer them fewer benefits, but because "hiring part-timers can be a way of union busting." He explains: "In the retail industry, for instance, the employers try to exclude as many of the full-time people as they can by calling them department heads or supervisors, so they're not eligible for union protection. Much of the rest of the work is done by part-timers, and since many of them are seasonal employees, they're difficult to organize."

Leon Harris, director of research for the Retail, Wholesale, and Department Store Union in New York City, agrees. Harris, who claims that between 85 percent and 90 percent of his union's thirty-five to forty thousand members are part-timers, also sees the hiring of part-timers as a union-busting tactic. Most part-timers "just need the extra money, or can't get full-time work," he claims. "They see the union as a liability." He offers an example: "If someone's only making $50 a week, he's not going to want to pay $2 each week to the union. The employer knows that if there's an election, these people will not vote to join the union."

The director of information for the Retail Clerks International Association in Washington, D.C., Walter Davis, speaks for 1.3 million members in some seven hundred locals. Sixty percent of the Retail Clerks' members are part-timers, he contends; thus only 40 percent work full-time. Davis's experiences with and attitudes toward part-time workers are slightly different from those of his counterparts at other unions. "We have no problem with those part-timers who want to work part-time," he says. "They are fully protected. They receive the same hourly salaries and prorated pension and health and welfare benefits as full-timers. And they're not reluctant to join the union if you can demonstrate the advantages. They understand what you're doing. Sure," he continues, "there's a prejudice about paying dues if you don't work full-time. But our part-time members don't pay full-time dues. What they pay depends on individual contracts. There *is* a logic to employing part-time workers, and many people want part-time work. There's a lot to be said on both sides. We try to do a good job for both."

David Cromer, assistant to the general organizer of the Service Employees International Union (SEIU) in the nation's capital, is also aware of the complexities involved in the union versus part-timers matter. His union, the sixth largest in the country, claims 625,000 members, who are divided equally among three divisions: health care, building services, and the public sector (state, county, and municipal workers). Even within the giant SEIU, he contends, part-timers and union officials have had different experiences.

"In the health-care field, more and more of the labor force is becoming part-time," Cromer says. "This enables hospitals to avoid paying benefits and put more money into wages. Part-timers often earn more — up to $2 or $3 an hour more than full-timers. But they get no benefits, which seems to fit in with their desired life-style. Women's attitudes are definitely changing," he continues. "They want to work two or three days a week and pursue other activities. They realize that they can control the employer, that they're in a good bargaining position. The hospitals need them more than the women need the work."

In the union's building services division, however, the situation is different. "The work involved there is generally cleaning," Cromer says, "and about 80 percent of the workers are part-timers who are holding down more than one job. There are many minorities: Latins, blacks, females. And a great many of them are union members." Interestingly, he adds, whereas there is no trouble organizing part-time workers in the health-care field, there is tremendous difficulty organizing building service workers, who tend to earn much less. "The places we have difficulty organizing are Atlanta, Baltimore, Houston, and San Antonio," he claims. "There is no 'pro part-timers' attitude there and the antiunion feeling is very deeply ingrained."

When Cromer refers to SEIU as a whole and considers all of its divisions, including the public service group, he agrees with his counterparts in other unions that hiring many part-timers can be an attempt at union busting. The difficulty, he maintains, is that "part-timers don't usually have the relationships with the full-time workers or with each other that create a feeling of solidarity." However, he concedes, "if the union operates correctly, it can organize part-time workers and get them the same benefits as full-timers."

Experts such as Dr. Stanley Nollen of Georgetown University have pointed out that in order for part-time work to gain greater acceptance among private-sector employers, cooperation from unions will be necessary. And in order to gain the support of unions, strong safeguards will have to be offered to full-time workers already on the job; workers will have to be guaranteed that they will be forced neither to work part-time nor to give up benefits they have already won in collective bargaining agreements.

For the time being, though, would-be part-timers must recognize that their acceptance in most unions and particularly in the skilled trades and other nontraditional fields is apt to be slow in coming. In the foreseeable future, they are likely to encounter situations similar to the one recently described by Ellen Gurzinsky, executive director of the Coalition of Labor Union Women in New York City: "A woman called here the other day and wanted to know how she can arrange to get benefits even if she works part-time. We told her to go to the people who are full-time, who are the negotiators, and ask *them* to lower the number of hours required to get benefits."

The Nontraditional Jobs: Some Resources

Most of the organizations working to help women break into the high-paying skilled trade jobs limit their activities to securing training and employment for those women who wish to work full-time. With that *caveat* in mind, you may find the following list of resources helpful.

Coalition of Labor Union
   Women
National Office
15 Union Square
New York, NY 10003

Women Working in Construction
1854 Wyoming Ave., N.W.
Washington, DC 20009

The National Association
   of Women in Construction (for women in the
   white-collar areas of the
   construction business)
2800 West Lancaster Ave.
Fort Worth, TX 76107

All-Craft Center
19 St. Marks Place
New York, NY
   10003

Publications Office
Women's Bureau
U.S. Department of Labor
200 Constitution Ave., N.W.
Room S3317
Washington, DC 20210

Wider Opportunities
   for Women, Inc.
1649 K Street, N.W.
Washington, DC
   20006
*Ask for "National
   Directory of
   Women's
   Employment
   Programs: Who
   They Are; What
   They Do," an
   excellent guide to
   140 programs for
   women throughout
   the United States,
   including services
   offered, contacts,
   and publications.
   Cost: $7.50.*

National Urban
   League, Inc.
Labor Education
   Advancement
   Program
500 East 62nd Street
New York, NY
   10021

Employment and Training Administration
Bureau of Apprenticeship and Training
U.S. Department of Labor
Washington, DC 20212
Ask for "Apprenticeship: Past and Present," which examines past and current programs, particularly for women and minorities. Free.

National Association of Trade and Technical Schools
2021 K Street, N.W.
Washington, DC 20006
Ask for "Handbook of Trade and Technical Careers and Training" and "How to Choose a Career . . . And a Career School." Free.

U.S. Department of Energy
Technical Information Center
P.O. Box 62
Oak Ridge, TN 37830
Ask for "Professional Energy Careers," a 45-page booklet describing careers in one of today's hot fields. Includes details about training, names of organizations that represent workers, and so on. A good guide to nontraditional careers.

The Public Sector

Opportunities in the Federal Government

Administrators of huge bureaucracies are hardly ever noted for their innovative or progressive thinking. Therefore, it is hard to imagine that with his 2.8 million employees, Uncle Sam would stand out as one of the most enlightened bosses in the nation. Yet it happens that he is. In fact, part-time workers have made some of their greatest inroads and advances in the offices of federal, as well as in state and local, government. Thanks largely to something called Public Law 95-437 — one of the happiest combinations of numbers ever put on paper — the federal government actually offers one of today's most far-reaching and progressive programs for men and women who would like to work part-time.

The material below provides a look at the law that Congress enacted in 1978, beginning with its impressive introduction.

PUBLIC LAW 95-437—OCT. 10, 1978   92 STAT. 1055

Public Law 95-437
95th Congress

An Act

To amend title 5, United States Code, to establish a program to increase part-time career employment within the civil service.

Be it enacted by the Senate and House of Representatives of the United States of America in Congress assembled,

SHORT TITLE

SECTION 1. This Act may be cited as the "Federal Employees Part-Time Career Employment Act of 1978."

CONGRESSIONAL FINDINGS AND PURPOSE

SEC. 2 (a) The Congress finds that—

(1) many individuals in our society possess great productive potential which goes unused because they cannot meet the requirements of a standard workweek; and

(2) part-time permanent employment—

(A) provides older individuals with a gradual transition into retirement;

(B) provides employment opportunities to handicapped individuals or others who require a reduced workweek;

(C) provides parents opportunities to balance family responsibilities with the need for additional income;

(D) benefits students who must finance their own education or vocational training;

(E) benefits the Government, as an employer, by increasing productivity and job satisfaction, while lowering turnover rates and absenteeism, offering management more flexibility in meeting work requirements, and filling shortages in various occupations; and

(F) benefits society by offering a needed alternative for those individuals who require or prefer shorter hours (despite the reduced income), thus increasing jobs available to reduce unemployment while retaining the skills of individuals who have training and experience.

(b) The purpose of this Act is to provide increased part-time career employment opportunities throughout the Federal Government.

Oct. 10, 1978
[H.R. 10126]

Federal Employees Part-Time Career Employment Act of 1978. 5 USC 3391 note.

5 USC 3391 note.

There it is: short, sweet, and very much to the point — the recognition by Congress that a lot of untapped talent exists out there, and that providing opportunities for part-time workers is one good way to get at it.

KEY PROVISIONS

Several major provisions of P.L. 95-437 affect all would-be part-timers. Here are some of the highlights of the bill, as they pertain to people already working for the federal government, and to those who would like to.[3]

◆ The law narrows the definition of part-time career employment from scheduled work of less than forty hours per week to scheduled work between sixteen and thirty-two hours per week. (Under certain circumstances, agencies are permitted to hire workers for fewer than sixteen hours per week.)

◆ It requires agencies to establish programs to expand part-time career employment opportunities in competitive and certain other positions from the GS-1 level through GS-15 or its equivalent in offices throughout the country (see page 273–75).

◆ It requires agencies to set specific goals and timetables for establishing part-time positions, based on such considerations as work-load fluctuations, geographic dispersion of employees, affirmative action, potential for improving service to the public, and interest in part-time work, among others.

◆ The law calls for the establishment of systems whereby employees can request to switch to a part-time schedule, and for the development of ways in which to notify the general public of part-time vacancies.

◆ Effective October 1, 1980, the law changed the method of determining agency personnel ceilings. Formerly, agencies counted only the number of people working. Now they base the count on the total number of hours worked, thereby providing the opportunity for workers to divide the forty-hour work week among them.

THE PARTICIPATING AGENCIES AND WORKERS

Under the recent law, almost every branch of the government — specifically, all executive agencies, all military departments, agencies of the judicial branch, the Library of Congress, the Botanic Garden, and the Office of the Architect of

---

3. See "The Part-Time Career Employment Act of 1978 — An Agency Guide on P.L. 95–437," FPM Bulletin 340–1 (Washington, D.C.: Office of Personnel Management, April 11, 1979).

the Capitol — is directed to meet these requirements. Which agencies are not? Government-controlled corporations, such as the Federal Deposit Insurance Corporation or the Government National Mortgage Association, are not, for example. The Tennessee Valley Authority, the Alaska Railroad, the Federal Bureau of Investigation, the Central Intelligence Agency, and the National Security Agency are also exempt.

Not all government employees are covered by the law, either. Those people who worked part-time prior to April 9, 1979, are unaffected by the legislation. They may continue to work the same schedules they worked before or, for that matter, *any* under-forty-hour-per-week schedule. Nor are those men and women who work on a temporary basis covered by the legislation.

We should also note that under Public Law 95–437, part-time work is an option, not an obligation, for government employees. If for any reason a worker's hours are decreased against his or her will, that employee has the right to appeal the change. On the other hand, there may be limited times during the year when an agency may *increase* the number of hours an employee works. This might happen, for example, when there is an extremely heavy work load or when an employee is required to participate in a special training course.

FRINGE BENEFITS
All part-timers can earn annual leave. Moreover, if a holiday happens to fall on a day when a part-timer would have worked, he or she is paid for the number of hours he or she would have put in. Part-time workers are also eligible for retirement benefits, life insurance, and health insurance. In fact, one of the provisions of the law is that the government can now prorate its contribution toward health insurance for employees who became part-timers after April 9, 1979. Contributions are made according to the fraction of a full-time (forty-hour) work week that the employee puts in. The employee contributes the rest.

JOBS NOW OPEN TO PART-TIMERS
The range of part-time jobs now available is enormous, from

the GS-1 through the GS-15 level. Most government service (GS) jobs at the GS-1 level are beginning clerical positions. Those at the GS-15 level are extremely responsible and high-paying jobs (for example, head of policy analysis, public information, or the budget office of an agency). According to Ellen Russell, a staffing specialist at the Office of Personnel Management (OPM), numerous high-paying jobs are now open to part-timers. Most are in the GS-5 to GS-14 range. Some examples are personnel specialist, service specialist, budget analyst, program analyst, accountant/auditor, computer specialist, economist, public information specialist, loan specialist, librarian, writer, and editor.

SALARY LEVELS

The following list provides an overall look at the various government service job groups open to permanent part-time workers. As you can see, the grades are grouped according to both the relative level of responsibility and the 1980 starting salary. Wage figures given at the right are starting salaries for *full-time* employees, who work forty hours per week. The actual earnings of an employee would of course be based on the number of hours he or she worked. Also, keep in mind that there are often nine or ten "steps" within each grade level. A move from one step to the next would mean higher earnings than those listed below.

Clerical

GS-1	$ 7210
GS-2	8128
GS-3	8952
GS-4	10,049

Clerical supervisor (some positions require college degree)

GS-5	11,243
GS-6	12,531
GS-7	13,925
GS-8	15,423

Mid-level administrative (require both education and experience)

GS-9	17,035

GS-10	18,760
GS-11	20,611
GS-12	24,703

Senior positions

GS-13	29,375
GS-14	34,713
GS-15	40,832

GETTING AHEAD AS A PART-TIMER

The Part-time Career Employment Act doesn't deal specifically with the question of promotions for part-time workers. As the Office of Personnel Management pointed out in its guide to the new law, measures developed by each agency to determine both promotion and special training opportunities for part-timers would be "not required . . . but highly desirable."

In the past, good jobs and continuing promotions and pay increases have been available to part-timers in some agencies. In other agencies, opportunities have been quite limited. To see how job satisfaction and promotion opportunities can vary, let's look at the experiences of three women who currently hold high-level jobs in the federal government on a part-time basis.

Winifred Gilmore, position specialist, Federal Railroad Administration, Department of Transportation; GS-13. A forty-year-old mother of two, Winifred has worked part-time for the U.S. government since 1975. She has done personnel work at the Office of Personnel Management and also at the Defense Logistics Agency. Winifred puts in thirty hours a week and earns about $23,000 a year. "I've gotten regular promotions as a part-timer and haven't had any problems whatsoever working part-time." Of course, if she did, Winifred says she would know exactly what to do: "Working in personnel, I know where to shop around for a good job. And in my area there's always a need."

Bonney Sheahan, assistant program director, History and Philosophy of Science Program, National Science Foundation; GS-11. Bonney, thirty-seven, has been able to work out a schedule that allows her to be home when her two children arrive from school. When the position she now holds was created, she recalls, her employees were very forward-thinking. "The job was set up with a working mother in mind," she says. Bonney's schedule is somewhat unusual: "I average twenty hours a week, but it works out that I actually put in twenty-five hours a week during the academic year and take the summers off." Bonney earns about $12,000 a year. In addition to enjoying good pay, she has found far less difficulty in being a part-timer than she originally anticipated. "I expected some kind of anti–part-timer discrimination, but I haven't found any," she reports. "They treat me just like a full-timer — sometimes better. For example, occasionally when important meetings are scheduled at a time not within my five hours a day, they try to accommodate me." When it comes to promotions, Bonney says she has been fortunate. "I didn't think I'd advance," she recalls, "but I've been given both promotions and awards."

Lois McHugh, foreign affairs analyst, Congressional Research Service, Library of Congress; GS-12. Thirty-four-year-old Lois has a job that most people would envy. She does research on demand for Congress and writes reports and speeches on a wide variety of subjects. Lois has worked twenty-eight hours a week since 1976. "I wouldn't trade my job for the world because it gives me more time with my two kids," she claims. However, in exchange for gaining time with her preschoolers, Lois does feel that she has had to give up opportunities for advancement. "You're not taken seriously," she contends. "Especially in this town, where people who work 'full-time' put in eighty to ninety hours a week. I think a lot of people around here think I just come in to tidy my desk." Lois believes that being a part-timer has hindered her career in the past and will in the future. "Certain projects were not given to me because I'm a part-timer. There's discrimination and there's resentment. I'm definitely not getting promoted as fast as other people are. I've been told it would be 'difficult' for me to be promoted. What's more, if you complain, you're likely to hear, 'You'll get paid more when you work more.' "

Undoubtedly, within the next few years guidelines will be

set forth that will open up the advancement paths already available to Winifred Gilmore and Bonney Sheahan to such part-timers as Lois McHugh. For now, however, recognize that promotion opportunities vary from one federal agency, and often from one supervisor, to the next.

GOOD NEWS FOR OLDER WORKERS

How does the recent law affect those who are about to retire or who are already retired? A fact sheet called "Part-time Employment and the Older Worker," put out by the Office of Personnel Management in June 1979, deals specifically with this issue. The sheet points out some of the particularly attractive options now available to men and women nearing or already over the customary age of retirement. Among them:

Phased retirement. Government workers may continue to hold the jobs they already have and simply limit the number of hours they work each week. Of course, the amount of salary any worker earns will be based on the proportion of a forty-hour week that he or she continues to put in. However, when the employee does decide to retire, he or she will get credit for having worked the additional amount of time.

Returning to work after retirement. People who return to federal jobs after having retired from them are called "re-employed annuitants." Although the pay earned by such workers is reduced by the amount of the "annuity" (the federal government's term for *pension*) they receive during the same period, there are incentives for them to continue working. Under certain conditions — for example, if a worker comes back on a part-time basis — he or she may later be eligible for a supplementary annuity. Also, if the employee works an additional five years on a part-time basis, his or her annuity may be recomputed. As the OPM fact sheet points out, "adding five years' service to an employee's time base, with an average salary of $12,000, can increase the employee's annuity by approximately $100 a month."

Retirees outside the federal government. Those who have never held federal jobs are also eligible to work on a permanent part-time basis. Since an older employee may now earn up to $6000 a year without reducing his or her Social Security benefits, a part-time job with Uncle Sam may be just the ticket for a retired person to earn extra income and find stimulating work while continuing to collect a Social Security check each month. A bonus that OPM highlights: Working for Uncle Sam enables an employee to enroll in federal health and/or life insurance programs, which "can be continued after your federal career ends."

WHERE THE JOBS ARE

Two encouraging statistics are worth noting. The first is that right now there are over fifty thousand part-timers in Uncle Sam's employ. That may not seem all that impressive, since part-timers represent only about 3 percent of the total U.S. government payroll. However, the second statistic makes the first seem much more promising. Between September 1977, when President Carter first spoke about the need for increased opportunities for part-timers within the federal government, and February 1980, over twenty thousand *new* permanent part-time positions were created in federal agencies.

Ellen Russell of OPM is quick to indicate that no quotas are involved under the new legislation; agencies are responsible for reporting their own goals and progress. Neither, she adds, is OPM making any projections about the future. However, since 1978 over six thousand new part-time positions have been created *each year*. Barring any unforeseen changes in government hiring policies, there should be far more opportunities in the future, despite an anticipated reduction of about 2 percent, or some 43,000 positions, in the federal government by the end of 1982.

Which agencies now hire the most part-timers? Obviously, the larger the agency, the more employees and the greater the potential for conversion of full- to part-time positions. The following table, based on information published by the Office of Personnel Management, can give you a good idea of which agencies have been hiring the largest numbers of part-timers, as well as of those that have increased their proportion of part-time workers by the greatest percentage.

Permanent Part-Time Employment in Federal Agencies AGENCY	Total Part-time Personnel as of 12/31/79	Part-timers as Percent of Total Agency Employment	Percentage Change* 1/31/79 to 12/31/79
Agency for International Development	248	4.1	+20
Agriculture	5090	4.2	+6
Air Force	1197	0.5	−41
Army	1864	0.6	+15
Commerce	4105	9.7	+219
Defense (other)	136	0.2	+24
Energy	486	2.3	+60
Environmental Protection Agency	761	5.5	+82
Equal Employment Opportunity Commission	1	0.0	−66
General Services Administration	871	2.3	+121
Health, Education and Welfare	8044	4.9	+5
Housing and Urban Development	131	0.7	+5
International Communications Agency	39	0.4	−13
Interior	4727	5.9	+2
Interstate Commerce Commission	33	1.5	+6
Justice	372	0.6	+4
Labor	543	2.3	+108
National Aeronautics and Space Administration	122	0.5	+22
National Labor Relations Board	24	0.8	+60
Navy	1744	0.6	+3
Nuclear Regulatory Commission	38	1.2	−12

AGENCY	Total Part-time Personnel as of 12/31/79	Part-timers as Percent of Total Agency Employment	Percentage Change* 1/31/79 to 12/31/79
Office of Personnel Management	703	8.6	+13
Railroad Retirement	7	0.4	+250
State	139	0.6	+153
Transportation	601	0.8	+21
Treasury	2551	2.1	−33
Veterans Administration	14,374	6.2	−1

*From SF-113, Monthly Report of Federal Civilian Employment.
Source: Office of Personnel Management, 1980.

The graph on page 281 shows the relative growth in part-time opportunities at the various pay levels within the government. Note that although the number of part-timers is greatest at the lower GS-1 through GS-6 levels, the rate of increase in new part-time jobs has been greater at the GS-7 through GS-9 levels, and greater still in GS-10 to GS-12 jobs. Things are indeed looking up!

The Office of Personnel Management has also compiled figures on the number of part-timers added to agency staffs. In terms of sheer numbers of new part-time employees, the leaders are the Veterans Administration, the Department of the Interior, the Department of Health, Education and Welfare (recently divided into the Departments of Health and Human Services and Education), the Department of Agriculture, and the General Services Administration. Which agencies have hired people at the highest job levels? In terms of numbers, the Department of Health, Education and Welfare (272 jobs at GS-10 to GS-15), Department of the Interior (83), Environmental Protection Agency (68), Department of Labor (54), Department of Agriculture (44), General Services Administration (41), and Department of Energy (40) lead the field.

Finally, in terms of the highest proportion of top new part-time jobs, it turns out some of the smaller agencies have added proportionately more than some of the large agencies have. For example, at the International Communications Agency, 27 percent of all the new part-time positions have been at or above the GS-10 level. Other top agencies include the Department of Labor (29 percent), Nuclear Regulatory Commission (29 percent), National Aeronautics and Space Administration (33 percent), and the Small Business Administration (41 percent). The undisputed first place is held by the Department of Housing and Urban Development. HUD,

Federal Part-Time Permanent Employment: Trends by Grade*

Grades/Annual Pay*

Grade/Annual Pay	Year	Value	Change
(GS 1–3) $7210–$11,634	1978	7169	
	1979	8846	up 23%
(GS 4–6) $10,049–16,293	1978	12,889	
	1979	15,710	up 21%
(GS 7–9) $13,925–$22,147	1978	3112	
	1979	4121	up 32%
(GS 10–12) $18,760–$32,110	1978	1884	
	1979	2548	up 35%
(GS 13–15) $29,375–$50,112	1978	738	
	1979	890	up 21%

*Does not include Postal Service data as of July 31, 1978, and July 31, 1979.
Source: Central Personnel Data File.
**Pay reflects full-time annual salary ranges as of October 1979.
Source: Office of Personnel Management, May 1980.

one of the smaller federal departments, employs only sixteen thousand people nationwide. However, between August 1978 and September 1979, it created fifty-eight new part-time jobs, 62 percent of which were at or above the GS-10 level.

Undoubtedly, the impressive efforts at HUD represent a continuation of a progressive program begun way back in 1965. At that time, the department set up a model Part-time Professionals Program to attract well-trained women in Washington and in its regional offices throughout the country. Over the years, the majority of HUD's part-timers have been highly educated and well-paid professionals.

Typical of these is Marion Gerhardt, a twenty-six-year-old divorcée and the mother of a young baby. Marion, who lives in Manchester, New Hampshire, works thirty-two hours a week as a multifamily housing representative. She earns almost $13,000 a year. Her job is to review and process applications for various types of public housing. Marion's supervisors, both of whom are men, had originally requested that her job be made part-time because they knew about Marion's other responsibilities — as a single parent and as a full-time law student at the Franklin Pierce Law Center in Concord, New Hampshire.

A direct beneficiary of past and current HUD efforts to help women obtain career-oriented part-time jobs, Marion will undoubtedly find more professional women working in jobs comparable to hers. According to Priscilla Lewis, personnel management specialist at HUD, the agency plans to expand its part-time program significantly once new goals and guidelines are clearly established. "The increase will probably be about 35 percent to 45 percent," she says.

WHERE TO GET INFORMATION
Whether the job you seek is a clerical position or a post as a top computer specialist, the first step is to call your local Federal Job Information Service, listed in the white pages of the phone directory under "U.S. government." You may also want to check the *Federal Research Service,* a biweekly listing of job openings within the federal government. This should be available at larger public libraries.

Next, contact the agency you wish to work for. Under a two-year experimental program begun in early 1980, selected federal agencies will be able to fill part-time jobs under streamlined conditions. "Instead of having their names added to lists in Washington, applicants can contact agencies directly," explains Ellen Russell of OPM. "No testing procedures will be waived, but the application process will be simpler. More important, it will save time."

Here is a list of addresses for the various federal agencies in Washington that have initiated national part-time and placement programs. If you get no satisfactory answers when you call the Federal Job Information Service, by all means write and inquire about part-time opportunities in your area. Also note that many agencies are now operating a special direct-hire program for jobs that are particularly hard to fill. Ask about the program when you write.

ACTION
Personnel Operations
ACTION
Washington, DC 20525

Agency for International Development
Agency for International Development
Department of State
Washington, DC 20523

Agriculture
Office of Personnel
Department of Agriculture
14th & Independence Avenue, S.W.
Washington, DC 20250

Air Force
Personnel Management Branch
Directorate of Civilian Personnel
Department of the Air Force
Washington, DC 20314

Army
Headquarters
Department of the Army
DAPE-CPS
Washington, DC 20310

Central Intelligence Agency
Office of Personnel
Central Intelligence Agency
Washington, DC 20505

Civil Aeronautics Board
Personnel Division
Civil Aeronautics Board
Room 416 N
1875 Connecticut Avenue,
     N.W.
Washington, DC 20428

Commerce
Office of Personnel
Department of Commerce
Washington, DC 20230

**Community Service
     Administration**
Organization and Manpower
     Development
Community Services
     Administration
1200 19th Street, N.W.
Washington, DC 20506

**Consumer Product Safety
     Commission**
Employment Branch
Consumer Product Safety
     Commission
Washington, DC 20207

Defense
Personnel Division
Department of Defense
Pentagon
Washington, DC 20301

Defense Logistics Agency
Office of Civilian Personnel
Defense Logistics Agency
Cameron Station
Alexandria, VA 22314

Defense Mapping Agency
Civilian Personnel Division
Defense Mapping Agency
Building 56, U.S. Naval
     Observatory
Washington, DC 20305

Energy
Division of Personnel
Department of Energy
1000 Independence Avenue,
     S.W.
Washington, DC 20545

**Environmental Protection
     Agency**
Personnel Management
     Division
Environmental Protection
     Agency
401 M Street, S.W.
Washington, DC 20460

**Equal Employment
     Opportunity Commission**
Personnel Division
Equal Employment
     Opportunity Commission
Washington, DC 20506

Export-Import Bank
Personnel Office
Export-Import Bank
811 Vermont Avenue, N.W.
Washington, DC 20571

Farm Credit Administration
Office of Personnel
Farm Credit Administration
490 L'Enfant Plaza, S.W.
Washington, DC 20578

Federal Communications Commission
Personnel Division
Federal Communications
Commission
1919 M Street, N.W.
Washington, DC 20554

Federal Deposit Insurance Corporation
Personnel Division
Federal Deposit Insurance
Corporation
550 17th Street, N.W.
Washington, DC 20429

Federal Emergency Management Agency
Personnel Division
Federal Emergency
Management Agency
1815 North Lynn Street
Arlington, VA 22209

Federal Home Loan Bank Board
Personnel Division
Federal Home Loan Bank
Board
320 First Street, N.W.
Washington, DC 20552

Federal Maritime Commission
Office of Personnel
Federal Maritime
Commission
Washington, DC 20573

Federal Mediation and Conciliation Service
Office of Personnel
Federal Mediation &
Conciliation Service
2100 K Street, N.W.
Washington, DC 20427

Federal Reserve
Division of Personnel
Board of Governors of the
Federal Reserve System
Washington, DC 20551

Federal Trade Commission
Personnel Division
Federal Trade Commission
6th and Pennsylvania Ave.,
N.W.
Washington, DC 20580

General Accounting Office
Office of Personnel
Development & Services
U.S. General Accounting
Office
Washington, DC 20548

General Services Administration
Staffing and Career
Development Division
General Services
Administration
18th & F Streets, N.W.
Washington, DC 20405

Government Printing Office
Personnel Division
U.S. Government Printing
 Office
Washington, DC 20401

Health and Human Services
Office of Personnel and
 Training
Department of Health and
 Human Services
300 C Street, S.W.
Washington, DC 20201

**Housing and Urban
 Development**
Office of Personnel
Department of Housing and
 Urban Development
451 7th Street, S.W.
Washington, DC 20410

Interior
Division of Employment and
 Personnel Management
Department of the Interior
Washington, DC 20250

Internal Revenue Service
Personnel Division
Internal Revenue Service
111 Constitution Ave., N.W.
Washington, DC 20224

**International
 Communications Agency**
Office of Personnel Services
International
 Communications Agency
Washington, DC 20547

**International Trade
 Commission**
Personnel Division
U.S. International Trade
 Commission
Washington, DC 20436

**Interstate Commerce
 Commission**
Personnel Division
Interstate Commerce
 Commission
12th & Constitution Ave.,
 N.W.
Washington, DC 20423

Justice
Personnel Division
Department of Justice
10th and Constitution Ave.,
 N.W.
Washington, DC 20530

Labor
Office of Program Analysis
 and Development
Department of Labor
200 Constitution Ave., N.W.
Washington, D.C. 20210

**National Aeronautics and
 Space Administration**
Personnel Division
National Aeronautics and
 Space Administration
400 Maryland Ave., S.W.
Washington, DC 20510

National Credit Union Administration
Division of Personnel
National Credit Union Administration
2025 M Street, N.W.
Washington, DC 20456

National Endowment for the Humanities
Personnel Division
National Endowment for the Humanities
Washington, DC 20506

National Gallery of Art
Personnel Division
National Gallery of Art
Washington, DC 20565

National Labor Relations Board
Personnel Branch
National Labor Relations Board
1717 Pennsylvania Ave., N.W.
Washington, DC 20570

National Science Foundation
Division of Personnel Management
National Science Foundation
Washington, DC 20550

Navy
Office of Civilian Personnel
Department of the Navy
Washington, DC 20390

Nuclear Regulatory Commission
Personnel Operations Branch
Division of Organization and Personnel
Nuclear Regulatory Commission
Washington, DC 20555

Office of Management and Budget
Personnel Division
Executive Office of the President
Office of Management and Budget
Washington, DC 20503

Office of Personnel Management
Personnel Labor Relations Division
Office of Personnel Management
1900 E Street, N.W.
Washington, DC 20415

Overseas Private Investment Corporation
Personnel Division
Overseas Private Investment Corporation
1129 20th Street, N.W.
Washington, DC 20527

Pension Benefit Guaranty Board
Personnel Division
Pension Benefit Guaranty Board
2020 K Street, N.W.
Washington, DC 20006

Postal Rate Commission
Personnel Division
Postal Rate Commission
2000 L Street, N.W.
Washington, DC 20268

Small Business Administration
Office of Personnel
Small Business Administration
1441 L Street, N.W.
Washington, DC 20225

Smithsonian Institution
Personnel Division
Smithsonian Institution
900 Jefferson Drive
Washington, DC 20225

Social Security Administration
Personnel Division
Social Security Administration
Room G, 408 West High Rise
Baltimore, Maryland 21235

State
Office of Services and Career Development
Department of State
Washington, DC 20520

Transportation
Personnel Division
Department of Transportation
400 7th Street, S.W.
Washington, DC 20590

Treasury
Office of Personnel
Department of Treasury
2412 Main Treasury
15th & Pennsylvania Ave., N.W.
Washington, DC 20220

U.S. Arms Control and Disarmament Agency
Personnel Division
U.S. Arms Control and Disarmament Agency
Washington, DC 20451

Veterans Administration
Office of Personnel
Veterans Administration Central Office
810 Vermont Ave., N.W.
Washington, DC 20527

A WORD ABOUT THE U.S. POSTAL SERVICE

The U.S. Postal Service is one of the agencies that are exempt from the provisions of the Part-time Career Employment Act.

Yet, as everyone knows, postal workers are among the most visible and numerous part-timers employed by the U.S. government.

Jeannie O'Neill of the Postal Service explains that just about everyone employed by the service starts out as a so-called part-time flexible. That means the beginning employee has no structured schedule, has no forty-hour-per-week guarantees, and works the hours necessary depending on the work load and the area in which the person is assigned. "Everyone hired as a part-time flexible must take a competitive exam," she says. By passing the exam, workers can become letter carriers, mail sorters, baggage and parcel handlers, and customer service representatives. Part-time flexibles earned $8.50 an hour at the end of 1980. They accrue both sick and annual leave and receive prorated health and retirement insurance.

Besides those who work year-round on part-time schedules are "casuals," who work between two and forty hours a week for no more than ninety days' duration (for example, during the Christmas season). These people, O'Neill says, earn $4.76 an hour and receive no benefits.

O'Neill suggests that those men and women interested in part-time work with the Postal Service go directly to their local post office personnel office to inquire about or apply for jobs. "Opportunity depends on current needs," she says. "The larger the community, the greater the chance for success."

State and Local Governments

"I think at a time when the family is subjected to serious strains in this society, government has the responsibility to be innovative, to be creative in trying to find ways to allow both parents who work to do their jobs and do them well . . . within nontraditional, innovative settings."

— HARRISON J. GOLDIN, comptroller, City of New York. Quoted in *New York Times*, October 9, 1980.

During the past five or six years, various states and a few municipalities have made concerted efforts to increase the number of part-timers on their payrolls, or at least to give part-time scheduling a try. In Wisconsin, for example, one of the earliest experimental programs, Project JOIN, opened certain middle- and high-level positions to part-time workers. That is how Mary Mullen and Dorothy Schmitz got the job as research analyst they now share (See "Personnel," page 187).

Not all of the more progressive states have such comprehensive programs, even on an experimental basis. However, among the more innovative state plans is one mandated by a 1975 law in Maryland. The Permanent Part-time Employment Act set a target: 5 percent of all state jobs should be open to part-time workers. Similarly, Pennsylvania, New York, and Massachusetts have passed bills that encourage the hiring of more part-time workers throughout the ranks of the state governments. In California, an experimental program for part-timers in the Department of Motor Vehicles was so successful that the Reduced Worktime Act was passed in July 1980, opening almost all state jobs to part-time scheduling.

JOBS AT ALL LEVELS
Although "mostly clerical" is still the most frequent response to the question "Which jobs are open to part-time workers?" some states, such as Pennsylvania and Washington, employ part-time teachers, technicians, physicians, engineers, and even psychiatrists. An example of one of the more successful high-level part-time situations is a job-sharing arrangement currently in effect in the state of Oregon. Ann Lau and Phyllis Elgin share the position of administrative assistant to one of Oregon's highest elected officials, Secretary of State Norma Paulus.

As is the case with other outstanding part-time positions available in state and local governments, Ann and Phyllis's top-level job was made possible in large part by the good intentions of their boss. During the three terms that Norma Paulus served in Oregon's House of Representatives, Ann Lau worked part-time as her legislative secretary. In 1977, Paulus was elected secretary of state. She offered Ann the administrative assistant post on a full-time basis. Ann replied that she preferred working part-time. "There's a lot to life," says Ann, explaining why she declined the full-time position. "My two children were grown and I wanted time to participate in civic organizations, to play tennis, and to travel with my husband."

Paulus knew she needed someone in the office all the time, so she suggested that Ann might share the job with someone else. She explains: "I have long been active in the women's movement and in women's political caucuses and have tried to promote the concept of job sharing." It was only logical, therefore, for Paulus to try to set up such a situation in her own office. She and Ann Lau were both willing to give it a try.

At first, they met with extreme skepticism. The assistant secretary of state was openly opposed to the concept. He even went so far as to speak to Paulus's husband, hoping that some good-natured intervention from a sensible spouse might dissuade the new secretary of state. Likewise, Paulus's female friends and associates — women who normally favored alternative work patterns — were doubtful. "Even the women who were the most supportive said that job sharing wouldn't work at this level," Paulus recalls. "Also, it was difficult to get the state payroll office to okay it, what with the split benefits and all."

Undaunted, Norma Paulus held on to the job-sharing idea. Ann contacted Phyllis Elgin, another legislative secretary whose four children were grown and who also wanted time to pursue leisure interests. The rest, as they say, is history.

The two women have held the position of administrative assistant since 1977, sharing not only their title but a desk, a typewriter, and even a parking space. They both handle everything from mail and other correspondence to setting up the secretary of state's meetings with the governor and other top state officials. They also schedule her numerous speaking engagements. The two women earn $9.21 an hour each, and both receive full benefits, including pension based on salary. Their vacations and sick leaves are split.

Ann and Phyllis work out the logistics of their job according to each one's needs. At the beginning of each month they get together, make their schedules, and mark their "days on" on a big calendar in their office. They try to work the same number of days each month. Whenever possible, they alternate long weekends.

What about problems? In the years in which they have shared a single job, there have been few difficulties, the women contend. Of the problems they have encountered, most concern communication. Ann and Phyllis speak to each other every night, sometimes for as long as ninety minutes. Nevertheless, gaps in the information they exchange do occur, and their boss confirms that occasional difficulties arise. "Both people must know exactly what has transpired," says Norma Paulus. "I don't like to have to repeat myself, but sometimes I must."

Other, minor communications difficulties occasionally crop up with coworkers. "Sometimes it's a little hard for individuals who have to take orders from different people day to day," says Phyllis. "I'm afraid it can be a bit confusing." Yet considering the potential for turmoil and disorganization that exists in their job — if *one* person were to hold it — Ann and Phyllis have proven to the skeptics that job sharing can work at even the highest administrative levels. "We have never fouled up yet," says Phyllis proudly.

NOT ALL SO PROGRESSIVE

Finding good examples of states and of particular officials who have tried to broaden opportunities for would-be part-timers in state government is getting easier all the time. On the other hand, unfortunately, locating states that have done little or nothing to help part-time workers is even simpler.

Incredible as it might seem, some state spokespersons cannot provide any current information on the number of part-timers working in their governments, nor do they know what policies and regulations govern part-timers' schedules or what benefits they receive. For example, when asked how many part-time employees worked in his state government, one official at the Texas State Employment Commission in Austin answered that his state has no statistics whatsoever on part-timers other than those provided by the U.S. Census Bureau. "Texas has some two hundred different agencies; each is self-regulated," said the official. "The information is all in the computer, but no one has ever programmed it to find out." Similar responses were forthcoming from a number of different officials who were asked about the current and projected numbers of part-time jobs in their own states. Many personnel officers could only hazard a rough guess as to the number of part-timers currently on the payroll.

The same is true of local governments. There are a few good programs for part-timers, but the overwhelming majority of local governments apparently have not even considered making jobs available to those who would like to work fewer than thirty-five, or even forty, hours per week.

Among the best part-time innovations at the local level are those in several California jurisdictions. The city of Palo Alto and the county of San Diego have both begun programs for clerical workers, supervisors, and managers, and the city of Berkeley initiated a job-sharing program that involves over seventy municipal employees, including some police officers.

On the opposite side of the country, in New York City, there were no programs for hiring part-time workers until recently. In June 1980, a spokesperson for the New York City Department of Personnel seemed somewhat taken aback when asked about the city's policies regarding part-time workers. "There *is* no part-time civil service," she responded. "I guess if you want to work part-time you should contact the agency you want to work for, and maybe you could work something out." Yet on October 8, 1980, Mayor Edward Koch publicly announced a sweeping program to open jobs in all nonuniformed city agencies to every type of alternative scheduling. Koch said that he was taking this step, which stands to benefit over a hundred thousand city workers, "to improve productivity" and "to make it easier to work for the city."

LOCATING A JOB
The following table reviews some of the states that currently have the most progressive programs for part-timers.

Top State Programs for Hiring
Part-Time Workers

State	Type of Jobs	Salary/Benefits
Alabama	Mostly clerical, but there are no restrictions	—.* All benefits, prorated, for those employees working more than 20 hours per week
Alaska	Mostly clerical; some professional and job-sharing positions. Seasonal work also available.	—. Same as full-time workers, prorated, except that those working under 15 hours per week do not get health insurance. Those working 15–30 hours can pay one-half.
California	All jobs except state peace officer are open to part-time scheduling.	All ranges. Pension and health benefits previously established by law. All other benefits now prorated.
Colorado	Clerical to professional; from custodian to finger-print identifiers to service workers. Any classification a possibility.	—. Permanent part-timers get full benefits, prorated. Temporary workers get no fringe benefits.
Delaware	Clerical; teachers; technicians; attendants. Divided evenly among clerical and professional positions.	—. All benefits, prorated.

*The symbol. "—." means information was not available.

Percent Part-Time/Projections for Future	Address
Under 1%. No change seen.	State Personnel Department 402 Administration Building Montgomery, AL 36130
1%. Legislation allowing job sharing passed several years ago. So far, though, "little pressure to expand."	Director of Administrative Services Department of Administration Juneau, AK 98911
—. Legislation passed in 1980 should greatly increase number of part-time workers.	Public Information Section Employment Development Department 800 Capitol Mall Sacramento, CA 95814
—	State Department of Personnel 1313 Sherman Denver, CO 80203
Under 1%. —.	Secretary of Labor 801 West 14th Street Wilmington, DE 19899

State	Type of Jobs	Salary/Benefits
Maryland	Mostly clerical, although jobs range from guard to administrator.	$3.90 to $25 per hour. Most benefits prorated for those working half-time or more. Those working less than half-time do not receive health insurance or pension.
Massachusetts	Mostly clerical and hospital staff. Some professionals. About 2000 temporary summer positions.	Average: $3.90/hour. Those working half-time and over receive prorated sick and vacation leave.
Nevada	Clerical; highway inspectors; some professionals, including doctors and psychiatrists	$4.01/hour to $23.70/hour. All benefits prorated. No retirement for those workers putting in less than half time.
New York	Mostly clerical and stenographic. Some professional and clerical job sharing.	$4000 to $12,500 per year, based on half-time employment. — .
Oregon	Mostly job-sharing positions. Clerks; human resource aides; accounting clerks; employment specialists; graphic artists; adjudicators.	$300–$450 per month based on a 20-hour week. — .
Pennsylvania	Mostly professional, engineers, physicians. Job sharing at both professional and administrative levels.	Average: $7500 per year for those working half-time. — .

Percent Part-Time/Projections for Future	Address
2.5%. Definitely expected to increase.	Department of Personnel Application Control Unit 301 West Preston Street Baltimore, MD 20201
Under 1%. Should increase. In 1974, a law promoting part-time career opportunities was passed.	Personnel Department Massachusetts Division of Employment Security Charles F. Hurley Employment Security Building Government Center Boston, MA 02114
Under 1%. — .	Nevada State Personnel 209 East Musser Street Carson City, NV 89710
5%. Expected to increase.	New York State Department of Civil Service State Office Building Campus Albany, NY 12239
Under 1%. Should increase.	Employment Division Post Office Box 571 Salem, OR 97310
1.6%. Expected to increase, particularly in job-sharing positions.	Civil Service Commission State Office Building P.O. Box 569 Harrisburg, PA 17120

State	Type of Jobs	Salary/Benefits
Washington	More professional than clerical. Job sharing widespread. Any position eligible.	$323 to $1030 per month based on half-time employment. All benefits prorated.
Wisconsin	Positions ranging from clerical to professional, including personnel specialists, accountants, social workers.	—. All benefits prorated.

Included in the table are the jobs offered on a part-time basis, salary and benefits (if provided by state officials), the current percentages of part-time workers on the state payrolls, projections for the future, and, finally, the address of the personnel divisions in the various states.

By far the best way to land a part-time job in almost any state government, it seems, is to hold that job already on a full-time basis and request a shift to a part-time schedule. Having a supervisor who is receptive to the idea is a big plus. He or she can go to bat for you and help convince the personnel or payroll department that the switch is for the good of the state, as Norma Paulus did in Oregon.

If you don't already work for your state government, head for your local office of the state personnel or state employment agency. Better yet, go to the agency's headquarters, if possible. If you are lucky enough to live in any of the more progressive states and you happen to offer a skill the state needs, you might just connect with a good job. Of course, if laws calling for new or additional part-time jobs are already on the books, you will have an even easier time.

In either case, whether you're an outsider or insider, remember that in any bureaucracy, one office frequently has no idea what the next office is doing. If you have no success with the centralized personnel office, ask which state, county, or municipal agencies you might contact directly, and get in

Percent Part-Time/Projections for Future	Address
4%. Expected to increase.	Department of Personnel Post Office Box 1789 Olympia, WA 98504
—. Expected to increase.	State Division of Personnel 149 East Wilson Madison, WI 53702

touch with them. With determination, patience, and the realization that it may take several phone calls to find out what opportunities are available, you might be able to find the job you have been looking for.

Landing
a Good
Part-Time Job

HOW DO PEOPLE find part-time jobs? To get an idea of how many ways there are, let us consider for a moment how a few of the successful part-timers cited in the chapter "Today's Best Part-Time Jobs" found the positions they hold today.

◆ A prominent physician announced that she would only consider a part-time schedule when she was offered a job at a major university medical school.
◆ A typesetter decided to list her name in a journal for people in the graphics field. She has had free-lance assignments ever since — often more work than she can handle.
◆ A fashion designer asked his boss to let him switch to a part-time schedule. He implied that the change was only going to be in effect for a while, knowing full well that that wasn't the case. Since then he has convinced the boss that he can handle all of his work on a reduced schedule, and he has worked part-time for several years.
◆ A bank officer, recently returned from maternity leave, announced that difficulties with baby sitters made it impossible for her to continue working. Her boss suggested that she switch to a part-time schedule, which she did.
◆ An engineer has worked twelve years for the same temporary agency. She contends that as a temp she is able to change

employers at will and work whatever schedule she chooses. She says she would never consider a full-time job.

◆ A vocational counselor applied for a position at a home for learning-disabled adults. It turned out that the job, which she had thought was full-time, was actually half-time. Reluctantly, she accepted the position. Today she is thrilled to be working a part-time schedule.

Some part-timers demanded their schedules at the outset. Others fell into their jobs almost accidentally. Still others finagled their way into part-time jobs they never would have obtained otherwise. Some people have opted to work for many bosses or for themselves, assuring constant diversity and flexibility. Clearly, today's 23 million part-timers got the jobs they hold in any number of ways. Yet because this is still basically a full-time world, the fact remains that landing a good job is a decided challenge for today's would-be part-timer.

Job-Hunting Basics

"Once you learn to drive a car, it doesn't matter what car you drive. Those people who learn the mechanics of a thorough job campaign will get a job."

— JOHN E. STEELE, director of career planning and placement, Boston College. Quoted in *New York Times,* June 17, 1980.

What's Special About the Part-Time Job Hunt?

You already know the answer: It's hard work. Looking for a good part-time job involves the same skills as hunting for a job at which you would spend thirty-five to forty hours each week does. The only difference is that it takes more preparation, more time, and usually more effort.

O.K., so you know part-time work won't be available everywhere you would conceivably like to be employed. It won't exist in all fields and in all companies. Regardless of the skills and experience you offer, it is unlikely that Exxon will invite you to head its overseas operations division on a three-day-a-week basis. But if opportunities are somewhat more limited, that doesn't mean that you have to settle for the minimum wage, pushing papers into file folders or standing behind a sales counter in a discount department store — unless that is what you want to do.

As we've seen over and over, there are good jobs in dozens of fields today, part-time jobs that combine a high level of responsibility with good pay. You *can* land one of them, provided you are willing to pursue that part-time job with the same effort and determination with which you would seek a full-time position — only with more ingenuity and even more persistence.

Planning Your Strategy

If you are looking for a new job or heading back to work after a long absence, remember that the key to the successful part-time job hunt is *focus.* You must first decide what it is you want to do and be sure you will be able to do it well. If you don't have marketable job skills, you must get them. If your skills are rusty, you must sharpen them up. Next you have to identify the fields in which you are likely to find the greatest opportunities to put your skills to use, then narrow your search to the types of companies or organizations that might be able to use your talents and that are likely to be amenable to alternative scheduling. Finally, you must locate the person who has the power to hire you and convince her or him that you are the one who can do the job that needs to be done — and that the company or organization is darned lucky to get you for twenty or thirty hours a week!

If you already hold a full-time job, your task will be easier. Starting out as a valued full-time employee is far and away the best method of switching to a part-time schedule or changing your present job to a shared one. But more of that later. For now, let's consider the job hunt from the perspective of the person just starting out or returning to the labor market. Here is a quick and basic guide to finding any job.

Any number of excellent full-length books that deal extensively with the subject of how to get a full-time job are available. Most begin with sections on how to assess your interests and wind up with such pointers as how to handle a tough interviewer or how to negotiate a good salary. All of the following are good and useful, and can be helpful regardless of the type of job you seek:

* Richard Nelson Bolles, *What Color Is Your Parachute? A Practical Manual for Job-Hunters & Career-Changers* (Berkeley, Calif.: Ten Speed Press, 1979).
* John Crystal and Richard Nelson Bolles, *Where Do I Go From Here With My Life?* (Berkeley, Calif.: Ten Speed Press, 1971).
* Richard K. Irish, *Go Hire Yourself an Employer* (New York: Anchor Press/Doubleday, 1973).
* Tom Jackson and Davidyne Mayleas, *The Hidden Job Market* (New York: Quadrangle/New York Times Book Company, 1976).
* Richard Lathrop, *Who's Hiring Who* (Berkeley, Calif.: Ten Speed Press, 1977).

Taking Stock

Presumably, if you have already worked at any paying or volunteer jobs, your experience reflects the kind of interests you have — or have had. Of course, you may have worked years ago and want to do something different now. Or if you have only taken routine jobs to make ends meet, you may want to think in terms of beginning a career. If you're not sure what it is you want to do or what you would be good at, perhaps some in-depth self-assessment is in order.

If so, there are several routes you can take. The easiest, and most costly, is to march into a local vocational guidance office or women's center and ask for vocational testing. You may be lucky enough to stumble onto a well-funded program that offers free counseling. More likely than not, however, you will be charged anywhere from $25 to $100, and sometimes much more, for the testing and counseling. Unfortunately, there is no guarantee that any money you shell out will be money well spent. Since there are few if any requirements for the establishment of vocational counseling centers in most states, the quality of the services you receive may vary considerably from one place to the next.

If you feel that professional help is absolutely necessary (and it probably isn't!), minimize your risks by going to the vocational guidance center at your local college or university. Or contact one of the organizations listed in the "Catalyst National Network of Local Resource Centers," available free from Catalyst, 14 East 60th Street, New York, NY 10022.

Another idea, and probably a better one, is to launch your own self-evaluation program, using the excellent *What Color Is Your Parachute?* or *Where Do I Go From Here With My Life?*, both of which are listed on page 303. As Richard Bolles recommends, you may want to get hold of John L. Holland's classic "The Self-directed Search," which originally appeared in his book *Making Vocational Choices: A Theory of Careers* (Englewood Cliffs, N.J.: Prentice-Hall, 1973). This self-evaluation guide is now available to professionals such as vocational counselors or placement officers, and can be obtained from Consulting Psychologists Press, 577 College Avenue, Palo Alto, CA 94306.

Getting the Skills or Training You Need

"The higher a skill level you can legitimately claim, the more likely you are to find a job."
— RICHARD NELSON BOLLES, *What Color Is Your Parachute?*

Once you have identified the field that interests you most or the type of work you think you would be happiest doing (taking note, of course, of projected demand as indicated in the chapter "The Jobs of the Future"), the next step is to start investigating opportunities to obtain the training and experience you need to enter the field and do the job. Each of the listings in "Today's Best Part-Time Jobs" highlights the most common training requirements for jobs typically adaptable to part-time scheduling. If the field you want to enter or the work you wish to do isn't included among those listed, that doesn't mean that you don't have a chance to get such a job on a part-time basis, though it may indeed be tougher for you than for someone who wants to enter the health-care field, for instance. Nevertheless, head for your library, look up the job that interests you in the *Occupational Outlook Handbook,* and find out what educational requirements exist for the position you seek. For further information or suggestions about suitable training facilities in your area, write to the organizations listed at the end of each job description.

> *"If you're going to go for retraining, why not go for a field that offers better employment prospects? While I'm in class, I'm not only learning the field, but I'm making contacts with potential employers through people in my classes, and I'm lining up prospects for a job when I'll be looking for it, in about four months or so."*
>
> — CAROL PARKER, former sixth-grade teacher now working toward a master's degree in computer sciences at American University, and codirector of Job Sharers, Inc., Arlington, Virginia.

While you are waiting for replies from the professional or trade organizations, begin checking out resources in your area. Ask local four-year, junior, or community colleges for catalogues or descriptions of the courses they offer in the field that you're interested in. If you are not willing or able to put in a year or more at college, or if the job you want doesn't require long-term training, get in touch with continuing education or adult education program directors to see if courses are available in your field of interest. Also, if publicly funded BOCES (Board of Cooperative Education Services) or CETA (Comprehensive Employment Training Act) education and job training programs still operate in your area (funding for many programs is currently in jeopardy), a phone call to your local office of the State Employment Service or even your local college vocational guidance office should help you track them down.

You still have the option of attending a private vocational school or studying at home. For information on accredited vocational schools, write to the National Association of Trade and Technical Schools, 2021 L Street, N.W., Washington, DC 20036. Information on home-study courses can be obtained from the National Home Study Council, 1601 18th Street, N.W., Washington, DC 20009. And if the way to get training and experience is through apprenticeship programs, the organizations that represent workers can advise you on the best ways to obtain it.

Financing Your Education

The December 22, 1980, issue of *Time* magazine brought us the depressing news: Stanford University announced that in the fall of 1981, the cost of tuition, fees, room and board for a single year would rise 13.3 percent to an astronomical $10,105. As the *Time* item pointed out, Stanford usually charges *less* than such Ivy League schools as Harvard and Yale, or M.I.T. Williams College has projected that by 1990, tuition and other expenses will total $16,890 a year! Though state schools and of course community and junior colleges charge substantially less, you will still have to come up with a bundle of money if you wish to further your education.

To make matters worse, as this book goes to press, Congress is considering various changes in the availability of, and eligibility for, federally financed scholarships and loans. If sweeping budget cuts mean that government aid is severely curtailed, finding money for advanced education will be even more difficult than it has been in recent years.

Whether you are in your late teens or late sixties, if

you plan to continue your studies the place to begin looking for financial assistance is the financial-aid office of any college or school you want to attend. However, to get a head start in locating sources of educational funding, you should go to your local library and check out current guides to financial aid. You may also wish to obtain some of the publications listed below.

◆ "Paying for Your Education: A Guide for Adult Learners." A sixty-five-page booklet put out by the College Board which details a wide variety of resources for adults, including special programs for women, minorities, those over age sixty, the unemployed, the disabled, veterans, and public employees. It also discusses the wide availability of employer-paid tuition, plus income-tax deductions permitted adult students. The guide costs $3.50 and is available from the College Board, Department C-88, Box 2815, Princeton, NJ 08541.

◆ "The A's and B's of Academic Scholarships." Lists more than forty thousand academic opportunities. Also, "Don't Miss Out," a general guide to meeting college costs. Each costs $2 and is available from Octameron Associates, Box 3437, Alexandria, VA 22302.

◆ "Meeting College Costs." Another good general guide. Available free from College Board Publications, Box 3815, Princeton, NJ 08541.

◆ "Need a Lift?" Published by the American Legion, this booklet lists dozens of different sources of both scholarships and loans. Costs $1. Write to the American Legion, Need a Lift, P.O. Box 1055, Indianapolis, IN 46206.

Finally, you may be interested in an organization called Scholarship Search. For $45, the organization takes your application and puts it through a computer. The goal is to match you with a variety of scholarships and loans, some of which you might never have found on your own (such as scholarships for left-handed students or grants for students who don't drink or smoke). For further information, write to Scholarship Search, Suite 627, 1775 Broadway, New York, NY 10019.

As you search for education funds, remember that many unions, fraternal organizations, business and professional associations, and other groups offer grants and loans. If you or a family member belongs to such an organization, it is certainly worth checking to see if you may be eligible for assistance.

If you are long on training and rather short on experience, consider taking a volunteer or an entry-level position to get your feet wet. In and of themselves, volunteer positions are not likely to lead to high-paying jobs. However, when any paid positions open up, people who have worked as volunteers almost always get the first shot at them. What's more, a volunteer job can give you the opportunity to develop strong skills in administrating, fund raising, supervising people, managing finances, or any of a number of skills that are directly transferable to the profit-oriented business world, if that is where you think you eventually want to work.

"I used to say, 'Don't volunteer. Don't work for no pay,'" says Carol Parker of Job Sharers, Inc., in Arlington, Virginia. "Now I believe that if you want to work in any of the humanitarian fields in particular, you *should* volunteer. Volunteering can work if you use it wisely. Keep your ears open. Make yourself known. Be on the lookout for paid jobs on a part-time basis and be right there ready to apply."

Taking a paid entry-level job as an alternative to volunteering is a good idea, particularly if you need to be earning money right away. That doesn't mean that you should settle for any dead-end position that happens along. Choose a job that will advance your standing in your chosen career. Work in a field or a company that can provide you with useful experience plus a feel for what goes on every day — and again, one that offers a source of contacts for the future.

Understand that any entry-level job will pay you very little. But realize that as long as you are not going to earn much, you might as well invest your time in a job that at least holds out the promise of long-range benefits. If it's a secretarial job that lets you get your foot in the door, be selective about where you work. Secretaries are in such high demand that you should have no difficulty getting a position almost anywhere you want.

Another possibility is to take the temporary employment route for a while. Tell the placement representative that you will only work in, say, advertising companies, brokerage firms, or whatever companies interest you. Register with more than one temporary agency if you live in a large city. (They are listed in the Yellow Pages under "Employment Agencies — Temporary Contractors.") Take a look at the display ads of various agencies. That way, you can get an idea not only of the agencies' specialties but of the benefits they may offer, such as health insurance or paid vacations.

Be choosy about any beginning positions you take. Think of a first job not as something you have to take because you can't get any other work but rather as the first step in realizing your overall career goals.

Finally, if you need both training and experience, remember that it is possible to obtain them simultaneously. Take a part-time job while you're studying. The placement office at any institution of higher learning can help you land a part-time job on or off campus. See "Money-Making Jobs for Students," page 217, for more ideas on how to combine earning with learning.

Lining Up Prospects

If you have looked at the chapter "Who Is Hiring and Who Isn't," you should have a pretty good idea of which types of companies are likely to be receptive to such alternative scheduling patterns as permanent part-time work or job sharing. Now use this list as a basic foundation on which to build your personal list of possible employers (see page 246). Think of the skills you have mastered and the abilities you possess. Then think of how many different kinds of organizations could use similar skills. For example, if you have demonstrated the ability to supervise people, manage finances, or raise money, your work would be valuable to virtually any type of employer in the nonprofit or business world.

Write down all the varieties of businesses that would be able to utilize your skills and that you might be interested in working for. Don't leave any out. The purpose of making an exhaustive list is to help you realize at the very outset that the number of potential employers in your area is a lot larger than you probably ever imagined — even if you limit the list to only those employers willing to hire part-time workers. If you do a thorough job of writing down the types of organizations that might be appropriate, you will be amazed at how many there are.

O.K. Let's assume for the moment that you have decided you want to do some sort of administrative work for a bank or brokerage house, a nonprofit organization, or perhaps a finance or credit card company. How do you find the names of companies in your field? How do you begin to track down the names of the officers at those companies or organizations who have the power to hire you?

The first step in all job-hunting is to head to your local library. Your librarian can be a most valuable source of information, a person who can lead you to an almost infinite list of resources. You may want to begin by asking for the *Guide to American Directories,* which can aim you at directories that are appropriate for finding leads in your chosen field. Among the many good guides that can help you locate possible employers and corporate officers are:

- *The Encyclopedia of Associations*
- *The Foundations Directory*
- Dun and Bradstreet's directories (to identify officers and give important details about company finances)
- *Standard and Poor's Register of Corporations, Directors, and Executives*
- *Moody's Industrial Manual*
- *Standard Rate and Data* (to identify specialized publications in every field)
- *Investor, Banker, Broker Almanac.*

The list of resources in your library goes on and on. So does the amount of work you will have to do if you are serious about finding a good job.

Other good sources of information on prospective employers are local newspapers -- specifically, stories about expanding businesses, major personnel shifts, plans to relocate headquarters. Trade and professional associations also put out magazines and newspapers that can be extremely helpful. For example, the *Chronicle for Higher Education* can alert you to openings in colleges and universities; *Publishers Weekly* is the bible of the publishing industry; *Advertising Age* carries all the news related to advertising, including details of proposed new ad campaigns and information on which agencies are moving up (and down) in terms of billings. Not only do specialized journals carry stories that could tip you off to good prospects, but some have classified sections that carry want ads for top-level jobs.

A WORD ABOUT NEWSPAPER WANT ADS AND EMPLOYMENT AGENCIES

Don't expect much from either one, unless you are looking for a clerical or other relatively low-level position. Under "part-time" in the Sunday classifieds you are likely to find an overabundance of ads for typists, telephone solicitors, bookkeepers, and inventory takers. Occasionally jobs for part-time social workers, registered nurses, and even research analysts are advertised in the Sunday papers. But in the two or three haphazard columns that most newspapers customarily dedicated to listings of part-time job opportunities, advertisements for clerk-typists and bank tellers are clearly the most abundant.

On the other hand, larger display ads for good full-time jobs, usually at much higher pay levels, can be found in such Sunday papers as the *New York Times,* the *Los Angeles Times,* and the *Cleveland Plain Dealer.* The display ads may be useful for the professional with impressive credentials who hopes to find a top-level part-time job, or for two people interested in convincing potential employers to let them share one job, particularly if the advertised job seems to lend itself to a ready division of time and tasks. However, for the most part, don't expect to see many top-level part-time jobs advertised in the

Sunday newspapers. Some experts estimate that as few as 20 percent of all good jobs are ever advertised. For good part-time jobs, the number is undoubtedly a lot lower. If help-wanted ads are likely to be a source of discouragement, so, too, are employment agencies. Part-time jobs listed in ads run by agencies are almost always clerical positions. What's more, few employment agency people are thrilled to learn that a job applicant is looking for part-time work. Why? Because part-timers are harder to place than full-timers. Moreover, agency representatives earn their commissions based on a portion of an employee's salary. If someone wishing to work part-time stands to earn, say, only one-half or two-thirds as much as someone willing to work full-time, which person do you think the representative is going to work harder trying to place?

An obvious exception to the try-to-stay-away-from-all-employment-services rule is any agency or job-help center that caters exclusively to part-time job-seekers or to women wishing to return to the work force after a long absence. Organizations that actively work to better part-time opportunities in their cities are topnotch places to go. Some even maintain job banks or keep résumés on file for interested employers. By all means get in touch with the group nearest you (see "Organizations that Help Part-Timers" in the "Resources" section, page 361). If there are no nearby advocacy groups, contact one of the organizations listed in the "Catalyst National Network of Local Resource Centers," mentioned on page 304.

Use Every Resource Available

Doing extensive research on companies that are likely to be hiring part-time workers is definitely the best way to begin any hunt for a good part-time job. Find out about their products or services, organizational structures, the size and make-up of their staffs, innovative programs, planned expansion, and so forth. Consult professional journals. Look for display ads in trade magazines. Skim books and read articles about various firms, and note the names of people interviewed as well as of the authors of any interesting and informative articles. That is how you build up a list of useful resources that can help you learn about companies.

While library research is extremely important, what is absolutely essential is that you begin making personal contacts. Find out who might be helpful to you, who may know of job openings or of situations in companies or organizations that might lead to job openings. Get your contacts to begin working for you, to lead you to still more potentially useful contacts and possibly even to people who can actually offer you a job. The point can't be emphasized enough: Tell *everyone* you know that you are looking for work as a whatever-it-is. Say, "I'm available to do such-and-such. Do you know of anyone I might talk to who could offer some pointers on how to get started looking for a suitable job?"

Should you mention that you are looking for part-time work? The answer is, sometimes. If the position you seek is one that is commonly done on a part-time basis, such as medical assistant, bookkeeper, dental hygienist, librarian, teacher, or a similar occupation, by all means change your opening line to "I'm available to do such-and-such on a part-time basis. Do you know of anyone . . . ?"

However — and here's the big IF — if the job you want to do is *not* customarily done on a part-time basis but you hope to be able to convince an employer to hire you part-time, then most experts agree that you would be well advised *not* to mention right away that you are looking for part-time work. " 'Part-time' is a red flag," warns Nancy Inui of FOCUS, Inc. "It can close off many avenues that might otherwise be open. It's much better to get as far as you can during a job interview and establish yourself positively in the interviewer's mind. The more the interviewer likes you, the more he or she is going to be willing to accommodate your needs."

Adds Barney Olmsted of New Ways to Work, in San Francisco: "Why set up obstacles right at the outset? Part-timers are better off proceeding as though they're looking for full-time work. There's plenty of time later to negotiate schedules."

Whether you decide to be open about your desire to work part-time or to keep it to yourself for the time being, use any and all contacts you have: your relatives, your friends, your spouse's friends, your friends' spouses or parents, your dry cleaner, the pediatrician, shopkeepers in your area, members of any clubs you belong to, your stockbroker, your insurance agent, members of any classes you attend, professors, your dentist, the children's teachers, your hairdresser, former employers and coworkers, members of professional organizations you belong to, placement counselors at postsecondary schools you have attended or now attend, your banker, and others.

The reason for talking to every person you can think of should be obvious. Each one of them knows dozens of other people. Your local pharmacist, Joe Jones, might remember that a customer works for the kind of company you are interested in working for. Or better yet, Joe Jones may mention that he plays golf with Sam Smith, the vice-president of a firm in your chosen field, and suggest that you give him a call. Then you are able to pick up the phone and say, "Joe Jones suggested that I speak to Sam Smith," which at least gets you past Sam Smith's secretary. Better yet, Joe Jones may offer you a personal introduction, which is even more likely to lead to a personal interview and in turn could lead to a job offer. Even if no offer comes or you feel that this isn't the company for you, at least you now know Sam Smith — another contact.

The Informational Interview

In *What Color Is Your Parachute?* Richard Nelson Bolles advocates using library research and personal contacts to begin a campaign of what he calls "interviewing for information." What that means is speaking to people within various companies — preferably those who have the power to hire you — to ask specific questions about their firms, about jobs in their industry, about what it takes for people to get ahead in their field, or about the big challenges that the industry faces right now — anything that helps you figure out what an employer's specific needs are at that moment and that permits you to begin thinking in terms of how your own skills and abilities can help the employer fill those needs.

The purpose of any informational interview is not to solicit a job, Bolles cautions, but simply to gather information and to let the potential employer "window shop" you. The informational interview takes the pressure off both the employer and the job-hunter. It lets each learn about the other without either feeling that any commitment must be made. In fact, Bolles suggests, if a job offer is made during an informational interview, the job-seeker should decline it politely. He or she should say something like, "Thank you very much for the offer. I'd be very happy to consider it and to talk with you again. But right now, I'm not quite sure exactly where I want to work." The job applicant should follow up with a thank-you note to the interviewer that refreshes his or her memory about the matters discussed during the interview, and that includes any pertinent further comments or material.

There is no denying that starting to line up contacts and going around to various people takes courage. Each of us feels that no busy executive at any company or organization is going to want to be bothered talking to us. Yet as Bolles points out, people are often flattered to be asked for their opinions — particularly if they are not being asked for anything else!

If you find you have cold feet when you begin approaching your first few contacts, Bolles suggests starting with such simple questions as "How did you get into this business?" or "How did you become interested in computers?" (or whatever it is that you are also interested in).

Once you begin to feel more confident, you can begin to move on to such questions as what kinds of jobs the person thinks might involve the activities you are interested in pursuing, or which positions might use skills such as those you possess. Let the executive tell you about the possibilities. If he or she doesn't know the answers to your questions, ask if he or she can think of someone else you might talk to. Then call up that person and say, "Fran Franklin suggested I call." There — you've done it again! You have gotten past the secretary and lined up still another potential interview.

Zeroing In on Your Target

Only after you have done extensive research, talked to knowledgeable people in a number of different companies, learned all you possibly can about the companies you would like to work for, and identified the problems that the various employers seem to have should you go back and talk to a particular person you would like to work for, advises Richard Bolles. At that point, and not before, tell the executive that his or her company is the one that impressed you the most, and why, and that it's the one in which you feel you can make the greatest contribution, and how. If a job offer is forthcoming, you are in a good position to negotiate all of the specifics. If no job offer comes, then you move on to the next company you would like to work for.

In brief, that is the job-hunting method described by Richard Nelson Bolles and advocated by a growing number of vocational counselors throughout the country, including those who advise would-be part-timers. Marcia Kleiman of Options for Women, in Germantown, Pennsylvania, emphasizes that doing all of the advance research into companies (including finding out their view of and their experience with alternative work scheduling) is by far the quickest and most direct route to finding a good part-time job. "If there's anything I'd want to stress it's the tremendous need for up-front preparation," says Kleiman. "Research who *you* are and then find out who's out there, how they operate, what their philosophy is. That way, when you walk in the door to sell yourself, you are very clear about who you're dealing with and what their expectations are.

"We find over and over again that people are resistant to doing the advance work that's necessary," she continues. "They say, 'Why should I bother reading?' and 'Why should I bother researching? I'll just sell myself at the interview.' We convince them that if they don't know exactly to whom they're talking, they're going to fall flat on their faces. In the long run, doing the up-front work is a time-saver. And it's a much more successful method of finding a part-time job.'"

But Can't You Just Send Out Résumés?

The research/contacts/informational-interview approach is the one most likely to help you find a job, yet there may be reasons that you want to use a more varied approach to job-hunting or to try a number of different methods to help you find the job you want, including presenting yourself on paper before you do so in person. Should you send out résumés? Richard Bolles might answer, "Sure, if that's what you really want to do. But don't expect much in the way of results." Other counselors would disagree. They maintain that the time-honored résumé is the customary and therefore the required method of presenting yourself to potential employers. Some, for example, argue that a *chronological* résumé, which highlights continuous employment and a succession of increasingly responsible jobs, is the best presentation that someone with a solid work background can possibly make. Others reply that a *functional* résumé, which stresses duties and responsibilities and which can camouflage a spotty work history, is the only way to go for job-seekers with little or no paid work experience.

Still other counselors argue that any résumé is probably the least effective way in which to present yourself and your credentials, because it is so common. They maintain that it is fine to put your qualifications on paper, but by all means choose another format. Which one? A letter tailored to the person who has the power to hire you — one that clearly presents you as the person who can best help that employer solve his or her problems.

Chief among the advocates of this method is Carl R. Boll, a noted employment adviser who maintains that the best way to attract attention and to get a prospective employer interested in meeting you is to write a letter that highlights specific, concrete achievements in a forceful, direct way but gives no details about where and for whom you did all of the achieving. Boll's premise is that any employer would be much more interested in meeting the person who wrote a compelling letter than in talking to someone who sent in a résumé that looked and read just like the 150 or 1500 other résumés that came in the same week.

I agree. Although I recognize that the old standby résumé may still be a necessity in some cases, I firmly believe that if you are going to present yourself on paper, rather than at an in-person informational interview, you are better off writing a solid, carefully written, and brief letter that sets you apart from all other job-seekers as a capable, forthright person who is making some interesting claims and who is willing to back them up *in person.* By writing an effective letter to the man or woman who has the power to hire you — Yes, you still have to do all of the research! — you can make even limited experience sound most impressive.

Here is an example of how someone without any paid work experience whatsoever might put together a letter that would make any potential employer take notice. As you are reading this sample letter, keep in mind that the writer mentions no previous employers, no dates of employment, no indication of whether the work was done on a full-time or part-time basis, or even of whether she got paid for doing it.

4 Ardsley Place
Bayside, NY 11368
July 26, 1982

Dr. Dorothy Burger
Administrator
United Community Services
1250 Hanson Place
Brooklyn, NY 11205

Dear Dr. Burger,

During the past six years, I have spent thousands of hours devising cost-effective programs and money-making projects that have directly benefited over 1200 families in the greater New York area.

Your agency may be in need of someone with my qualifications to develop and coordinate fund-raising and volunteer activities. If so, some of my accomplishments may be of interest to you.

As director of volunteers for a major community agency, I increased the number of unpaid staff members by 17 percent and reduced turnover among volunteers by one-third.

I developed innovative fund-raising programs that increased net revenues by $5000 over the previous year.

I started a quarterly newsletter to inform contributors of the work and progress of the agency. Within six months, donations from private sponsors increased by 12 percent.

If you believe that my experience could benefit your organization, I would be happy to discuss my background in greater detail at a personal interview. You can reach me at the above address, or by phone, during the evening, at (212) 497-8868.

Very truly yours,

Anita Levy

If you were Dr. Burger, would you be interested in meeting Anita Levy, even though she omitted any mention of where she has worked, what her educational background is, or anything remotely resembling personal data? Of course you would. That is the whole idea behind a tailored letter.

Now let's take a closer look at Anita's letter to see what makes it so compelling. The first thing you will notice is that the opening is an attention-getter: "I've spent thousands of hours . . . that have benefited over 1200 families . . ." This is an impressive claim. Now look at it again. When you consider what Anita is saying, you find that her efforts have merely helped the *agency* help the people it normally serves! It's the phrasing that makes her contribution seem so immense and interesting. No, Anita hasn't lied in any way. But she has begun to attract attention to her skills and to the concerns of virtually every employer, cutting costs and making money — all in fewer than thirty words.

Second, there is the matter of why she is writing the letter: not to ask "if you might have a position available," but to appeal directly to the administrator's self-interest ("you might be able to benefit from what I have to offer"). That, after all, is what any employer cares about — what can *you* do for *me?*

Third, to back up her implied claim that she is someone rather special, Anita immediately launches into several examples of concrete achievements. Notice that instead of writing that she was in charge of volunteers and leaving it at that, she specifically says that she increased the number of unpaid staff members by 17 percent and found a way to make them stay for a longer period of time than volunteers had previously served. Instead of writing that she ran fund-raising events, she says she devised ways to raise $5000 more than such efforts had netted during the previous year. Obviously, you don't make such claims unless they are true. But if you have such achievements to your credit, now is the time to take credit for them! Modesty is of little benefit when you are looking for a job.

Fourth, consider the closing. Note that once again Anita does not ask for a job or even for an interview. She merely states her availability and willingness to discuss her background in greater detail *at a personal interview* (the key!) and leaves the rest up to the employer. That's it.

Since 96 to 99 percent of all résumés are screened out immediately, a well-tailored letter can be very effective, particularly when compared to normally dull résumés. Whether you decide to use the letter format or simply to try to write a résumé that is better than most, make sure your presentation is strong, memorable, and to the point. Focus on very specific achievements and accomplishments. For example, even if you only worked as a cashier, make the position sound important. Try to remember how much money you handled, then write, "Responsible for over $6000 cash each night." If you sold misses' sportswear in a department store, you might write, "Sold an average of $200 worth of merchandise each day," or "Sold over $6000 worth of clothing and accessories during the first month." No one knows whether that is a lot or a little, but it certainly sounds good. More important, it helps a potential employer see you as responsible, profit-oriented, determined, or just plain enthusiastic — all qualities that he or she wants in any employee.

For in-depth advice on how to set up résumés, consult the career guidance books by Richard K. Irish and Tom Jackson and Davidyne Mayleas, mentioned on page 303. You may also want to obtain a copy of the Catalyst *Résumé Preparation Manual,* available for $3.50 from Catalyst, 14 East 60th Street, New York, NY 10022. For a complete rundown of how to devise customized letters to send to a number of potential employers or as answers to help-wanted ads (including those that specify résumés), see Carl R. Boll's excellent book, *Executive Jobs Unlimited* (New York: Macmillan, 1965).

How to Handle the Job Interview

Ah, yes. That ultimate head-to-head encounter. The make-or-break meeting. Thirty or forty minutes that can reduce the most self-composed individual into a clammy, sweaty mess.

How do you get through it with minimal damage to your chances for getting the job, or to your ego? All of the top career guides offer solid pointers. Among them: ask intelli-

322   *A Part-Time Career for a Full-Time You*

gent questions based on all of the research you have done; speak only in positive terms about previous employers or schools you have attended, since you want to give the impression that you get along with people and have learned a great deal from your previous work or educational experience; use every possible opportunity to stress your achievements and your strong points; always minimize the negative.

To help you prepare for an interview, many guides suggest that you plan your answers to probable questions well in advance and that you rehearse the interview with a friend posing as the interviewer (a good idea, even though you don't want to sound like a recorded message during your interview). If you want to do as much advance preparation as possible, consult the major career guides. Of particular interest may be a book that contains suggestions about how to answer some of the tricky questions interviewers sometimes throw at job applicants: *Getting a Better Job* by David Gootnick (New York: McGraw-Hill, 1978). There are some good tips for students on how to locate potential employers and how to handle interviews with them in William N. Yeomans's book *Jobs 80–81* (New York: Paragon Books/Putnam Publishing Group, 1979).

For anyone seeking any job — full- or part-time — the interview is the culmination of all efforts. It is at the interview that you actually get a job offer and settle details of salary and all the other benefits. Or you get a polite brush-off. (Actually, in some large corporations you may have to go through as many as three or four different interviews before anything is settled.)

The final interview can be particularly stressful for the part-timer, since it is often during this interview that your desire to work a reduced schedule first becomes known. You are not only selling yourself, which is hard enough for most people to do, but you are proposing something that may be unfamiliar to the employer. Worse, he or she may know all about part-time scheduling and have absolutely no desire to try it.

When is the right time to bring up the Big Subject? How do you convince a skeptical employer to try a part-time schedule? How can you approach your present boss to say that you want to switch to three days a week? How do you negotiate a good benefits package? All of these are of great importance to any would-be part-timer. Once again, advance preparation will help you gain confidence and will ensure that you present your case as strongly as possible.

When is the right time to mention that you are interested in working part-time? Some people can safely say so up front, when they first meet the person who has the power to hire them. Others should wait. It depends on your circumstances and on the job you are applying for. For example, if you're a student or over the age of sixty or sixty-five, an interviewer might well expect you to be looking to work fewer than thirty-five or forty hours a week. Your announcement will come as no surprise. Similarly, if the job you seek to obtain is one that is often done on a part-time basis (nurse, dental hygienist, teacher), it's fine to indicate your preference for part-time work at the outset.

You are probably also on safe ground if you know that a prospective employer is desperate for the skills you offer. Highly trained secretaries, computer programmers, scientific technicians, accountants (particularly during the tax season), engineers, and medical specialists of all kinds can probably indicate that they wish to work reduced schedules and find any number of employers eager to accommodate their needs.

On the other hand — and here's where it gets a bit sticky — if you know or strongly suspect that the employer is only looking for a person who will work full time and you want the job on a part-time basis, you would probably be wise to wait until he or she indicates that you're the person for the job before you begin to ease into the matter of a reduced schedule. Once again, Nancy Inui advises that "it's much better to get as far as you can during a job interview and establish yourself positively in the interviewer's mind" before broaching the subject.

How do you bring up the subject? A good way to initiate any discussion of a reduced schedule, Inui suggests, is to start talking about "flexibility" as one of the advantages you offer. "If you sense that the employer doesn't really have the job fixed clearly in his or her mind, or that the nature of the job could change after a while," she points out, "you might say something like, 'From what you're saying, it sounds like you may not really need someone here five days a week,' or 'It seems that it may be an advantage to you if we were able to work out a schedule that allows you some flexibility during the week. That would be good for me, too. In fact, I'd really prefer it.' "

Carol Parker of Job Sharers, Inc., offers some further advice: "Don't stress that *you* need a part-time job. Always say that you offer the employer the advantage of being able to accommodate *his or her* needs." For example, if the boss does a great deal of traveling or doesn't normally come into the office on Mondays or until 10:30 each morning, you might take advantage of that fact to call attention to your own willingness to adapt to his or her schedule. Of course, advises Parker, if you possibly can, you should say you would be able and willing to put in thirty-five to forty hours a week if it becomes necessary or during peak periods or office emergencies. Stating that reinforces the idea that your first commitment is to the job — that you are dependable and serious about working, even though you would prefer a reduced schedule.

If you don't have an opportunity to jump in with an offer to accommodate the employer's needs, and if it isn't readily apparent to you that the employer might benefit by your working part-time, broaching the subject is going to take a bit more ingenuity. You are going to have to phrase your desire to work part-time in slightly different terms.

Marcia Kleiman of Options for Women suggests that if that's the case, *wait until you are actually offered the job,* when the employer has made a definite commitment to you as the best-qualified person, before you bring up the subject. At that point, and not before, advises Kleiman, you might say something like, 'Now that we're negotiating the specifics, I think I can offer something that would benefit both of us. You believe that my qualifications are right for the job. I think I can make a significant contribution to this company. But I also feel that I can be even more productive than you might have realized. I believe I can handle all of the responsibilities of this job in twenty-five or thirty hours a week. I can do the job, do it well, and save you money at the same time. And in fact, I'd be happier if we could arrange a reduced schedule that's mutually agreeable."

Saying something to that effect is the best way to present your case. *Don't* issue a plea for the employer to accommodate your needs. Rather, present your proposal as something that will benefit the employer: You are offering increased productivity at a reduced cost in return for the employer's agreeing to a reduced schedule. No one is making any sacrifices; you both benefit. That's the point you want to make. "All this stuff about 'happy workers are good workers' is absolutely true," says Marcia Kleiman. "But if we're honest with ourselves, we have to recognize that all any employer is really interested in is the bottom line: 'What is such-and-such going to cost me? Or save me?' "

Tell the boss that you are not only good, but cost-effective. Say that he or she is getting not only a competent person, but one who is willing to eat a sandwich at her desk instead of taking a lunch hour, one who won't take three coffee breaks a day, one who won't sit around and waste time but will come in and get right to work, one who will therefore be as efficient as or even more efficient than someone working full-time. You might say, "Look at it this way. For only seventy-five percent of the salary we've discussed, you're getting someone who is well qualified and who is willing to give the job two hundred percent in order to make this arrangement work."

"If you can demonstrate to the employer that his or her bottom line isn't going to suffer but may actually benefit," Kleiman contends, "the employer may be willing to give it a try." If, despite all your logic, the employer still seems to feel some skepticism, then it's time to go for broke, says Kleiman. "Offer to work part-time on a trial basis," she suggests. "Say something like, 'You still seem to have some reservations, and I'm absolutely convinced that this can work to our mutual satisfaction. How about if we agree to give it a try for three or six months? After that, we'll sit down again and evalute how everything is going. If you feel that you're not satisfied with the arrangement, I wouldn't expect you to be committed to it, and I'd leave. Of course, that's a lot of extra pressure on me, as I'm sure you realize. But I'm willing to try it because I honestly believe that any doubts you have will be alleviated in less time than that.' " There's *your* bottom line. You can't make any employer a better offer than that.

Should you take a job on a full-time basis and plan to switch to a part-time schedule after you begin working? That is a matter between you and your conscience. There is no question that many people now holding top part-time jobs did sign on as full-timers and planned all along to switch as soon as possible. Is that taking the job under false pretenses? Some think yes; others, no.

"I have a lot of trouble with that concept," says Marcia Kleiman. "It's one thing to take a job and think in terms of changing schedules several years down the road. But it's another to take the job and pull a fast one on the employer after only a short time. I think that's dishonest. What's more, it's something that can backfire on you if the employer finds out you did it."

Nancy Inui of FOCUS and Barney Olmsted of New Ways to Work feel somewhat differently. Both know of many people who have taken full-time jobs, established themselves as extremely valuable employees within a short time, and asked for a change of work schedule without any difficulties. Neither woman, however, suggests that as the best method of obtaining a good part-time job, and both advise anyone contemplating such a move to exercise good judgment. "You should wait at least three to six months before asking to switch to a part-time schedule. A year is better," says Nancy Inui.

"Make sure that you're well established and considered a valued employee before you make the attempt to modify your schedule," cautions Barney Olmsted. The reason is simple: Unless you are a good worker who is well liked, the boss isn't going to try to arrange a work schedule you obviously could not get six or eight months ago. If you have become a highly valued employee, though, the boss is going to do what he or she can to keep you.

How do you go about switching from a full-time to a part-time schedule? The important thing is to deal from a position of strength. If you're good at what you do, if the boss has come to depend on you and to trust you — in short, if you're that often-mentioned "valued employee" — you have the best chance of convincing your employer to let you make the change and to fight for whatever approval is necessary for you to do so.

How do you present your case? The same way a new employee would: by emphasizing the benefits to the employer — namely, that by accommodating your needs, he or she gets to keep you. As you have seen in examples throughout this book, numerous women who became well established and highly regarded in their companies and who then decided to have children found it easy to negotiate reduced schedules after their children were born. Similarly, older workers who have done a good job over the years have been able to negotiate curtailed work weeks with little difficulty.

If you don't have such an obvious basis on which to ask for a part-time schedule, try approaching your boss with something like this: "I love this job and I really enjoy working for you very much. But I'm having tremendous problems finding reliable after-school child care (or handling my job and all of my schoolwork at the same time) and it's making it rough for me to continue working. Do you think we might be able to set up a schedule whereby I would give up lunch hours in return for being able to leave earlier in the afternoon?" Or perhaps, "If we could work out a reduction of, say, eight or ten hours per week, which I think I know how to manage fairly simply, it would make it much easier for me to continue working here. Of course, if I were able to reduce my schedule I'd expect to earn proportionately less salary, so it wouldn't cost the company any more money."

By making a pitch similar to these, you cover all bases. You establish that (1) working is very important to you; (2) working for your present boss is very important to you; (3) you have a good reason for wanting to switch schedules; (4) you have come up with a possible way to do it and still remain productive; (5) it won't cost the boss anything extra to accommodate your needs; and, perhaps most important, (6) this is probably the only way the boss *can* expect to keep you.

Go in with a concrete plan detailing how you would alter

your schedule and handle your responsibilities in fewer hours per day or fewer days per week. For example, if some duplication of efforts between you and another employee now exists — as it often does in offices — you might suggest a way to divide the tasks more clearly, by your assuming some responsibilities and the other employee handling the remaining duties. Perhaps you might come up with ways in which to streamline your own work, so that you can work even more efficiently. If you gave it some thought, you could undoubtedly find ways in which you could be more productive in less time, which is what you have to convince the boss you are willing to do.

A good employer doesn't think in terms of how many hours you actually occupy your desk each day, but rather in terms of whether you get your work done. You might fortify your request for a change of schedule with something like, "You already know that I work hard and that I produce. To make this arrangement possible and successful, I'm willing to give it extra effort."

Make your boss your ally. Make him or her *want* to help you get whatever approval you need (if changing your schedule is going to take some doing). As Carol Parker points out, "If someone is willing to go to bat for you, someone who already has authority within the company or pull with the people upstairs, that helps tremendously." Perhaps there is no better example of how a supportive employer can help establish an innovative work plan than the efforts put forth by Secretary of State Norma Paulus in Oregon. As I mentioned, Paulus fought opposition from coworkers, friends, the state's payroll department, and lots of well-meaning advisers who tried to get her to give up the idea of having two women share the position of administrative assistant in her office. But she stuck with it. Consequently, Ann Lau and Phyllis Elgin have successfully shared their current position since 1977 (see "State and Local Governments," pages 290–92).

Presenting the idea of a reduced schedule is obviously going to be easier if precedents already exist in your own company. Try to find out who else has switched to part-time schedules and ask how they have worked out their arrangements. If possible, find examples of people who hold similar jobs on a part-time basis in companies other than your own. Ask friends or business acquaintances if they know of any part-timers doing the same job you do. Also, contact some of the part-time advocacy groups listed in the "Resources" section, pages 361–67. Ask if they know of part-timers in your field or if they can put you in touch with someone who holds a similar position on a part-time basis.

Remember that people tend to be resistant to change. As Nancy Inui says, "No one wants to be the first one on the block" to try alternative scheduling. They want to know who else has done it and how it works. Show that it will work well for your boss, and you will be in the best possible position to negotiate the change you want.

What about benefits? How do you handle problems that may arise? "You can't expect to get full-time benefits if you work part-time," says Marcia Kleiman. "It shouldn't cost the employer anything extra to have you on a part-time basis," adds Barney Olmsted. All of the experts on part-time work agree that you have to be realistic and expect only what's fair from an employer, just as you expect the employer to be fair with you.

What *is* reasonable is for you to get prorated benefits. "You're working out an agreement that's mutually beneficial," explains Marcia Kleiman. "You're willing to invest your time and a lot of effort in your job. The employer should be willing to invest in you, too."

After you have established your credibility as someone who can do the job that needs to be done and you have begun to work out the details of a proposed part-time work arrangement, you might suggest to the interviewer that fringe benefits be prorated. If you have done your advance research, you should be able to come in with a ready plan to offer — perhaps one based on the guidelines outlined in the Catalyst booklet "Constructing an Employee Benefit Package for Part-time Workers: How to Calculate an Equitable Benefit Package at No Extra Cost to the Employer," available from Catalyst, 14 East 60th Street, New York, NY 10022, for $1.25.

Another possibility suggested by Marcia Kleiman is one

that, as she's quick to point out, is not necessarily feasible for all job-seekers but that may be for you. If you don't need such fringe benefits as health or life insurance (for example, if you're already covered under the policy of your spouse), you might offer to forgo such benefits as an added cost-saving incentive to your employer. Or you might suggest a "market-basket" approach whereby you would select from among the various benefits, choosing the ones you need most, with the total package based on the amount of company expenditures to which you would be entitled.

If you are already working full-time, you should be prepared to give up some of the benefits you now have. For example, suggest that you can decrease your vacation time or give up some paid holidays, or offer to contribute a portion of the cost of your health and life insurance coverage. Sometimes, if you are really lucky and you work for a particularly benevolent company, you may be able to keep a full package of benefits. But don't expect it. Just make sure that the result is equitable to you as well as to the company.

How do you guarantee that as a part-timer you will get raises and promotions? There are never guarantees that any employee will receive periodic raises unless such agreements are spelled out in a labor contract. Otherwise, only you and your boss can make that determination. What is absolutely essential is that you establish suitable guidelines for both salary reviews and promotion considerations *while you are setting up your schedule and working out your part-time agreement.*

Getting promoted is probably one of the most difficult problems faced by men and women in high-level part-time jobs. What you want to do, therefore, is establish at the outset just how your salary will be determined and how your suitability for promotion will be evaluated in the future. At the same time, you may also want to determine the conditions under which you could return to full-time employment if you should desire and be able to do so.

If possible, get everything in writing. Ask for a letter of confirmation of your agreement which spells out every detail you have discussed. By getting your employer to make a commitment now, you will be much happier, and better off, later.

Finding a Good Shared Job

Before you pick up the phone to call a friend or business associate to suggest that the two of you try to find a job that you can share, take a few minutes to consider whether your own personality and temperament make you suitable for a job-sharing situation. The point may seem somewhat odd, given the emphasis in this book on all of the positive aspects of shared positions. But thinking it through is really important.

"Ask yourself *honestly* whether you tend to be particularly competitive," suggests Barney Olmsted. "Some people need to 'own' their work and would be unwilling to share the credit for it. If you're one of those people, you may want to reconsider the job-sharing alternative."

For example, ask yourself how you would feel if your partner was credited with an achievement that was actually yours. "I recall a situation in which one woman received a compliment on a particular project that both had worked on," says Olmsted. "The woman didn't feel at all uncomfortable saying, 'Thank you very much,' and dropping it at that, knowing she and her partner had both worked equally hard. Nor did her partner feel slighted that the job-sharing point hadn't been made." How would you feel in the same situation? What would you have said if you had received the compliment? How would you have felt if your partner were publicly credited?

After you have considered a positive example, stop to think about a negative one. What if you were blamed for a serious mistake that your partner actually made? Would you be angry and feel compelled to point out that it wasn't your fault? Would you expect your partner to go in and accept responsibility for the error at the first possible opportunity? Or would you be willing to say something like, "We apparently had some misunderstanding, and we'll try not to let it happen again"?

On the other hand, what if *you* made the mistake and your partner was called to task? What would you expect her or him to say? Would you feel the need to exonerate her or him and apologize directly to the boss? Or would you be comfortable knowing that he or she would apologize for the two of you?

Answering these and similar questions before you consider job sharing can save you a great deal of time, trouble, and unhappiness later. If you decide you're not cut out for sharing, you always have the possibility of pursuing a part-time job on your own, as outlined in this chapter. If you still think job sharing sounds like a good idea, however, by all means read on!

Picking a Partner

Compatibility is obviously the basis of any job-sharing situation. "You have to respect each other or it can't work," says Carolyn Corbin, a personnel specialist and job sharer from Portland, Oregon. A willingness to be flexible, mutual trust, absolute honesty, and the ability to communicate well are essential ingredients of a successful job-sharing arrangement, say people who have counseled job sharers. According to Carol Parker, however, "You must remember that job sharing isn't a marriage." "When you decide to seek a job-sharing situation, you're not making a lifetime commitment," adds Nancy Inui.

Nevertheless, both these experts agree that you must discuss a wide range of subjects long before you present yourselves to any prospective employer as the ideal solution to his or her staffing problems. For example, you should talk about exactly how you both feel about the work you intend to do, experience and strengths you can bring to the arrangement, and the degree of commitment you expect from each other.

Needless to say, you can't know what is going to happen once you start working as a team. But it is important to explore your views, attitudes, and possible approaches to situations that are likely to arise in the future. Among the important considerations are these:

Complementary skills. Do you have different strengths, or are you both trained in the same specialty with similar amounts and levels of experience? This has a direct bearing on the kinds of jobs you would be best equipped to handle as a team. As a rule, it is easier to convince employers that two people are better than one if you offer diverse abilities and backgrounds rather than similar experience.

Division of labor. How would you divide the tasks that a prospective job entails? Would each of you be responsible for certain functions but not others? Would you both handle all job responsibilities but at different hours of the day or days of the week? The more readily identifiable the job responsibilities are, the more easily you can divide them. For example, in a partnership-teaching situation, one sharer might teach math and science, the other English and history. But if the job you share is that of a customer service representative for a credit company, odds are both members of the team will do the same work but at different times of the day or week. That is what you have to decide.

Coverage. How would you provide for such contingencies as one partner's car not working on a snowy morning, or the other's child being sent home from school with chicken pox? Would the other person be able to fill in? How about for several days, or a week or two, if need be? Could you work out an arrangement whereby someone would always be on the job?

Coverage is one of the key advantages that job sharers offer any employer, particularly if they are applying for a position that involves heavy public contact or peak periods during the week or year. You should be prepared to tell a prospective boss that he or she would never have to worry about absences because of illness or vacation. In fact, it would be an added advantage if you were able to say that during emergencies at the office, both of you could arrange to be there if necessary.

Job offers. If one of you but not the other was offered a job after separate or joint interviews, how would you react? Would you adopt a "both or neither" stance and say, "Thank you, but we are only interested in a shared position"? Or would the person offered the job be free to accept it without either party's feeling guilty or betrayed? Similarly, if you are seeking to restructure a full-time job you currently hold and your boss doesn't go along with your proposal, are you prepared to abandon the idea and continue as a full-timer? Or will you leave?

As Carol Parker indicates, sometimes a firm is looking for a job-sharing partner for someone already on the staff who wants to reduce his or her hours at work. That means that although both you and your partner may be well qualified, the firm only needs one person. How would you handle that situation?

Communications. If you were to get a shared position, how would you inform each other of what happened at work during the morning, or on Wednesday? Would you leave elaborate notes and messages all over the desk? Would you try to overlap schedules in order to maintain continuity during the day? Would you get together each night or once a week to go over details that need the attention of both? What would you do about staff meetings; would one attend, or both? What if the staff meeting was held when you're normally not in the office?

Promotions. What if one job sharer was offered a promotion but the other was not? How would you deal with that? That is a critical matter for both of you to consider.

Leaving the job. What if one person was unhappy at work? Or if the boss was unhappy with one of you? Would you both leave and attempt to find another shared position? Or would one be free to remain and try to find another partner?

As you can see, there are many possibilities to be considered. "There are no right or wrong answers to any of these questions," says Nancy Inui. "Each team must decide what's right for them, and work out their own solutions to potential problems." The point is, it is essential for you to talk about these and other possibilities ahead of time — openly, honestly, and with mutual consideration. Only when you have worked through all of these questions can you expect to convince a prospective employer of your sincerity and your commitment.

The Job Hunt

Just as job-sharing teams work out different arrangements regarding their responsibilities and schedules, so they adopt various ways of finding suitable jobs and of approaching prospective employers. Carol Parker points out some of the more common methods.

When the partners see an appropriate ad for a full-time job or decide to follow up on a lead they have heard about, they try to find the name of someone in the company to ask about the firm's part-time hiring policies. Or one will call the personnel office and ask about alternative work schedules used by the firm in the present or the past. "It's better to get a name, if possible," advises Parker. "A contact is always the best lead."

If you are applying for a specific job, call the person who has the power to hire you (using your contact's name, if possible). Failing that, call the head of personnel and say, "I'd like to talk to you about the company" or "I'd like to talk about the position." Say right away that you are interested in job sharing, that you think you are offering an innovative approach to filling the job, and that you would like to come in and discuss it with him or her. Some job-sharing teams send one member ahead to pave the way. That person discusses the job-sharing alternative with the employer before the two present themselves as a team.

Other pairs send one covering letter with two individual résumés. "This is particularly useful when it's a cold contact situation — no name, and no knowledge of the company's past hiring practices," Parker continues. "If you're sending a joint covering letter, explain briefly that the two of you would bring skills, compatibility, and enormous experience to the job. Also include a very brief description of how you envision sharing the position, and say that you would like to come in and talk about it."

Suggest that you are willing to be interviewed separately or together, depending on the employer's preference. "Of course, it's preferable for you to be interviewed as a team," Parker points out. "But some employers prefer to interview each candidate separately and then bring you together for a joint interview." By offering to be interviewed separately, you demonstrate tremendous confidence. You also take some of the stress off the interviewer, who may feel that he or she is being "ganged up on" in a two-to-one situation. (One thing you *don't* need is for the interviewer to feel pressured!)

Surprisingly, Parker points out, some people have landed jobs simply by showing up at the personnel office of a company that has placed an appealing ad or at a firm they have decided they want to work for, with no advance letter, no phone call, no nothing. Instead, she maintains, they arrive with their covering letter and two résumés in hand and ask to see the director of personnel. "They figure, 'What have we got to lose?' " Parker says. " 'We're offering something different, so why not try approaching the job hunt differently?' " Some teams have found particular success with this method *because* no one expects it. "The usual advice is to stay away from personnel people. In this case, though, the unusual approach can be the most successful."

> *"Job hunting is hard in itself. Looking for a job as a team is even harder. But at least you have company."*
>   — BARNEY OLMSTED, codirector, New Ways to Work, San Francisco.

The Interview

As Nancy Inui points out, once a team is invited for an interview, the partners have already overcome a major obstacle, namely:

YOU: "Would you consider filling that position with two people in a job-sharing arrangement?"

EMPLOYER: "What's that?"

"The very fact that they're willing to talk to you usually means that they have some idea of what job sharing is all about, which certainly helps," Inui says.

At the interview, she continues, the team must try to get across one message from the outset and constantly reinforce it throughout the discussion: "We offer two for the price of one." "It's essential to stress the different backgrounds, experience, and expertise each one brings to the job," adds Carol Parker.

It is equally important to give the employer the feeling that rather than being a source of continuing confusion and disorganization, you offer stability and competence. Show that you know exactly how you would handle the job on a day-to-day basis. "Be prepared to tell the employer how you plan to split the responsibilities and the scheduling," advises Parker. "If the tasks can't be readily identified, try to come up with something innovative, if possible. That way, you'll show that you're both resourceful and that you're both problem solvers. What's more, you'll be able to portray yourselves as serious and committed to your careers, a point you'll want to make when indicating that you would hope and expect to be considered for salary reviews and promotions."

When the question of benefits comes up, it's essential that you be well prepared. "The team must come in knowing the approximate cost differential for hiring the two of them as opposed to hiring one full-time worker," says Inui. "The company shouldn't have to pay more than it would for one person," adds Parker, "and the team members must be able to point out ways in which benefits could be handled."

For example, if the combined salary for the two individuals

is below the Social Security maximum, which is $32,400 in
1982 ($33,900 in 1983), the employer won't have to contrib-
ute any more in Social Security payments than he or she
would for one person. On the other hand, if it is more than
the Social Security maximum, the employer would have to
pay 6.70 percent (6.70 percent in 1983) on the difference.
"The team should offer to pay that difference," says Parker.
"Better yet," she maintains, "explain that one of the advantages you offer as a team is guaranteed coverage of the job.
If that represents, say, four or five fewer days of absenteeism
during the year, that would more than cover any additional
Social Security costs."

Interestingly, as Barney Olmsted points out, many employers have come to realize that the additional expenses of employing job sharers are at most minimal. Moreover, many
companies already realize that these expenses are more than
offset by such factors as reduced absenteeism, increased productivity, and improved employee morale. "Some firms aren't
even prorating health insurance," she adds. "They're just providing it to both people as a matter of course."

Needless to say, a company that offers full benefits to both
members of the team is ideal. But it is unrealistic to assume
that all employers are willing to be so generous. Nor should
you expect them to be. "Be flexible about benefits," advises
Inui. "Don't go in saying, 'We demand this or that.' Instead,
be prepared to agree to a partial benefit package, or proration
of all benefits, or the so-called market-basket approach
whereby each person chooses from among a number of benefits." Adds Parker, "You might also suggest that you're both
willing to contribute the difference in payments so that both
of you have complete health and life insurance."

It is probably a good idea to send for two publications:
"Constructing an Employee Benefit Package for Part-time
Workers: How to Calculate an Equitable Benefit Package at
No Extra Cost to the Employer," available from Catalyst, Inc.,
14 East 6oth Street, New York, NY 10022, for $1.25, and "Job
Sharing: General Information," a guide for employers of-
fered by New Ways to Work, 149 Ninth Street, San Francisco,
CA 94103, for $1.50. By reading both publications you can

familiarize yourself with the various benefit options. Moreover, you will be able to suggest possibilities and smooth the way for an employer who may not be familiar with providing benefits for job sharers. The point, as Nancy Inui so aptly indicates, is to make it easy, not difficult, to hire you.

If at all possible, try to line up an employer who has already had experience with job-sharing employees to speak with your prospective or current employer to discuss job sharing in general. If you don't know of any employers yourself, contact a local part-time advocacy group and ask for the name of someone who may have volunteered to be a resource for the group. "Whenever we place a job-sharing team, we ask the employer if he or she would be willing to serve as a resource for other potential employers," says Nancy Inui. "Most are happy to spread the word."

If no employers are available, you might suggest that your potential boss call someone at the advocacy group who is prepared to answer specific questions about job sharing. Even if the groups around are general women's counseling services or vocational advice centers, undoubtedly someone there is conversant with the specifics and advantages of job sharing as well as of part-time employment in general. Call ahead to find out who can field questions. Then present your interviewer with that person's name and phone number and information about when he or she can be reached.

Finally, if despite your well-prepared presentation there still seems to be some hesitation about trying the job-sharing arrangement, make the same bottom-line offer that individuals seeking high-level part-time jobs should make: "Try us for six months. If at the end of that time you are not convinced that our job-sharing arrangement has worked out, we'll quit."

Good, solid preparation plus a lot of enthusiasm is the winning combination, the key to convincing an employer to try an innovative and possibly unfamiliar work situation. "Many times we hear that what sold the team is the advance preparation they did, and particularly how well they presented themselves as a team," affirms Nancy Inui. "They came in and they were terrific together; the company just didn't want to lose them."

To make sure you are well informed and able to cite all of the benefits that a job-sharing arrangement can bring to an employer, you may want to invest in two excellent guides:

◆ Gretl S. Meier, *Job Sharing: A New Pattern for Quality of Work* (Kalamazoo, MI: W. E. Upjohn Institute, 1978). Available from W. E. Upjohn Institute for Employment Research, 300 South Westnedge Avenue, Kalamazoo, MI 49007, for $4.50. More an information source than a how-to guide, this book is based on extensive research into a large number of job-sharing arrangements. It is interesting as well as informative, and contains an exhaustive bibliography.

◆ Barney Olmsted and Marcia Markels, *Working Less But Enjoying It More* (San Francisco, CA: New Ways to Work, 1978). Available from New Ways to Work, 149 Ninth Street, San Francisco, CA 94103, for $4.25. This is a step-by-step how-to guide that includes details on how to pick a partner, how to set up a job-sharing arrangement in a company you already work for, and how to help an employer devise a benefit package that is fair to all of you. It also contains a list of suggested readings, which can help you present an even stronger case when you approach employers with your innovative plan.

9

The Work-at-Home Option

FOR MILLIONS of Americans, particularly women with young children, working at or from their own homes is the best of all possible part-time situations. Why? First, because working at home affords you maximum flexibility. You work only when you can or want to. Second, when you are your own boss, you work  as much or as little as you like; the amount of money you earn depends not on how many hours you have punched in on a time card, but on how much effort you decide to put into your job.

Another advantage is that working at home saves money. You don't need to worry about the costs of day care or of commuting. There is no reason to accumulate a wardrobe of business suits or dresses, nor are restaurant lunches an ongoing expense. (Of course, if you are a lawyer, accountant, interior designer, or any other professional who plans to establish a consulting business, you will incur these costs. But you will also be earning from $25 to $100 or more per hour.) When you set up a business at home, you usually have little or no overhead and a lot of tax deductions you can take advantage of. When you consider all of these factors, it's no wonder that so many people decide to set up shop at home.

From or In Your Home?

Basically, if you decide to forgo the customary office or retail-store job settings, you have two alternatives: first, to work *from* your home, using it more as a base of operations than as an actual place of business; and second, to work exclusively *in* your house or apartment. There are good opportunities with both alternatives. However, you'll probably find that you will enjoy your work more if you do have the chance to get out of the house every so often.

Some of the simplest home-based jobs involve little or no work experience and lots of opportunity to meet new people. Let's take a look at some of the easiest ways in which you can make money in a successful home-based business.

Shopping services. If you enjoy browsing in specialty shops, burrowing into department stores, or even heading to the supermarket, you can easily set up a shopping service and earn good money. One successful New York shopper service charges $25 an hour, paid in advance, for purchasing Christmas or special-occasion gifts for clients, or simply taking care of personal shopping needs for people who don't have the time or inclination to do it themselves. A San Diego woman built a thriving local business by grocery shopping for women who were away from home during the day and elderly people who were eager to have someone else fight the crowds and checkout lines. Two other women did quite well establishing a gift-buying service especially for fathers who are divorced or otherwise unable to get to the store to buy presents for their children.

Caring for plants. Another clever idea, and one with many potential offshoots, is plant care. Watering houseplants while their owners are away on vacation, or even taking care of lush tropical displays in offices or homes when people are there, can easily bring in from $10 to $15 per visit, or in the case of larger collections of greenery, $25 per visit or even a monthly retainer.

Party planning. Imagination, the ability to organize, and a willingness to tend to details are the prerequisites of party planning, a potentially lucrative home-based business. Organization fund raisers, office Christmas parties, "Sweet 16" celebrations, and even special occasions for private companies (opening new offices, launching new products, awards dinners) offer an infinite variety of ways in which to demonstrate creativity with invitations and decor, food and entertainment.

Most party planners charge from 10 percent to 15 percent of the total cost of the party as their fee. Others act as subcontractors, receiving the same percentage from the florists, bands, caterers, or printers they use and charging their clients nothing. Still others set a flat rate or a per-person fee for their services. By starting small and arranging local parties for a flat fee, you can easily build up experience, a list of satisfied clients, and your bank account.

Catering. If you can cook anything well, chances are you can prepare it for other people at a profit. You will probably find your business growing faster than you ever imagined, particularly if you live in or near one of the nation's larger cities. You don't need to offer elaborate selections, either. One Manhattan housewife and mother made quiches that her friends all agreed were sensational. Almost as a lark, she decided to go into business. Several years ago she began offering dinners consisting of hors d'oeuvres, quiche, salad, and dessert to party-givers, for $11 per person. She did quite well.

Two New Jersey women started a fabulously successful business offering hot dogs and assorted accompaniments to businesses and to homeowners having swimming parties around their pools. The women arrived with a gaily decorated cart which they pushed around from guest to guest. They were a smashing success almost immediately.

Preparing gift baskets is another good idea for the person with imagination. Either homemade or purchased items can be assembled in attractive baskets or other containers and sold at a markup. Even sandwiches packed in ribbon-tied paper bags with fresh fruit and home-baked cookies might be a big favorite with nonprofit organizations or companies holding lunchtime meetings or seminars. One Boston woman made a fortune charging $4.50 each for her gingham-tied bundles.

The only limitations to setting up a thriving catering business are your imagination and perhaps local zoning laws. It is a good idea to check with the Board of Health or other regulatory agencies before you embark on catering as a home-based business.

Entertainment. Children's parties are among the easiest types of festivities to brighten with colorful costumes and assorted songs and games. One woman from Stony Brook, New York, played clown at her four-year-old son's birthday party. Before long she had launched a full-blown career. So far she has performed at well over one thousand parties, has several people working for her, has written a book on conducting children's parties, and has begun designing a full line of children's party games geared to the interests and skills of youngsters at various ages. Other entertainers offer juggling, music, participation games, arts and crafts, and even puppet shows. The market is large and growing, as mothers have less and less time to plan and execute elaborate birthday parties. Anyone who loves children and has the ability to keep them amused for a couple of hours can earn from $30 to as much as $100 per party.

Tutoring. Teaching your own skills and hobbies to others is work that you can easily conduct either in or out of your home. If you speak a foreign language or play a musical instrument, you can certainly teach a beginner's-level course for between $8 and $15 an hour. Or if you're an accomplished cook and catering doesn't appeal to you, you can give cooking lessons at anywhere from $5 to $35 apiece. Virtually any skill or knowledge you possess, from the ability to do yoga to the art of Oriental flower arranging, can be passed on to others. If you can show people how to better themselves or expand their horizons, you will find there is lots of money to be made.

Sewing. It is hard to imagine ways in which to earn money by sewing other than by taking up hems or letting out seams.

But one Manhattan business executive who took a pattern-making course several years ago for her own enjoyment wound up starting a custom-made skirt and dress business that netted her $25 to $75 on each garment. Other at-home entrepreneurs design special appliquéd children's clothing or throw pillows. One Long Island woman designs and sews vests and tunics made of antique laces she finds in local thrift shops and at garage sales.

Perhaps the most lucrative home-based businesses that involve sewing also depend on a number of talented seamstresses. An Arizona woman began a small enterprise making canvas tote bags, relying on women from a local senior citizens' employment center to do most of the handiwork. And a Tennessee woman made a small fortune selling pillows and other hand-quilted items sewn by women in her community.

Like catering, sewing and related crafts such as knitting, crocheting, and needlework offer many opportunities for creative people, from making customized designs to creating ready-to-wear garments. In an age when quality handmade items are rapidly becoming relics of the distant past, your talent can be your fortune.

Many other opportunities. There is no limit to the types of businesses you can launch or the ways in which you can pick up extra cash in your spare time. For example, you can set up a typing service that caters to college students and local businesses; many successful at-home typists run a few local ads or rely on word-of-mouth contacts and have thriving businesses that net hundreds of dollars a week. Or you may wish to set up a flower-delivery service, such as the one started by two Texas women several years ago. They buy flowers from a wholesale market and deliver fresh bouquets to customers once a week or according to whatever schedule the customer prefers. They simply tack on a fee for their services.

Another possibility is taking pictures of children's parties. An enterprising fifteen-year-old from Long Island charges $20 for each roll of Super-8 film he shoots, and estimates his profit at about $10 per roll, for about a half-hour's work. (Those with video equipment can make substantially more money, although their initial investment is also much greater.)

Along the same lines, two clever women began a service that many people can use and that businesses seem to be happy to know about. They go into a home, office, or store and photograph everything inside, then prepare a detailed inventory of the contents in case the owner ever needs documentation for insurance purposes. In addition, one of the women is now studying to become a licensed appraiser so that the team can do more — and charge more!

Finally, if you think you have no marketable talents and no likely way to turn your time into cash, consider the business that one Manhattan woman started several years ago. It is basically an "anything service": The woman does everything from organizing clients' closets or files and shopping and gift wrapping to escorting elderly, ill, or handicapped people to their doctors' offices. She takes cats and dogs to the vet, carries documents anywhere in the country to have them signed, conducts garage sales, supervises painting, packing, or moving, pays clients' monthly bills, and even helps clients find suitable charities for their clothing and other donations. She charges a flat fee of $20 for the first hour and $15 an hour after that, and earns over $100 a day.

What It Takes

A good idea, of course, is the first ingredient of any successful business, wherever it is launched. However, as important as it is, a sound concept simply isn't enough by itself. Often fledgling enterpreneurs fail at the outset because they have not taken the time to think their ideas through. Take a few moments to consider the following points and to ask yourself these questions before you plunge into any business venture — at-home or otherwise.

Examine your interests. What do you enjoy doing? What do you dislike having to do? Do you like to work with other people, or do you prefer being alone? Would your proposed career suit your personal and family needs? Would it leave you time for other pursuits?

Assess your abilities. This doesn't necessarily refer to what you were trained to do, but rather refers to what you do well.

What are you good at? Do you have the ability to persuade people? To put them at ease? Do you work well with other adults? With children? Do you have a sense of design? A good imagination? Do you have a green thumb? A flair for decorating? Shopping? Sewing? Cooking? Are you good at details? Do you usually see projects through to completion? Do you have a great deal of patience? Self-confidence?

Scout your community's needs. Many successful home-based career women have found a need that existed in their communities and proceeded to fill it. What could your area use? What do your friends say they would like to see opening up in the near future? For example, could your town use more day-care facilities or after-school play groups? House checkers for vacationing families? Are there children who could use tutoring in math or English? Do members of your community entertain a lot? If so, do they hire caterers, party planners, or entertainers? Would they buy prepared foods to serve at parties?

Test your business expertise. What do you know about the business you would like to run from your home? If the answer is nothing, you need to do quite a bit of investigating. Ask your librarian to show you how to locate trade organizations, professional groups, and other sources of aid and information. Find out about local zoning laws that govern at-home businesses, or health regulations that may apply. Remember that the Small Business Administration and your own local Chamber of Commerce are two invaluable sources of aid and information.

Locate resources. Do you have friends or neighbors who would be willing to join you if your venture works out? Can you gain valuable advice from talking to people already in similar businesses? How much capital will you need to get started, and how can you raise it?

Get the publicity you need. Take advantage of all the free advertising you can get. Put up index cards in supermarkets, shopping centers, libraries, community centers, college lounges and dormitories, churches and synagogues — everywhere you can think of. If you can afford to do so, you may wish to mimeograph flyers and put them in mailboxes or under apartment doors. Or it might be a good idea to run an ad in a local newspaper or magazine or in any publication able to reach prospective clients or customers. If your work-at-home idea is particularly unusual, imaginative, or simply new to your area, contact the features editor of your local newspaper. If he or she is interested in your service, you may get some free publicity.

A WORD OF CAUTION: Unfortunately, there are many unscrupulous individuals who set up "work-at-home" schemes that exploit tens of thousands of Americans each year. Typical of these schemes is one cited by the U.S. Postal Service in a booklet it published on mail fraud several years ago: "A classified ad appearing in newspapers in many parts of the United States offering women an opportunity to 'Earn up to $1.68 an hour sewing baby shoes in your home' drew more than 200,000 inquiries. First, however, it was necessary for the prospective sewer to pay a small registration fee and demonstrate her skill in sewing a pair of the wool-felt shoes for infants. In this particular scheme, virtually every one of the 60,000 applicants failed to measure up to the promoter's high standards."

There are many such schemes. Be on the lookout for them. To protect yourself, be wary of any sales opportunities that require a substantial investment, or any supposed employment opportunity that necessitates your paying a fee. Take the advice of the U.S. Postal Service: "In considering a work-at-home plan, think twice before paying for the chance to work."

The best and most satisfying way to earn money at home is to use your time, talents, and creativity to benefit yourself, not some promoter. There are plenty of legitimate opportunities for making good money at home. All you need to do is take advantage of them!

Where to Get Help

Need help with money management, bookkeeping, legal questions? Low-cost, high-quality professional help is available nationwide.

The National Association of Women Business Owners is well on its way to creating an effective "new woman's network" to help women who want to go into business or who have already begun and need support. Based in Washington, D.C., with branch offices in eight cities and with many local chapters, the organization will help put you in touch with other women who run businesses similar to yours. Local chapters run topical programs in tandem with local media, the Small Business Administration (SBA), colleges, and universities. Subjects include finance, law, marketing, public relations, and more. In addition, they publish a national directory of female-owned businesses. For information on membership and how the association can help you, write to the National Association of Women Business Owners, 200 P St., N.W., Suite 410, Washington, DC 20036.

SCORE is the acronym of the Service Corps of Retired Executives, a national network of retired volunteers who will put their decades of business experience to work for you at absolutely no charge. Sponsored by the Small Business Administration, SCORE will assign you a personal counselor whose experience best fits the needs of your business. Many women have reported learning everything from bookkeeping and tax know-how to publicity writing from their SCORE counselors. What's more, counselors offer encouragement and moral support. Consult your phone directory for the nearest SCORE office, or contact the closest SBA office or your Chamber of Commerce.

The Small Business Administration is the best-known source of help for the beginning entrepreneur. As a government agency, it can offer counseling and loans as well as courses, workshops, and seminars, which are given in local libraries, colleges, hotels, and government offices. General prebusiness workshops are offered, as well as special women's courses and marketing seminars. Check your phone directory for the nearest office. For a list of the many free and low-cost publications the SBA offers, write to the U.S. Small Business Administration, 1035 15th Street, N.W., Washington, DC 20416.

Legal clinics may be the answer to getting legal advice at a reasonable cost. If you are unwilling or unable to pay for the services of a high-priced attorney, try this alternative. Legal clinics are springing up all over the country, and they are allowed to advertise their prices. Run on a low-overhead, high-volume basis, they can provide expert advice for as little as $15 per consultation. You may even get advice over the phone. Of course, fees vary with the complexity of your questions and the services you need. Check the Yellow Pages and classified ads for law firms advertising as clinics, or check with your local bar association.

For Additional Information

Here are some useful publications for any at-home entrepreneur; most should be available in your library.

♦ Claudia Jessup and Genie Chipps, *The Woman's Guide to Starting a Business* (New York: Holt, Rinehart & Winston, 1976).

♦ Donald M. Dible, *Up Your Own Organization* (New York: Hawthorn, 1973).

♦ *Small Business Bibliography,* a collection of SBA and government pamphlets on launching a wide variety of ventures. Some examples: "Handicrafts" (No. 1); "Home Businesses" (No. 2); "Restaurants and Catering" (No. 17); "Nursery Business" (No. 14). Available from SBA, Washington, DC 20416, or any SBA field office.

♦ Leta W. Clark, *How To Make Money with Your Crafts* (New York: William Morrow, 1973).

♦ Julian L. Simon, *How to Start and Operate a Mail-Order Business,* 2nd ed. (New York: McGraw-Hill, 1976).

♦ American Crafts Council, comp., *Contemporary Crafts Market Place* (New York: R. R. Bowker, 1977–78). Directory of crafts courses, workshops, suppliers, stores, and other outlets.

♦ *Thomas' Register of American Manufacturers,* an annual guide to the products and services of over 100,000 U.S. companies, including addresses and phone numbers.

♦ *Gale's Encyclopedia of Associations,* an annual list of trade, technical, educational, and other public and private groups that provide publications and services.

♦ Jean Ray Laury, *The Creative Woman's Getting It Together At Home Handbook* (New York: Van Nostrand Reinhold Co., 1977).
♦ Herb Genfan and Lyn Taetzsch, *How To Start Your Own Crafts Business* (New York: Watson-Guptill, 1974).

Direct Selling

If ever a part-time opportunity promised that you will get out of it what you put in, it's direct selling. Today some four million Americans, 80 percent of whom are women and 90 percent of whom work part-time, see direct selling as a direct route to good money. And it certainly can be. What's more, direct selling can bring with it elaborate sales bonuses such as appliances, fur coats, gold and diamond jewelry, all-expenses-paid trips, and the keys to company cars.

All across the country, women (and some men, of course) knock on doors during the day or hold parties in people's homes during the evenings. Seventy percent of them sell cosmetics; the rest, household cleaning products, vacuum cleaners, encyclopedias, jewelry, Bibles, crystal glasses, houseplants, plastic freezer containers, health foods and vitamins, and other products.

How much do they earn? From almost nothing to well over $100,000 a year. Typically, commissions range from 30 percent to 50 percent. According to a 1977 Louis Harris survey, however, the median earnings of direct salespeople was $27 a week; only 11 percent earned over $100 a week. But as the same survey revealed, over 60 percent put in fewer than ten hours a week, and 43 percent held other jobs that they considered their primary work. Clearly, the more time and effort people put in, the higher their income is.

Getting Started

The usual minimum investment in sample products and sales literature ranges from $15 to $75. Avon, for example, charges $15 for its starter kit; Mary Kay, $75. The average seems to be the $60 that Amway charges for its demonstration packages and brochures.

Training can range from an impromptu session with a local director to attendance at several home parties with an experienced salesperson before you are sent out on your own. In most companies, either the sponsor who recruited you or the director in charge of your sales unit is responsible for making sure you can present products properly, conduct a party, close a sale, fill out order forms, and deliver the merchandise you have ordered once it has been shipped. Ongoing sales meetings provide support, additional training, and constant reinforcement of the "you can do it!" theme. In fact, many of the weekly or monthly meetings held by such companies as Tupperware and Stanley Home Products begin with inspirational prayers and include the singing of songs designed to get everyone into the proper spirit.

What the Companies Require

Most direct selling companies permit their salespeople to sell products wherever they choose to do so. Others assign territories. For example, the familiar Fuller Brush man (in 75 percent of all cases, a woman) starts out with a territory consisting of five hundred houses. She or he can increase the territory later. Avon's territories consist of 150 homes. But companies such as Mary Kay and Stanley Home Products encourage their salespeople to sell everywhere they can.

Although direct salespeople are actually not company employees, but rather independent contractors, the companies may require adherence to certain rules of etiquette or to dress codes. "We're told never to eat or drink in a customer's home, and not even to ask if we may use the bathroom," says Patricia Dorsey of Houma, Louisiana, who has been with Stanley Home Products for over two years. Women who are Mary Kay beauty consultants are instructed not to wear slacks while they are working; only skirts or dresses are deemed acceptable.

As for sales quotas, most companies have them in one form or another, even though they prefer to call them "expectations" rather than "requirements." For instance, Sarah Coventry fashion show directors are supposed to conduct two shows within each three-week period, but are expected to run at least one show per week. And if an Avon representative doesn't place an order of at least $100 at a time, she must pay an extra $3 service charge, which obviously reduces her net profits.

Earning Big Money

Regardless of how many jars of skin cream or bottles of laundry spot remover a person sells, odds are she or he won't find either fame or fortune. Why not? Because in direct selling, high income is more a result of recruiting other salespeople than it is of selling merchandise. The way it works is this: When you bring in someone else, you earn a company-paid commission of between 4 percent and 8 percent on that person's sales. When and if you become a director (either a paid or a nonsalaried position, depending on the company), you may earn as much as 13 percent on the sales of everyone in your group. If you are truly successful and start other people on the road to becoming directors, you may earn 4 percent on everything *their* groups sell as well.

To see just how a part-timer can make good money in direct selling, consider the case of Patricia Dorsey. A divorced mother of five children ranging in age from fourteen to three, Patricia was working the 2 A.M. to 10 A.M. shift as a waitress in a local Louisiana restaurant when she decided to sell Stanley Home Products "to make a little extra." Actually, she confesses, she was more interested in getting a wholesale account of her own on products she was already using and liked. With five children in the house, Patricia used a lot of household cleaners.

So she signed up, got her wholesale account, and began to attend sales meetings. Soon she was hooked. Not by the prospect of high earnings, however; instead, Patricia was lured by one of the premiums being offered to the top salesperson during a particular campaign Stanley was running at the time — a free trip to Disney World. "I knew I could never afford to take the kids," she recalls. "But I am ambitious. So I decided I was going to win that trip." After putting in eight hours on her feet each night, Patricia ran as many as six Stanley parties during the day. Within three months, she had won not only the trip for two but enough extra money to enable her to bring two more of her children along.

Since that time, Patricia has kept up the Stanley venture on a part-time basis. She puts in between fifteen and twenty hours a week. "In addition to my own 35 percent commission, I earn 7.5 percent on the earnings of each of the twenty-seven people I've brought into the company," she says proudly. "And I've also trained one woman to be a unit sales leader, and I now make 4 percent on her group, too." Patricia's earnings: over $15,000 a year.

Although Patricia spends only fifteen to twenty hours a week in direct selling, those hours are packed with activity. On Mondays, she travels seventy-five miles to New Orleans for sales meetings. On Tuesday mornings, she drives dealers in her company car "to an intersection somewhere. They get out of the car and head in different directions, knocking on doors and trying to line up appointments for parties." Tuesday afternoons she conducts local sales meetings.

On Wednesdays, Patricia works on recruiting — setting up appointments with people who have answered her newspaper ads or following up on past party contacts. Wednesday evenings, Thursdays, and Friday mornings are reserved for parties. And on Friday evenings, Patricia gets on the phone and confirms the parties scheduled for the following week.

"I prefer to do parties during the day," she confides. "But

pretty soon I'm going to have to do them at night." The thirty-two-year-old mother recently remarried, and explains, "That's when my husband, Pat, is home and able to watch the children." Pat's services are clearly going to be needed if Patricia is to continue her successful part-time venture: she is expecting her sixth child soon.

What It Takes to Succeed

During the initial training that every salesperson gets, she or he learns how to demonstrate, model, or apply company products, either before a group of four to forty potential customers or on a one-to-one basis. A pleasant disposition, poise, and self-confidence are keys to direct-selling success. But it takes more than just knowing how to smile and fill in order blanks to make good money. To help ensure success and minimize your chance for disappointment, you should:

Consider your goals carefully. Know why you are going into direct selling. Is it to get out of the house for a few hours each day, or to build a career, or to earn a bit of extra money? If you can clearly identify what it is you want to get out of direct selling, you will be able to measure your progress more readily.

Check out any company before you sign up. Find out company policies on initial investments, training, territories, sales quotas, and commissions. Most reputable firms belong to the Direct Selling Association, a federation of 140 companies whose members adhere to a strict code of ethics. If the firm you are interested in working for isn't a member of the DSA, check with your local Better Business Bureau. It is a good idea to speak with several other salespeople and to ask about their experiences with the company. Never sign with a firm that requires an initial investment of more than $50 to $100 and that doesn't offer a written money-back guarantee if you should decide to return your starter kit. Your earnings should be based on sales commissions, not on someone else's investment. Beware of pyramid schemes!

Be persistent. Give selling a fair chance. According to the Louis Harris survey, the salesperson who lasts one year with a company is likely to stick with it. Only half of all direct-sales people have been in the business for more than two years. They are usually the ones who make the most money. Recognize that building up a business of any type takes time. It's hard work.

Plan to recruit others if you expect to make big money. If you don't want to become involved with recruiting other salespeople, be realistic about your potential earnings.

Adopt a positive attitude. Enthusiasm is probably the most essential ingredient in direct-selling success. You have to like the company you're selling for, the products you're selling, and the chance to get out and meet people. As one highly successful direct-sales person puts it, "You can do everything wrong. But if you have the right attitude, you'll succeed."

For more information about direct selling, including a free directory of the members of the Direct Selling Association, write to the DSA at 1730 M Street, N.W., Washington, DC 20036.

Resources

Index

Resources

Organizations That Help Part-Timers

In cities throughout the country, groups of dedicated people are doing what they can to promote the idea of part-time work at the professional and managerial levels and to help place qualified people in rewarding part-time jobs they might not otherwise have been able to find. Some of these organizations have been around for years; others, for only a short while. Most are providing services to both prospective employers and eager job-seekers.

Keep in mind that many of the part-time advocacy groups operate on a shoestring. Some may have gone out of business since *A Part-Time Career for a Full-Time You* went to press. However, others may have sprung up in their places. If you have no luck getting in touch with one of the organizations listed below, contact other local groups (such as those listed in the Catalyst "National Network of Local Resource Centers"; see Catalyst, below) or call or visit a local university's women's center or placement office. Ask for an advocacy group that can help in your search for a good shared or part-time job.

Note: An asterisk (*) after the name of a part-time advocacy group means that the group belongs to the National Job-Sharing Network.

Alternative Employment Opportunities Study
Lansing Women's Bureau
303 W. Kalamazoo, Suite 204
Lansing, MI 48933
Attn: Paula Bladen

Alternative Working Arrangements: R & D
College for Continuing Ed/Women's Programs
Drake University
Des Moines, IA 50311
Attn: Marie C. Wilson

Association for Part-Time Professionals*
P.O. Box 3632
Alexandria, VA 22302
Attn: Diane Rothberg

Catalyst, Inc.
14 East 60th Street
New York, NY 10022

Founded in 1962, Catalyst is the nation's foremost organization dedicated to helping women "choose, launch, and advance their careers." The organization maintains and publishes a pamphlet called "National Network of Local Resource Centers," which is available, free, from the national headquarters. The listing contains names, addresses, phone numbers, office hours, and a guide to services and fees of 196 organizations throughout the country that help women in their various roles as students, working mothers, job-seekers, and displaced homemakers. Also free on request are "Bibliographies List," "Occasional Papers List," "Case Histories and Profiles List," and order forms. For people living or working in the New York metropolitan area, Catalyst maintains an excellent library, open to the public.

Flexible Careers*
37 So. Wabash
Chicago, IL 60603
Attn: Joyce Drake

Flexible Careers Project
P.O. Box 6701
Santa Barbara, CA 93111
Attn: Pam Ostendorf

Flexible Ways to Work
c/o YWCA
1111 Southwest Tenth
Portland, OR 97205
Attn: Judy Buffo

FOCUS, Inc.*
509 Tenth Avenue East
Seattle, WA 98102
Attn: Nancy Inui

Since 1974, FOCUS has served over 7500 residents of the Seattle area, most of them mothers or women re-entering the work force. The organization maintains a "talent bank" which lists some seven hundred people who are interested in part-time work, and recently launched a program aimed at helping senior citizens. FOCUS puts out a quarterly publication on alternative work patterns that it circulates to 1200 local employers and public officials. Other FOCUS publications: "Employing Professionals Part-Time" ($2.00), "Part-Time Careers — An Introductory Sketch" (50¢), and "Part-Time Careers in Seattle" ($5.95).

Innovative Career Options*
Metropolitan State College
School of Business
1006 11th Street, Box 13
Denver, CO 80204

Job Sharers, Inc.
P.O. Box 1542
Arlington, VA 22210

Organized in 1977, Job Sharers has worked to educate employers in the Washington, D.C., area about the advantages of hiring part-time workers, and to place members in professional-level positions. The group has achieved success in helping job-seekers find work with local employers as well as with the federal government.

National Council for Alternative Work Patterns, Inc.
 (NCAWP)
1925 K Street, N.W.
Suite 308 A
Washington, DC 20006

NCAWP functions not as a personal counseling group but as an educational organization. It sponsors conferences, seminars, and various publications, among which is the notable *Alternative Work Schedule Directory: First Edition,* edited by Gail S. Rosenberg, Marion C. Long, and Susan W. Post. The directory, which lists some three hundred public and private employers who utilize alternative work patterns such as job sharing and permanent part-time work, was published in 1978. Additional funding may permit the group to update this valuable resource. The directory sells for $25.00, but it may also be available as a reference in libraries or career counseling offices.

The *NCAWP Newsletter,* published quarterly ($25.00 per year), covers federal and state activities, legislation on alternative scheduling, summaries of recent research, notices of forthcoming conferences, and case studies. Also planned are a book of case studies on work sharing (including job sharing and permanent part-time work) and a manual on alternative work-scheduling programs in the various state governments. For an up-to-date publication list, write to NCAWP at the address given on page 361.

New Ways to Work*
149 Ninth Street
San Francisco, CA 94103

Established in 1972, New Ways to Work has become the most well known part-time advocacy group, as well as a national clearing-house for information on part-time work and a guiding force in establishing the National Job Sharing Network. The group has also been quite successful in promoting part-time opportunities throughout northern California. Following is the New Ways to Work publications list, revised at the end of 1980. For a current publication and price list, write to the organization at the above address.

> *Job Sharers: Working Less but Enjoying It More.* A step-by-step guide to negotiating a shared job, plus profiles of current job sharers.
> *Job Sharing: General Information* (1980). A general information handbook for employers.
> *Job Sharing in the Schools* (1980). A practical handbook for teachers and administrators on the use and implementation of job sharing in school districts.
> *Job Sharing in the Schools* (1980). (Companion handbook to publication listed above.) A guide to policies and contracts.

Job Sharing in the Public Sector (1979).

Job Sharing: A New Pattern for Quality of Work and Life, by Gretl S. Meier, published by the W. E. Upjohn Institute for Employment Research, Kalamazoo, MI (1979). Reviews the development of and current usage of job sharing; analyzes data of a national survey of 238 job sharers.

A Selected Bibliography on Job Sharing and Permanent Part-Time Employment (1979).

Articles and Reports on Job Sharing. Reprints from *Personnel Journal, Personal Report to the Executive, Wall Street Journal, Kiplinger Magazine, Work Life,* Stanford University *Manager,* and others.

Options for Women
8419 Germantown Avenue
Philadelphia, PA 19118
Attn: Marcia Kleiman

Since 1970, this organization has offered services to job-seekers and employers alike. Counseling and workshops are offered, as are vocational and educational testing. For those who can't afford the full fees, a sliding scale structure and some funding are available. For would-be part-timers, there is counseling on how to sell employers on the idea of part-time scheduling.

Phoenix Institute
383 South 600 East
Salt Lake City, UT 84103

Project JOIN
State Bureau of Human
  Resource Services
Department of
  Administration
One West Wilson Street
Madison, WI 53702
Attn: Mary Cirilli or Diane
  Lindner Jones

Wider Opportunities for
  Women (WOW)
755 Eighth Street, N.W.
Washington, DC 20001

Most of the efforts of WOW are geared to helping people in search of full-time employment, but since 1964 the group has also worked to improve opportunities for part-timers. WOW in 1979 published the *National Directory of Women's Employment Programs,* an extremely valuable listing of 140 organizations, their programs, publications, and the names of people to contact. Among the other useful WOW publications: *Women in Non-traditional Jobs: Information and Resources* ($1.00); and *Job-Finder's Kit,* a self-help guide for beginners, complete with tips on how to organize a job search (1979). Write to WOW for an up-to-date publication and price list.

Women's Center of Dallas*
2800 Routh Street, #197
Dallas, TX 75201
Attn: Judy Laube

Women's Management
  Development Program
Goucher College
Towson, MD 21204
Attn: Winifred C. Borden

Women's Work Project
1 Harris Street
Newburyport, MA 01950

Work in America Institute,
  Inc.
700 White Plains Road
Scarsdale, NY 10583

Another excellent source of information, the Work in America Institute describes itself as an organization that "directs its efforts to improving the workplace and the nature and organization of work for the purpose of bettering work performance, productivity, and the quality of life." Its *World of Work Report* newsletter ($48.00 per year) highlights developments in this country and abroad that pertain to those goals. The organization also publishes a number of outstanding books, among which is Dr. Stanley Nollen's *New Patterns of Work* ($25.00), which explores many alternative work patterns. For a copy of the publications list, write to Work in America Institute at the above address.

Work Options for Women
321 N. Market
Wichita, KS 67202

Work Time Alternatives*
1016 Acequia Trail NW
Albuquerque, NM 87107

Work Options Unlimited*
645 Boylston Street
Boston, MA 02116
Attn: Fran Gardiner

Recommended Reading

Career Guides and Job-Hunting Manuals

Boll, Carl R. *Executive Jobs Unlimited.* New York: Macmillan, 1965. The advice contained in this book is as valid today as it was the day the book came out. A must for anyone with solid work experience who's looking to move up. Offers an alternative to the usual "how to write a résumé" instructions.

Bolles, Richard N. *What Color Is Your Parachute? A Practical Manual for Job-Hunters and Career-Changers.* Berkeley, CA: Ten Speed Press, 1980. Revised annually. The best job-hunting manual available. Contains an exhaustive list of resources for women, minorities, the handicapped, high-school and college students, and other special interest groups. Excellent.

Catalyst. *Career Opportunities Series.* Twenty-seven different booklets on various careers, including fund raising, recreation, and urban planning. Booklets should be available in your local library, or can be obtained for $2.00 each from Catalyst, 14 East 60th Street, New York, NY 10022. (Write for a free "Bibliographies List" which specifies the booklets and all other Catalyst publications.)

———. *Education Opportunities Series.* Eleven booklets, including "General Information for the Returning Student." Should be available in your local library, or from Catalyst at the address above. $2.00 each.

———. *Résumé Preparation Manual: A Step-by-Step Guide for Women.* Basic and useful for those who've never written a résumé before. $4.95.

———. *Self-Guidance Series.* Two booklets: "Planning for Work" ($2.50) and "Your Job Campaign" ($2.50).

Crystal, John C., and Bolles, Richard Nelson. *Where Do I Go from Here with My Life?* Berkeley, CA: Ten Speed Press, 1974. A classic strategy guide.

Donaho, Melvin W., and Meyer, John L. *How to Get the Job You Want: A Guide to Résumés, Interviews, and Job-Hunting Strategy.* Englewood Cliffs, NJ: Prentice-Hall, 1976.

Holland, John L. *Making Vocational Choices: A Theory of Careers.* Englewood Cliffs, NJ: Prentice-Hall, 1973. How to match your interests and aptitudes to the right job. Contains the famous "Self-Directed Search," the most comprehensive guide for determining the type of work you'd be happiest doing. A classic in vocational guidance.

Irish, Richard K. *Go Hire Yourself an Employer.* New York: Doubleday, 1973.

Jackson, Tom, and Mayleas, Davidyne. *The Hidden Job Market: A System to Beat the System.* New York: Quadrangle/New York Times, 1976.

Lathrop, Richard. *Who's Hiring Who.* Berkeley, CA: Ten Speed Press, 1977.

Lederer, Muriel. *Guide to Career Education.* New York: Quadrangle/New York Times, 1975. Focuses on careers that require fewer than four years of post-secondary study. Salary figures out of date, but information solid and useful.

————. *New Job Opportunities for Women.* Skokie, IL: Publications International, Ltd.; distributed by Simon & Schuster, 1975. Dated salary figures, but good introduction to careers that require only one or two years of study.

Lembeck, Ruth. *Job Ideas for Today's Woman.* Englewood Cliffs, NJ: Prentice-Hall, 1974. Contains some good ideas for various approaches to familiar at-home jobs. References to salaries and fees are outdated. Even though the book focuses primarily on the so-called "traditional" female jobs, it's still a good resource.

Lieberoff, Allen J. *Good Jobs.* Englewood Cliffs, NJ: Prentice-Hall, 1978. Basic and general, yet helpful.

Marketing Yourself: The Catalyst Women's Guide to Successful Résumés and Interviews. New York: G. P. Putnam's Sons, 1980. New and good.

Mitchell, Joyce Slayton. *I Can Be Anything.* Princeton, NJ: College Entrance Examination Board, 1978. Focuses on non-traditional occupations, such as truck driver, welder, statistician. Aimed primarily at young women planning for their first jobs.

National Directory of Women's Employment Programs: Who They Are; What They Do. Published by Wider Opportunities for Women, Inc., 1649 K Street, N.W., Washington, DC 20006, 1979. $7.50. A listing of 140 organizations, including descriptions of programs (mostly for full-timers), contacts, and publications. The only problem with directories of this kind is that organizations listed in them may be out of business before the books are in print. What's more, cuts in federal funding threaten to put many others out of commission. Therefore, when you write or call listed organizations, keep your fingers crossed.

Schwartz, Felice N.; Schifter, Margaret H.; and Gillotti, Susan. *How to Go to Work When Your Husband Is Against It, Your Children Aren't Old Enough, and There's Nothing You Can Do Anyhow.* New York: Simon & Schuster, 1973. A classic in the women-going-back-to-paid-work movement.

Splaver, Sarah. *Nontraditional Careers for Women.* New York: Julian Messner/Simon & Schuster, 1973. Basic job descriptions and sources of information, with emphasis on construction trades, engineering, auto repair, etc.

————. *Paraprofessions.* New York: Julian Messner/Simon & Schuster, 1972. Good introduction to work in architecture, education, social work, technological fields, law, medicine, mental health, accounting, and other fields that lend themselves to part-time scheduling. A good starting point for those seeking careers as paralegals, paramedics, etc.

Steele, Max. *Seasonal Jobs on Land and Sea.* New York: Harper Colophon Books/Harper & Row, 1979. Everything you need to know if you want to head to the vineyards of California or France for a while, or to land a job in a logging camp, on a fishing boat, or a grapefruit grove in Florida or Texas. Tips for ski bums and anyone else with a good case of wanderlust and no particular desire to get rich. Fascinating reading, even if you're not inclined to be a migrant worker.

U.S., Department of Labor, Bureau of Labor Statistics. *Exploring Careers*. Bulletin 2001. Washington, DC: Government Printing Office, 1979. Written primarily for junior high school students, the book provides a good introduction to various careers. Occupations are discussed in terms of young people's interests and school activities. Includes essays, questionnaires and games to make vocational counseling interesting. Check your local public or school library.

————. *Occupational Outlook Handbook,* 1980–81 Edition. Bulletin 2075. Washington, DC: Government Printing Office, 1980. The most comprehensive guide available to hundreds of different jobs. Should be the first source you consult in considering any occupation. Available at virtually every library or high school or college placement office.

What to Do with the Rest of Your Life: The Catalyst Career Guide for Women in the '80's. New York: Simon & Schuster, 1980. Brand new, up-to-date, and extremely useful.

Yeomans, William N. *Jobs 80–81.* New York: Paragon, 1979. Good section on job-hunting techniques, up-to-date details of salary and opportunities for new college graduates. Good for any job-hunter.

Sources of Information on Part-Time Work

Catalyst. *Part-Time Social Workers in Public Welfare.* New York: Catalyst, 1971. (Address listed in previous section.) The famous study of 50 Massachusetts women who worked part-time as social workers and an evaluation of advantages and disadvantages of part-timers. The study revealed that part-timers handled 89 percent as much of a caseload as did those on staff full-time.

————. *Part-Time Teachers and How They Work: A Study of Five School Systems.* New York: Catalyst, 1968. A detailed, positive study on school systems ranging from New York to Iowa. More testimonials than statistics.

Cohen, Allan R., and Gadon, Herman. *Alternative Work Schedules.* Reading, MA: Addison-Wesley, 1978. One of the few studies that examines part-time work from the perspective of the employer.

Davis, Herbert J., and Weaver, K. Mark. *Alternative Workweek Patterns: An Annotated Bibliography of Selected Literature*. Published by National Council on Alternative Work Patterns, 1925 K Street, N.W., Suite 308 A, Washington, DC 20006, 1978. Some 160 entries, including news releases, Department of Labor studies, and Congressional papers, among other things.

"Employing Professionals Part Time." Published by FOCUS, Inc., 509 Tenth Avenue East, Seattle, WA 98102, 1977. $2.00. Evaluation of numerous professional jobs done on a part-time basis by people in the Seattle area. Particularly good section entitled "Conversation with a Skeptical Employer," which can help both employers and job hunters.

Eyde, Lorraine D. *Flexibility Through Part-Time Employment of Career Workers in the Public Service*. Washington, DC: U.S. Civil Service Commission, Personnel Research and Development Center, 1975. A strong argument for using part-timers, including a good section on the pros and cons of job sharing.

Lazar, Ellen. "Constructing an Employee Benefit Package for Part-time Workers: How to Calculate an Equitable Package at No Extra Cost to the Employer." New York: Catalyst, 1975. $1.25. A worthwhile investment for job-seekers and employers alike.

Lazer, Robert I. "Job Sharing as a Pattern for Permanent Part-Time Work." New York: The Conference Board, October 1975. Written for employers, this article is a good introduction to the pros and cons of job sharing, complete with statistics and tables.

Matthews, Kathy. *On Your Own: 99 Alternatives to a 9–5 Job*. New York: Random House, 1976. Some of the money-making possibilities are a bit unusual, such as breeding earthworms for profit. Still, some good ideas for clever and enterprising individuals.

Meier, Gretl S. *Job Sharing: A New Pattern for Quality of Work and Life*. Published by W. E. Upjohn Institute for Employment Research, 300 South Westnedge Avenue, Kalamazoo, MI 49007, 1978. An exhaustive study of job sharing and job sharers. Excellent.

Nollen, Stanley D. *New Patterns of Work*. Published by Work in America Institute, 700 White Plains Road, Scarsdale, NY 10583, 1979. $25.00. An excellent review of the current literature on the subject of part-time work and other alternatives to the full-time schedule.

———; Eddy, Brenda B.; and Martin, Virginia H. *Permanent Part-Time Employment: The Manager's Perspective.* New York: Praeger, 1978. A thorough examination of the experiences and attitudes of employers who do and don't use part-time workers. Contains an excellent bibliography.

——— and Martin, Virginia H. *Alternative Work Schedules, Part 2: Permanent Part-Time Employment.* New York: AMACOM, a division of American Management Associations, 1978. An exhaustive survey of 481 users and 228 nonusers of permanent part-time workers. Examines the pros and cons, and offers concrete projections for the future.

Olmsted, Barney, and Markels, Marcia. *Working Less but Enjoying It More.* Published by New Ways to Work, 149 Ninth Street, San Francisco, CA 94103, 1978. $4.25. Contains a valuable guide to restructuring a full-time job to a shared position. Workbook format is particularly helpful.

Research Institute of America. *Improving Productivity with Part-Time and Temporary Help,* 1979. Available from The Research Institute of America, Inc., Department 111, Mt. Kisco, NY 10549. $7.50 to members; $15.00 to nonmembers. Extremely thoughtful and thorough exploration of the advantages to employers of using part-time and temporary workers. Good discussions of the jobs which part-timers can fill, the use of professional part-timers, job sharing, and other creative employment options. Written for employers.

Robison, David. *Alternative Work Patterns: Changing Approaches to Work Scheduling.* Published by Work in America Institute, Inc., 700 White Plains Road, Scarsdale, NY 10583, 1976, 1978. $5.00. Discusses alternative work patterns of all types and offers case studies as examples.

Rosenberg, Gail S.; Long, Marion C.; and Post, Susan W., eds. *Alternative Work Schedule Directory: First Edition.* Published by National Council for Alternative Work Patterns, Inc., 1925

K Street, N.W., Suite 308 A, Washington, DC 20006, 1978. $25.00. This first-of-its-kind directory contains about 300 listings of both public and private sector employers who have adopted such alternative schedules as flexitime, job sharing, and permanent part-time work. Specifies the jobs, company addresses, and contacts. Very useful.

Index

373

Update

---◆---

TO:

JoAnne Alter
c/o Houghton Mifflin Company
Two Park Street
Boston, MA 02108

◆ I suggest you make the following change in the next edition of *A Part-Time Career for a Full-Time You*. (List resources you weren't able to find, counseling services that no longer exist, public or private employers who have changed hiring policies in regard to part-time workers, along with new listings to be added to the book.)

◆ Here's a progressive company (or federal, state, or local government agency) you should know about:

Company or agency name, address, telephone number:

_____

_____

How it is accommodating would-be part-timers: _____

_____

Person to contact for further information (name, title,

dept.) _____

_____

◆ This person has a terrific part-time or at-home job:

Name _____

Address _____

Telephone number _____

Position, title, or at-home venture _____

_____

Employer's name and address, if any _____

_____

_____

_____

◆ I'd like to make the following comments (criticisms or suggestions) or relay my own experiences seeking or holding a part-time job:

Thanks for your help!

FROM:

Name _____

Address _____

_____